FROM COTTON FIELDS TO
UNIVERSITY LEADERSHIP

FROM COTTON FIELDS TO UNIVERSITY LEADERSHIP

All Eyes on Charlie, A Memoir

Charlie Nelms

Foreword by Walter M. Kimbrough

WELL HOUSE
BOOKS

AN IMPRINT OF
INDIANA UNIVERSITY PRESS

This book is a publication of

WELL HOUSE BOOKS

an imprint of Indiana University Press
Office of Scholarly Publishing
Herman B Wells Library 350
1320 East 10th Street
Bloomington, Indiana 47405 USA

iupress.org

Manufactured in the United States of America

First printing 2019

Cataloging information is available from the Library of Congress.

ISBN 978-0-253-04015-2 (cloth)
ISBN 978-0-253-04016-9 (paperback)
ISBN 978-0-253-04019-0 (ebook)

*This book is dedicated to the memory of
my mother, Carrie D. Nelms; my father, Eddie Nelms Sr.;
my sister Carrie C. Nelms; my brothers Harvey and Willie Nelms;
my mother-in-law, Julia Sherrod; my best friends Ernest Smith,
Kenneth Christmon, Jimmy Ross, and Tendaji Ganges; and
all members of the village who surrounded me with love,
encouragement, and support.*

*And to my family: my wife, Jeanetta; my son, Rashad;
my siblings and their spouses; my nieces and nephews; and
members of my extended family, all of whom have shown me
unconditional love.*

CONTENTS

FOREWORD

ON MANY OCCASIONS, PEOPLE CAN RECALL THE EXACT time and place they met someone. Maybe you were introduced by a mutual friend at a conference (which is how I met my wife—I guess I should remember that if I expect to go home). It could be a college classmate from freshman orientation or your first roommate. Whatever the situation, we all have conversations where we can recount the story of where we met someone, especially someone we have known for years.

I can't tell you when, where, or how I met Charlie Nelms. I have racked my brain for weeks and weeks trying to remember where I met him. I can tell you when he spoke for our faculty-staff institute when I was president at Philander Smith College in Little Rock, Arkansas, and even that he talked about the idea of being stone cutters that build cathedrals. I'll never forget it because the imagery he used was so vivid.

I can recall that I also asked him to speak for our faculty-staff institute when I got to Dillard. He helped to discuss what it means to work at a historically Black college and university (HBCU) and how sacred is the responsibility we have for the work we do. I remember being invited to speak as part of the centennial activities at North Carolina Central University (NCCU) when he was chancellor, as part of a panel to discuss the future of HBCUs. I also remember another speaking engagement I had at NCCU when he worked in time for lunch with me and Dr. Ontario Wooden, who was the Student Government Association vice president when I became vice president at Albany State and was then an administrator at Central. I can see the restaurant, in a warehouse district of some sorts, and the way we were just able to share ideas.

More recently, I fondly remember a late-night discussion we had with a colleague trying to figure out if he was called to do this work. While I offered some ideas, I was more interested in Charlie's, as a three-time university president with a wealth of experience. In fact, there are many times at conferences and meetings where we have been together where I just listened. The passion for his work, the ability with which he could color a story to make it vivid and real, and his frank, matter-of-fact nature all appealed to me.

But I can't for the life of me recall when or where we met. In reading *From Cotton Fields to University Leadership: All Eyes on Charlie, A Memoir*, I had an epiphany. I have known Charlie all my life. No, I don't mean that he knew my parents and has been a family friend. We probably met within the last fifteen years or so. But his story speaks to me on so many levels.

His humble beginnings in Arkansas and willingness to work hard in school mirrors that of my parents. His story is their story, and I have heard those stories my entire life. He was an active student and engaged in leadership early, which is my story. He knew early on that he wanted to serve as a college president and found himself engaging university leaders to begin to explore this career path. This is my story too.

Time and time again in the book, I found myself connecting to his story, one that will resonate with so many professionals who find themselves on a journey in higher education. But the story is one that could inspire young people with any career aspiration. He often speaks about his low American College Testing, or ACT, score and the way he overcame it. There are many young people who need to see the possibility of overcoming low scores as long as they have high motivation. Charlie is that possibility.

Maybe one day I will figure out when and where I met Charlie Nelms. Right now, I have no clue! But I know him now, and reading his story in full has at least explained for me why I have felt a connection to him and his career. It makes me even more thankful for times when I could just hang out with him and listen.

When you read this book, just imagine that the two of you are hanging out and, in his distinctive voice and tone, he's telling you his life story.

And just listen.

Dr. Walter M. Kimbrough
President, Dillard University

PREFACE

THE POMP AND CIRCUMSTANCE ASIDE, THERE IS SOMETHING extraordinary about the inauguration of a new college or university president that defies description—especially if you are the person being inaugurated. In the hours preceding my inauguration as North Carolina Central University (NCCU)'s tenth chief executive, my spouse, Jeanetta, and our only child, Rashad, welcomed family, colleagues, and friends to the historic home of the founder of the university, Dr. James E. Shepard.

My mind was flooded with memories: Mama and Papa, my teachers and mentors, and even the naysayers, who were all responsible for me reaching this seminal milestone in my professional career. Having previously served as chancellor of two predominately White universities, I knew firsthand what it was like to serve as a university president, but being inaugurated as CEO of a historically Black college and university, or HBCU for short, was another story.

As I donned my academic regalia with the assistance of my chief of staff and the university's grand marshal, I could not suppress my memories of chopping and picking cotton, milking cows on the college farm at Arkansas Agricultural, Mechanical, and Normal College (Arkansas AM&N), and using the colored-only water fountains and restrooms during the era of the 1950s and 1960s. Most importantly, I could hear Mama's sweet, reassuring, and comforting voice reminding me that I could be anything I wanted to be. In that moment, it occurred to me that I had come full circle. I was about to be installed as chancellor of an HBCU, the same type of institution that produced me.

The ten-minute walk to the inauguration site, McDougald-McLendon Arena on the NCCU campus, was lined with well-wishers of all ages, colors, and backgrounds. They all had two things in common. First, they respected the historic role that NCCU had played in the uplift of Black people. Second, they sought to convey their confidence in my leadership and their unswerving commitment to the university. Just as I had come full circle, so had North Carolina University, in hiring its first CEO from a predominately White institution (PWI), one who had not lost sight of his beginnings and the way that he made it over.

Coming full circle was more than a phrase to me; it reflected a reality of enormous proportions. This book is about the dreams and aspirations of a Black youngster who grew up in the Arkansas Delta during America's apartheid era, who had the audacity to dream of a better life for himself and those whose circumstances seemed hopeless. There were three turning points in my formation as a person. First, I decided that I was capable of doing more than working for the White man from sunup to sundown. Second, I chose education as my weapon of choice for fighting against the evil forces of racism and inequality. Third, I accepted the counsel and mentorship of sages who could assist me on my life's journey.

Although I've deliberately chosen not to spend time reflecting on what might have happened if I had not taken the road less traveled, it's certain that I would not have had the opportunity to do as well and as much good as I have by choosing the road that I did. Had I not taken that road, I most assuredly would have ended up in the Vietnam War or working in an automobile or steel plant in Cleveland, Chicago, Gary, or Flint.

The single most important constant in my life has been the presence of mentors—people who cared enough about me to tell me what I needed to hear, whether I wanted to hear it or not. They were teachers, preachers, barbers, college professors, and presidents who saw my potential and took personal responsibility for my growth and development. The most notable of these was Milton Mozell, my vocational agriculture teacher in grades ten through twelve, who convinced me that I had the potential to earn a college degree. He didn't just encourage me; he became my chief advocate and helped me to get a job on the AM&N College farm to work my way through college. Through modeling and mentorship, Mozell taught me the importance of passion, persistence, and hard work.

This book is about the power of aspirations, preparation, hard work, and mentorship. With these four, anything is possible; but without them, nothing is possible. For those of you reading this book, I want you to come away believing that you, too, can achieve your dreams, and I want you to have the courage to make a concerted effort to become the person you are capable of becoming.

This is the story of my journey, and I hope it will inspire you on yours.

ACKNOWLEDGMENTS

ALTHOUGH IT DID NOT QUITE TAKE A VILLAGE to write this book, writing it would have been far more difficult and less enjoyable without the expert assistance of my writing coach, personal editor, colleague, and friend, Dr. Nadine Pinede. She pushed me to dig deeply into the recesses of my soul in writing about the relentless effects of racism, bigotry, and discrimination I experienced while growing up in the Arkansas Delta during America's apartheid era. Writing about experiences long covered up by the scar tissue of my repressed memory was painful, but it resulted in a richer, more compelling story about my leadership journey. In addition, doing so proved to be a cathartic and liberating experience.

I am indebted to Gary Dunham, director of the Indiana University Press, who agreed to publish this memoir and to personally take on the task of serving as my editor. The feedback provided by Gary on my first draft proved invaluable as subsequent drafts of the book emerged. Likewise, I am grateful to Dr. Peggy Solic, acquisitions editor for Well House Books at Indiana University Press, who became my editor as Gary's responsibilities at the press increased. Working with Peggy and the entire team at Indiana University Press in general and Well House Books in particular has been a real joy.

Storme Day, executive assistant in Indiana University's Office of the Vice President for Diversity, Equity, and Multicultural Affairs (DEMA), and Roberta Radovich, program coordinator in DEMA, two of the university's most resourceful employees, always responded affirmatively to my request for assistance, and they did so in a timely manner.

My spouse, collaborator, and confidante of more than fifty years, Jeanetta Sherrod Nelms, encouraged me to keep writing as I dealt with the pain unleashed by my memories of life in the Deep South during the 1950s and 1960s. Likewise, my brother Eddie Nelms Jr., the patriarch of the Nelms family, provided invaluable assistance by filling in the details with names, dates, and events associated with life in the Arkansas Delta. If he didn't know the answer to a question I posed, he could always tell me where to find it.

Finally, while I had the support of many people in helping to make this book a reality, the story that unfolds in the pages that follow is my own, as are the errors and omissions. With sincere and heartfelt gratitude, I say thank you to everyone who helped me on my leadership journey so that I would have a story worth telling.

FROM COTTON FIELDS TO UNIVERSITY LEADERSHIP

1

"I'LL FLY AWAY"

THERE ARE A HANDFUL OF THINGS I NEVER want to forget. I don't ever want to forget what it was like working from sunup to sundown in the cotton fields of eastern Arkansas during the 1950s and 1960s. Since farm practices and social conditions have changed dramatically since that era, it is nearly impossible for me to be doomed to repeat those experiences should I forget them. Yet for more than four decades, I kept a jar of cotton on my desk. I have even held on to my cotton sack and the hoe used to chop the weeds from around the stalks during the height of the growing season.

Except for the foul smell of the chemical defoliates used to knock the leaves off the cotton stalks, the cotton itself had no smell. However, the sharp edges of the cotton bolls and burs were known to cut up one's cuticles to the point of drawing blood. Raw cotton, complete with seeds in the locks, was a lovely sight to behold, once it was picked and loaded onto the truck or tractor-driven trailer. For poor people like my parents, who owned neither a truck, nor tractor, nor trailer, the cotton was packed into a tin roof cotton house, located in the back of the shack we called home, until we accumulated enough to make a bale, which ranged from thirteen hundred to fifteen hundred pounds. My uncle, or a nearby Black farmer who owned a truck, would be hired to haul the cotton to the gin, where it would be ginned and sold to a White cotton dealer, often at a price well below the fair-market value.

Every farm boy or girl I ever knew had a job starting as early as four or five years of age. The job ranged from watering the cows, slopping the hogs, gathering eggs, delivering armloads of wood to the porch, or gathering kindling to start a fire in the cooking stove or the potbelly, cast-iron heater used to warm the house. But the one job we all had in common was picking cotton.

My earliest memory of being in the cotton field was September 1951, just a week following my fifth birthday. There I stood on that hot and humid day in my cotton flannel shirt and my patched and faded overalls. I was handed a burlap "croker" sack by Mr. Walter, the Black straw boss responsible for supervising the pickers and weighing the cotton. A regular sack was six or nine feet long, while a child's croker sack was approximately three feet long. I felt a certain amount of excitement and trepidation all at the same time. I was excited to be in the field with the big kids and the adults, but I was fearful of not being able to keep up with them and of getting lost in a cotton field, whose stalks were considerably taller than me. Although it was a field of only a few acres, at the time it seemed like a thousand. By the end of that first day, I was proud of myself for having picked nearly fifty pounds and being congratulated by Mr. Walter for being a good cotton picker with great potential.

Mr. Walter's prediction was spot on; by the fall of 1964, my last year of picking cotton, I had developed into one of the best cotton pickers in Crittenden County. On September 11, 1964, my eighteenth birthday and my final year of picking cotton before heading to college, I picked 468 pounds, nearly half a bale. Yet with all of that picking, I earned less than fifteen dollars!

The trick to being a great cotton picker was twofold. First, you had to develop a rhythm, and second, you had to pick your first sack while the dew was still on the cotton. A heavy dew meant that the cotton was wet and weighed more. Your first sack could easily weigh as much as 95 to 105 pounds. My brother Willie, who was three years older than me, was an even better picker. We often had cotton picking contests, and I recall winning only once. Of course, Willie was known for not exercising as much care in removing burs, whole bolls, and leaves from the cotton before placing it in his sack.

It was in the cotton field that I learned how to dream. I know that may sound crazy to some, but it's the truth; my body was in the field, but my mind was never there. Like the characters in Virginia Hamilton's *The People Could Fly*, a collection of African American folktales, I dreamed of a more equitable America where my parents and siblings (indeed all "Negroes," as we were called back then) could enjoy a quality of life beyond anything they could imagine. Thank goodness my parents never discouraged any of their children from dreaming, even if they weren't sure our dreams could become a reality.

In retrospect, I think it was because Mama and Papa had their dreams too: to own a farm and not to have to kowtow to White plantation owners. Sixty-three years after they made that $800 down payment on forty acres of farmland and woods, I can proudly say that we still have that little farm. Not only that, but my cousins and I still have our grandmother's eighty-acre farm too. Out of respect for the sacrifices made by my parents and grandparents, we'll never yield to the offers from wealthy physicians in the Memphis area who want to buy the land and establish a hunting lodge.

When I looked at the jar of cotton on my desk, it reminded me of struggle, dreams, and aspirations; the value of hard work, focus, and love; and the support I received from my parents. It reminded me of the fact that we are all more than our titles, our salaries, or the fancy houses in which we now reside. The cotton jar reminded me daily of the fact that we are more than our possessions, and it reminded me of the transformative impact of education. Time and again, I've used that jar and my cotton sack to talk with students of all ages about the importance of dreams, focus, and hard work.

As a cotton picker and chopper, my dream was simple: to escape our leaky tin roof house, the outhouse, coal-oil lamps, sunup-to-sundown hours in the field, dusty and muddy roads, and life without electricity or other modern conveniences. It was not until my junior year of college that my parents got electricity. Only after the death of one of the plantation owners who wanted to buy my parents' farm, which they refused to sell, did the Arkansas Power and Light Company get permission from his nephew to place a utility pole on their land in order to get electricity to our house. The plantation owner's descendants have rented our farm for more than forty years.

* * *

Like nearly all Blacks of my generation who grew up in the Arkansas Delta, our foreparents did not immigrate there. We were there because our great-grandparents were either slaves or direct descendants of slaves. My maternal grandfather, Isaac "Ike" Stokes, whom we called Papa Ike, was born to former slaves on a plantation near Crawfordsville, Arkansas, in 1873, and he died in 1952 not far from his birthplace. My maternal grandmother, Corrie Anderson Stokes (Mama Corrie), was born to former slaves in 1875 near Tunica, Mississippi, and as a young girl, she moved with her family to a plantation near Earle, Arkansas, where she met and married Ike. To this union were born eight children: Minnie, Alma, Lee Bertha, Frank, Ressie Mae, Carrie, Celeste, and Hattie, six of whom lived well into their eighties.

How my maternal grandparents managed to successfully transition from being sharecroppers to owning a farm is mindboggling to me, even to this day. They purchased sixty acres of bottomland inhabited by snakes, mosquitoes, raccoons, and other wildlife and struggled to eke out a living by growing large vegetable-truck patches to feed the family as well as a few acres of corn to feed the farm animals and cotton to sell as a cash crop, when it wasn't destroyed by floods, draughts, ferocious boll weevils, or other equally destructive insects. My grandparents married off their sons and daughters to the children of other farm families, who, like them, were trying to live off the land rejected by White plantation owners. Realizing that the backbreaking, sunup-to-sundown fieldwork left them in debt and in poverty at the end of the year, many of my aunts and uncles sold their little farms and moved north to Chicago, Flint, Cleveland, or Gary, to live in one-room, cold-water flats. There they toiled in the steel mills and automobile industry, or they worked as maids and janitors to provide for their families.

Life for my paternal grandparents was nearly identical to that of my maternal ones. My paternal grandfather, Charlie Presley Nelms, known affectionately to us simply as Grandpa, was born in 1893 on a plantation near Walls, Mississippi, while my paternal grandmother, Dulcia Little Nelms, was born in 1895 on a plantation near Augusta, Arkansas. They were married in 1914 and had six children who lived to adulthood and had careers as subsistence farmers, all save one who made his way to the army followed by a career with US Steel in Gary, Indiana.

Grandma was known to have a temper, a mean streak, and the attitude that it was her way or the highway. Grandpa, on the other hand, exuded warmth and a willingness to embrace people without judgment. Their styles clashed, and they divorced after thirty years of marriage. Grandma married a preacher, Reverend David Carter, who was later killed in a train-crossing accident when his truck stalled in a little hamlet known as Gilmore, Arkansas. With funds from her settlement with the railroad, Grandma paid off the balance due on their eighty-acre farm and spent the next forty-plus years overseeing the farm and dishing out orders to my uncle and aunt, who felt beholden to her and never left her side until the day she died in 1987 at age ninety-two.

To make sure that the farm remains in our family and to honor Grandma's womanist and independent streak, several years ago I bought out my siblings, and another cousin bought out two other cousins. I'll plant trees on my share and create a land trust specifying that the land will never be sold. I am sure that Grandma would approve of this decision, since she held on to her land despite recurring challenges that would have caused most people to capitulate. She said that she never wanted the White folks to have her land. Although she was not literate, she understood the power of owning land and the independence it accorded.

Grandpa Charlie remarried and lived happily as a sometimes farm-hand and day laborer. He never learned to drive, but for as long as I can remember, he owned a car and was chauffeured around by his youngest son, Irvin. Some of my fondest memories include him visiting us on occasional Sunday afternoons and bringing with him bags of groceries and pepper-mint or caramel candy treats for my siblings and me. Grandpa was an easy-going man who always had a word of encouragement for each of us. I could not help but feel his pride and see the twinkle in his eyes when my brother Willie went off to college, followed by my sister Carrie, me, and my sister Ruth, all before he succumbed to cancer at seventy-six years of age. Were he still alive, he would surely marvel at the fact that his namesake earned a doctorate degree and became a national leader in higher education.

My parents, Eddie Nelms Sr. and Carrie Stokes Nelms, were born on farms in the Arkansas Delta in 1915, and they went on to spend their lives in this environment. Married at age twenty-four, late by the customs of their day, they became sharecroppers like their parents before them. Short in stature, kind, passionate, and hardworking, Papa was one of the smartest, if not the smartest, people I have ever known. Mama, heavyset but shapely, with high cheekbones and warm brown eyes, was equally as smart but more strategic in her planning and execution. Had it been left up to Papa, he probably would have sold the farm and moved up north to pursue job op-portunities. But Mama wouldn't have any of it. She kept meticulous notes about crop harvesting and the amount of money they borrowed from the nearby plantation owner, Mr. Ed Copeland, to make the crop and to make ends meet until harvesting time. Papa was far more trusting of others than Mama was.

Family planning was not in vogue in the Black community in my par-ents' day. They had eleven children who lived to adulthood. While they loved us dearly and considered us a blessing, I really don't think they wanted that many children. In fact, I'm sure they didn't, and I still marvel at how they had enough time and love to attend to our needs without suffering a ner-vous breakdown. Clearly, Mama was the difference. A master disciplinarian and teacher, she had her child-rearing system down pat and never hesitated to swiftly and lovingly invoke her authority. Mama never said, "Wait until your daddy gets home." She disciplined us on the spot and always took time to remind us that she was doing so because she loved us and didn't want the "law" to do it. The "law" in my day was the White sheriff or one of his deputies whipping you with his blackjack, billy club, or pistol. Say what you may about my mama's approach, none of her brood ever ended up in jail or prison for committing a crime.

While it's not clear why my parents who had so little formal schooling believed so profoundly in its value, my siblings and I were the beneficiaries of this unswerving faith. Except for a King James version of the Bible with births and deaths of family members recorded in the front; a tattered copy or two of church hymnals; old copies of *The Weekly Reader* from school; a textbook one of us children failed to turn in at the end of the school year; and the *Farmer's Almanac*, which served as a guide for everything ranging from when to plant the crop or garden to when to have a tooth extracted, there were no books in our house. Occasionally, Mr. Copeland, the White plantation owner who made farm loans to my parents at greatly inflated interest rates, would drop off bags filled with old copies of newspapers: the *West Memphis Evening Times*, *Memphis Commercial Appeal*, and *Arkansas Gazette*.

It was a real treat when the bag included a copy of the *New York Times* or *Newsweek* magazine—no matter how old it was. From time to time, one of my older brothers, who had tractor-driving jobs, would buy copies of *Jet* or *Ebony* magazines, which were owned and published by African Americans for African Americans. Seeing all of those color photographs of Black people dressed in fancy clothes inspired me to keep dreaming and to work harder to escape the chains of poverty and the stranglehold of segregation designed to snuff out any hope of escape. However, except for artists like Louis Armstrong, Miles Davis, Cicely Tyson, and James Brown and politicians like Shirley Chisholm, all of the persons shown in the magazines were light skinned. Even so, this did not deter me from dreaming.

Amid an environment that was, for all intents and purposes, devoid of books and reading materials, my parents still had this phenomenal belief in education. Unlike parents who read to their child while still in the womb, my parents never read a story to any of us before or after birth. Their limited literacy skills aside, they were endlessly consumed with trying to make ends meet while navigating the drama and turbulence associated with the dual evils of racism and poverty.

Since my grandparents on both sides owned small farms, it's easy to understand my parents' penchant for land ownership and the independence it accorded them, but their commitment to voting is even less clear than their commitment to education. I say that because of the difficulties imposed by southern segregationists and the potential of physical violence if Blacks attempted to vote. As if the threat of physical harm was not enough, the nonsensical literacy test and the poll tax were additional impediments to Blacks voting. To Mama's protestations, Papa went from house to house, Black community to Black community, at night and encouraged sharecroppers and subsistence farmers to vote. Always polite and seemingly differential, Papa was smart enough to give White people the impression that they were in charge, all the while engaging in his covert community organizing.

I vividly recall overhearing a conversation between Papa and one of his brothers, Uncle Wes, a sharecropper, about how Blacks could influence the quality of education their children received if they would only turn out to vote. Papa argued that since Blacks outnumbered White voters by a substantial margin, they had the power to change the composition of the school board from totally White to at least 50 percent Black.

Although we were all poor, Uncle Wes and other sharecroppers had far more to lose by challenging the status quo than my parents did. My parents owned a small farm of their own and could grow enough food to feed our family. Uncle Wes's fear, along with that of my other relatives and area sharecroppers, did not deter Papa from trying to get them registered to vote. If anything, their fear seemed to embolden him to try even harder. More than forty years after Papa's covert voter-registration activities and just a few years before his death, two of his friends, Jack Jackson and Henry Valentine, were elected to the Crawfordsville, Arkansas, school board. By that time, however, the budget appropriations and tax revenue from the Arkansas legislature were insufficient for the school board to do anything to improve the quality of kindergarten-through-twelfth-grade (K–12) education in Crawfordsville.

My parents were phenomenal for several reasons. One is their unwavering faith in the power of education, although they possessed little themselves. Their belief in education's power to transform lives has inspired me since childhood. My parents were also deeply committed to land ownership and voting. Among those who have been dispossessed and disenfranchised, their profound belief in the trinity of education, voting, and land ownership motivated my siblings and me to commit ourselves to all three without questions.

For my parents, as for many African Americans, "forty acres and a mule" was more than a promise for agrarian reform (and reparation) made to slaves by General William Tecumseh Sherman on January 16, 1865, in Special Field Order No. 15, approved by President Lincoln. The promise of forty acres (the mule came later) was born in a meeting in Savannah, Georgia, where abolitionist leaders asked twenty Black ministers what Blacks would want for themselves. They said, "The way we can best take care of ourselves . . . is to have land, and turn it and till it by our own labor . . . and we can soon maintain ourselves and have something to spare. . . . We want to be placed on land until we are able to buy it and make it our own."[1] If this visionary promise had been kept, the history of the United States would no doubt have been quite different. As it was, this promise was never kept, yet it continued to symbolize the desire to achieve self-reliance and freedom from servitude, both mental and physical.

Few of us know that Black-owned farms once made up 14 percent of the nation's farms, peaking at nearly a million in 1920. Their combined area of fifteen million acres was the size of New Hampshire, Massachusetts, and New Jersey. However, blocked at every turn by the kind of discrimination my parents and countless others experienced, Black farmers spent the following decades in decline. In 1982, their numbers had dropped to thirty thousand, a mere 2 percent of the nation's total.[2]

Discrimination within the Federal Housing Administration (FHA) was so persistent and pernicious that, eventually, Black farmers filed a lawsuit against the agency, which was granted class-action status by the courts. Hundreds of Black farmers filed the class action lawsuit *Pigford v. Glickman* against the US Department of Agriculture (USDA) for racial discrimination between 1981 and 1996. The lawsuit was settled on April 14, 1999, by Judge Paul L. Friedman of the US District Court for the District of Columbia. To date, almost $1 billion has been paid or credited to more than 13,300 farmers under the settlement's consent decree, under what is reportedly the largest civil rights settlement to date. As another 70,000 farmers filed late and did not have their claims heard, the 2008 Farm Bill provided for additional claims to be heard.

In December 2010, Congress appropriated $1.2 billion for what is called Pigford II, the settlement for the second part of the case. Pigford became one of the largest civil rights settlements in history, although it came too late for many of those who suffered decades of discrimination.[3] This is indeed a bittersweet victory, given the never-fulfilled promise of forty acres and a mule, as well as the history of generous government subsidies for White farmers.

Although my parents were among those discriminated against, we did not have copies of the paperwork required by the agency to prove that they were denied a loan. Thus, we could not file a claim for damages endured. However, my siblings and I have the satisfaction of knowing that, despite the endless financial challenges faced by our parents, they held on to their little forty-acre farm and we continue to hold on to it long after their deaths. This runs counter to the national trend. Only ten years ago, a mere 1.5 percent of the nation's more than two million farms were owned by African Americans, and only 31 percent of Black farmers received some government payment, compared to half of all White farmers.[4]

Fortunately, the number of Black-owned farms began increasing under President Obama's administration and new policies by the USDA, which partnered with the National Black Farmers Association to help rectify past discriminatory practices, but who knows if these advances will be dismantled or reversed.[5] Given centuries of such tremendous struggle and perseverance in the face of disheartening obstacles, it should come as no surprise that the ownership and farming of land is and remains a vital part of the African American heritage.

* * *

My parents never sold their land or headed north seeking a better way of life, like many of my relatives and many African Americans in the Great Migration, a mass exodus of approximately six million Blacks from the South to urban centers in the Northeast, Midwest, and the West. In fact, my parents borrowed money against that little forty-acre farm on countless occasions to make sure we had the essential things for participating in 4-H and other clubs while we were in high school.

When Mr. Ed, the White farmer from whom my parents borrowed money to make a crop, told Papa that my brother Willie should be at home helping pick cotton rather than away at some "damn college," Papa simply said, "Yes, sir," and kept moving forward. Willie's dream was to become a physician, and Papa and Mama were determined to do their part to make that happen. But Papa had a saying: "When your hand is in the lion's mouth, you can't make any sudden moves."

Papa died in 1985, three months shy of his seventieth birthday, while Mama died at age ninety. Papa died of a heart attack, and Mama died from a series of strokes and related medical issues. Except for her last five years, the quality of Mama's life was excellent. A passionate gardener, quilter, and fisherwoman, Mama was a member of the Mother's Board at Shiloh Missionary Baptist Church and had an angelic singing voice. Her favorite hymn was "Some Glad Morning, I'll Fly Away":

Some glad morning when this life is o'er,
I'll fly away;
To a home on God's celestial shore,
I'll fly away (I'll fly away).

My most prized possession is the tape of an interview I did with Mama at age eighty-seven. We concluded the interview by singing that song together. When faced with a stressful situation during my tenure as chancellor at the University of Michigan–Flint (UM–Flint) or vice president at Indiana University (IU), I'd play that tape of the interview with Mama. Her clear, strong voice remains with and encourages me, as does my parents' legacy of hope and courage.

* * *

Not only was I fortunate to have parents who believed in their children's dreams, but I was also surrounded by a large band of loving siblings. We often joked with each other about the fact that there were enough of us to form our own football team! To my parents' credit, they did not expect my four sisters to perform all of the domestic chores. All seven boys in my family were expected to wash dishes, iron clothes, churn the milk, clean the house, and help with the cooking. It would require volumes to do justice to the lives of my amazing brothers and sisters. Instead, I'd like to sketch a portrait of four of my siblings: Roy, Harvey, Willie, and Carrie.

Every large, Black, southern family I've ever known had at least one set of twins and a preacher. While there were no twins in the Nelms family, there is a preacher: my brother Roy. Born in 1954, Roy is a quiet, serious, and devout person who has pastored a church in the rural Arkansas city of Wynne, with its eight thousand inhabitants, for twenty years. He worked in the construction-supply industry before accepting his call to the ministry in the mid-1990s.

Except for a few classes in religion and divinity, Roy did not continue his education beyond high school. Yet he has managed to develop and offer a number of award-winning summer and after-school children's programs in reading and computer technology. His congregation is slightly over three hundred parishioners, which is large for a rural community. Roy and his spouse do not have any biological children, but they have "adopted" untold numbers who have gone on to college around the country. He inherited our mother's angelic singing voice, quiet demeanor, and commitment to changing the world.

Roy and I are nearly ten years apart in age, but we are amazingly similar in physical appearance. My siblings and I have come to rely on Roy for non-judgmental spiritual guidance and advice. He exudes confidence and calm in even the most turbulent times.

My eldest sibling, Harvey W. Nelms, was born in 1939. He was a fearless and industrious person who was determined, according to him, "not to be no White man's cotton picker or tractor driver." Although I was afraid that his fearlessness might cause him to be harassed or harmed by the Klan, Harvey was my hero.

Harvey left school at age sixteen and began working construction with our uncle, Ellis Gillum, a self-taught contractor who could build or remodel nearly anything from a verbally conveyed description provided by his customers, since he was barely literate and unable to read blueprints. While working for Uncle Ellis paid far more than chopping and picking cotton from dusk to dawn, Harvey migrated to Memphis, Tennessee, in search of greater opportunities. When he was twenty years old, my parents signed their permission so that he could marry a beautiful girl, Mildred, who became pregnant in eleventh grade. They had two children but then divorced after nearly twenty years of marriage.

In addition to construction work, Harvey held an array of jobs that paid far more than the miniscule wages earned by farmworkers. He tried his hand at driving eighteen-wheeler trucks but settled on being an automobile mechanic. He could fix anything and owned his own garage for the better part of two decades. Following encounters with colon and throat cancer, Harvey died at age sixty-six of emphysema. I visited him for the last time on a hot summer day in 2005 at St. Francis Hospital in Memphis. As he lay dying, his breathing labored, I asked if he was afraid of dying, to which he replied yes.

Through tears, I thanked Harvey for the fine example he'd been for me and assured him that everything would be OK with our family and we'd always keep him in our memories. In his first inaugural address,

Franklin D. Roosevelt said, "The only thing we have to fear is fear itself," but it was my fearless brother, Harvey, who taught me the true meaning of these words in both life and death. Thanks to him, as an adult, I have never been afraid of failure, and I've always believed that I was just as capable of success as anyone else—Black or White, wealthy or educated.

I cannot say enough about the critical role my teachers and mentors played in my decision to go to college, especially my agriculture teacher, Mr. Mozell. However, for first-generation students like myself, I can think of nothing more important than having older siblings who attended college. Two of mine, Willie and Carrie, introduced me to a world of educational opportunities that I had no idea existed. Although neither was a bigwig on campus, they both enjoyed a reputation for being good students academically and quiet leaders in their own right.

Born in 1943, my brother Willie was very gifted intellectually and was the first of my siblings to go to college. Armed with the dream of becoming a physician, Willie attended and graduated from Mississippi Industrial College, a small, church-affiliated historically Black college and university (HBCU) in Holly Springs, Mississippi. It eventually merged with Rust College, also located in Holly Springs. Willie's intellect notwithstanding, he lacked the self-discipline and resolve to do what was required to go to medical school. He became a biology teacher in the public schools of Flint, Michigan, as well as a community education director under a program started by the Charles Stewart Mott Foundation in the 1960s. The program later became a national model for engaging all segments of the community in educating students for productive living.

Willie had a real knack for business and owned several business ventures during the 1970s and 1980s, including a grocery store, a restaurant, and several ice cream trucks that brought joy to neighborhood children throughout Flint. Willie married his high school sweetheart and was the father of one child, Regina, who graduated from Chicago State University. Willie mentored hundreds of students and took them into his own home when they had no place to go. He paid for college-application fees, tuition, ancillary fees, and books for countless young people who eventually earned college degrees and returned to teach in Flint or to work in management positions in the automobile industry in Michigan.

Like many young Black men today, Willie faced injustice in the American criminal justice system. As an eleventh grader, he was jailed for nine months for allegedly assaulting a White teacher on a rainy night in

Crawfordsville, Arkansas, a town about five miles from where we lived. It was a White woman's word against his, and she won.

Willie and I slept in the same bed, so I know that he did not get up and walk five miles in the rain to assault his accuser and make it back home before dawn. We didn't have a car, and we lived on a dirt road about a mile from the nearest gravel road. The justice system was so corrupt that neither my parents, nor my grandparents, nor any other Black farmers were able to put up their farms as collateral or bond to secure my brother's freedom pending his trial.

There was never a trial. Willie was released after an assault occurred against two Black teachers and the perpetrator was apprehended. That man confessed to the assault on the White teacher as well and was sentenced to life in prison in 1959. Without that confession, Willie's life would have been completely different. Despite being jailed for a crime he did not commit, Willie did not allow that incident to dim his spirits or his desire to make a difference in a world where race and racism colored everything. If anything, it was a source of motivation.

Willie and I were very close. He regaled me and my siblings with stories of college life. This was in the days before student financial aid, so our entire family made great sacrifices in order for Willie to go to college. Willie was an inspiration not only to us but also to many rural children and their families. Willie retired from the Flint Community Schools and passed away unexpectedly in Memphis, Tennessee, at age seventy.

My older sister, Carrie, was the best friend and sibling a person could have. She was smart, witty, passionate, loyal, and a feminist long before the term was in widespread use. Carrie and I both attended Arkansas Agricultural, Mechanical, and Normal College (Arkansas AM&N), an HBCU known as "the Flagship of the Delta," and we overlapped by two years. Together, we solved a lot of the world's problems! I quickly became known as Carrie's little brother and was expected to excel academically. Although I never quite met the academic bar she set, between being a campus politician and student leader, I gave it my best effort!

Carrie majored in institutional dietetics and nutrition and became one of the first Black registered dieticians in the country. She earned a master's degree in public health from the University of Michigan (UM) and directed the Special Supplement Program for Women, Infants, and Children (WIC) in Detroit-Wayne County, Michigan, for nearly twenty years. Carrie was diagnosed with stage IV lung cancer in 1997 and died nine months later.

A nonsmoker, avid golfer, photographer, and fitness enthusiast, Carrie never married and was a woman of many talents who traveled the world. I miss her still.

The Nelms family is not just large; it's also close knit. We call each other frequently and gather on a regular basis for reunions, holidays, birthdays, and graduations. We don't wait for someone to die to get together. And when we do get together, there are lots of stories, lies, laughs, and home-made cakes and pies! Our parents were a source of inspiration for all of us. Their faith in God as well as their belief in the power of education, hard work, and paying it forward has been a legacy we proudly carry on and bequeath to the next generation.

In a recent conversation with my only child, Rashad, who has lived and worked abroad for the United Nations for more than a decade, he asked if I ever think about my parents. I replied, "Yes." He then asked what I would say to them if they were alive today. I told him, "I'd thank them for being master teachers, although they never completed a college course. I'd thank them for modeling resilience and the true meaning of love. I'd thank them for nurturing the dreams of my siblings and me." Thanks to my parents, although my body was in the cotton fields, I was already learning to dream, to fly, fly away.

2

HOW I GOT OVER

SMITH PERKINS, MY LITTLE SCHOOL, WAS LOCATED ON Buck Lake Road, about three miles west of my family's homestead. In 1917, long before "Negroes" had access to public K–12 education, Julius Rosenwald, the president and part owner of Sears, Roebuck and Company, established the Rosenwald Fund, which would eventually provide financial support to construct over five thousand schools in fifteen southern states, including my native state of Arkansas.

An estimated five hundred thousand Black baby boomers like me benefitted from Rosenwald's generosity. In addition to funding K–12 education, Rosenwald was a major benefactor of the Tuskegee Institute (now Tuskegee University). Tuskegee's founder, Booker T. Washington, was an advocate for practical education, and this resonated with Rosenwald, just as strongly as Spelman College's commitment to the liberal arts resonated with Nelson D. Rockefeller and his spouse, abolitionist Laura Spelman Rockefeller, whose substantial financial contributions made possible the founding of what was originally named the Atlanta Baptist Female Seminary in 1881. Little did I know on my first day of school just what a tremendous role philanthropy would play throughout my life.

* * *

I remember Smith Perkins as if it were yesterday. The most remarkable thing about it was not its architecture, site, topography, or landscape; it was its redbrick construction. Why this particular building was constructed of brick when the overwhelming majority of the structures in and around Crawfordsville, Arkansas, were constructed of clapboard and painted white is still not clear to me.

Except for its redbrick exterior, there was absolutely nothing else that stood out about this little structure. With its outdoor toilet and rusted water pump, it stood on approximately one acre of land lush with Johnson grass, wild blackberry bushes, and toad frogs. There was no sign of a playground with the usual merry-go-round, swing, or slide. The building was in serious disrepair, and only one room could be used for instruction. The roof covering the second room had long ago rotted; the holes in the roof were so gaping that no one even bothered to put buckets under them when it rained. No yellow-and-black hazard tape warned us kids of any of these potential dangers. Just once did Mrs. Beatrice Johnson, our teacher, admonish us to stay away from the room—and once was more than enough!

In the middle of the one useable room stood a potbelly cast-iron heater, about three feet tall. It burned coal when it was available or wood, if it had not been stolen from the stack out back by a schoolhouse neighbor or passerby. Needless to say, there were many days when we had no heat and kept our coats on. Suspended from the ceiling was a lone light bulb, which emitted just enough light for us to read the three chalkboards at the front of the room.

Board one contained the parts of speech, a sample diagrammed sentence, and examples of block- and cursive-style writing. Board two displayed multiplication facts, basic math formulas, and examples of solved math problems. One-half of board three held the next day's spelling and math assignments, while the other half was left clear for students to solve math problems or diagram sentences.

Expecting a single teacher to instruct as many as fifty to sixty students at eight different levels—preprimer, big primer, and first through sixth grades—defied rationality or logic. Yet my teacher at Smith Perkins managed to do just that, even though on some days, she reeked of alcohol. In retrospect, I can understand why she imbibed from time to time! Those Rosenwald teachers pulled it off by deputizing older students who were fast learners to serve as teacher aides; they would instruct the students in preprimer, big primer, and first grade. They lined us up along the walls of the room according to grade level and age and led us through drills reciting our alphabets, times tables, and the parts of speech. We even read out loud to these aides. Even though our feelings fluctuated from disdain to envy, we secretly respected the important role these aspiring teachers filled.

Everything at Smith Perkins School had been previously used by White children, except the chalk. Those little twin-seat desks with flip-up tops to store books we didn't have were hand-me-downs from the White school uptown, as were the outdated textbooks with missing pages. Our writing tablets were of two types: refined white paper or cornbread paper. The former was slick, while the latter was a rough, yellowish paper in which you'd easily create a hole when trying to erase an error. Typically, white-paper tablets cost twenty-five cents, while cornbread paper could cost as little as ten or fifteen cents.

No matter what type of paper one's parents could afford, the tablet was used to copy the next day's assignment from the chalkboard and to complete overnight homework, which the teacher would check for accuracy and thoroughness. We even got a grade for handwriting and comportment. Anything less than an A in comportment led to Mama treating us to an "attitude adjustment." Although I hated those whippings, I must give Mama credit for her purposeful approach to discipline. She always made her expectations clear and let you know in no uncertain terms where you missed the mark.

* * *

The plantation owners controlled the school board, and they organized the school year around the planting and harvesting season. Their primary objective was to ensure the availability of a source of cheap labor. Thus, the school curriculum was designed to equip Negroes with basic literacy skills—reading, writing, and arithmetic—not to prepare us for college or for jobs beyond the cotton fields.

The two-room schoolhouse was bare bones. So it should come as no surprise that there was neither a library nor any science lab at Smith Perkins School. The only books I remember reading while in elementary school were Paul Laurence Dunbar's *Candle Lighting Time* and Booker T. Washington's autobiography, *Up from Slavery*. I still have copies of both of these classics, and I pause occasionally to read excerpts from each. Perhaps it was a lack of an early exposure to books and other reading materials that led me to create in my home a library that holds literally thousands of books.

As the fifth of eleven children, I aspired to be like my older siblings and was a proficient reader by the time I was four or five years old. Although the reading materials available to me were neither broad nor sophisticated, I loved reading and demonstrated my skill to my parents and anyone else who would listen. Since we didn't have a television set and the battery in our old upright Delco radio was too weak to pick up a broadcast signal, there weren't many distractions to compete with my predilection for reading.

Even to this day, reading materials can be found in every single room of our house. My wife and I bequeathed to our only child, Rashad, the joy of reading. Books, as well as magazine and newspaper subscriptions, continue to be gifts of choice for us, even in a digital culture dominated by sound-bite breaking news and social media.

* * *

A split school session only made sense if the needs of its designers took precedence over the learning needs of its pupils, and that is exactly what happened. The local school board was comprised exclusively of White plantation owners, whose highest priority was to make sure that they and their fellow planters had a ready supply of cheap labor. The availability of laborers when farmers needed them meant that school was in session those months between the planting, growing, chopping, and harvesting seasons. The weather, not the number of instructional days prescribed by the state, dictated when the school session started or ended for Negroes. However, this was not the case for White children, who typically started the new school year the first week of September and ended it the first week of May.

If the weather was favorable, Blacks in the Arkansas Delta typically started school the first Monday following the Fourth of July. For us, July 4 was more than a patriotic holiday recognizing America's founding and the Declaration of Independence. It marked a hiatus in the growing and chopping season, when the crop was "laid by" because attempts to chop (weed) the crop would result in damage to the young cotton blooms and green bolls that would eventually yield fluffy white cotton.

Off to school we'd go around July 5 and remain until the cotton was ready to pick, which was typically the third week of September. The fall recess lasted from the third week of September until after Thanksgiving. This period was set aside for picking or harvesting the cotton before the arrival of December rains and winter freezes. The winter session of the school year began approximately December 1 and continued through the first week of May, when the school year officially ended and the cotton chopping, growing, and harvesting cycle began all over again.

Since major planters and plantation owners did not settle up with their sharecroppers and the subsistence farmers to whom they loaned money until after Christmas, the school absentee rate could be as high as 75 percent. Like in my family and other Black families in the Delta, dollars from the settlement, when there was one, were used to buy school clothes and to stock up on food staples of flour, sugar, beans, corn meal, canned goods, and other essentials needed to tide us over until spring, when money was borrowed to make a crop, purchase a few clothing items, and restock depleted food pantries. For all intents and purposes, this meant that many of us did not return to school until after Christmas. Cotton came first.

* * *

It goes without saying that there is a vast chasm between the dilapidated two-room country schoolhouse where I commenced my education as a four-year-old preprimer student in the Arkansas Delta in 1950 and the midwestern research university where I completed my doctoral studies twenty-seven years later. When I reflect on the daily three-mile walk to and from school along dirt and gravel roads with cotton fields on both sides, the words from the song "How I Got Over," popularized by Mahalia Jackson, ring persistently in my ears more than a half-century later:

> *You know my soul look back and wonder*
> *How did I make it over.*

* * *

The grip of racial segregation and American-style apartheid was so pernicious during the 1950s and 1960s that it instilled in many of its victims a deep sense of fear, and it robbed them of their sense of hope and self-confidence. Like caged birds who often lose their ability to fly, many of the inhabitants of the Delta lost their ability to dream and to envision a life beyond the cotton fields. Chief among the measures used to suppress and to curtail our aspirations and preparation for life beyond the farm were poorly funded, staffed, and equipped schools; the public nature of Ku Klux Klan activities; the seizure of land owned by Blacks under the pretense of unpaid loans; the enforcement of Jim Crow laws related to public accommodations; and the occasional killing of a Black male for allegedly "acting White" or getting out of his place.

Make no mistake about it, there was a clear pecking order associated with Jim Crow cultural practices in the Delta. At the very top of the circumscribed hierarchy of respect stood the plantation owners, who controlled all aspects of the economy, directly or indirectly. Following close behind the plantation owners were the White merchants, who sold everything required to make a crop. Included in this group were the bankers, grocery store owners, dry goods dealers, preachers, and teachers, all of whom were White. The third tier of the racial hierarchy was the White overseers, who supervised the farms on a daily basis and operated the cotton gins and grain elevators, all the while enforcing the will of the plantation owners.

Poor Whites, who stood near the center of the racial order, always occupied a position higher than Blacks of any socioeconomic group. They could eat at restaurants and small diners, while economically well-off Black farmers and teachers, for example, were forced to order from the carryout window or from the kitchen itself.

Black farmers—large landowners as well as subsistence farmers—occupied the fifth rung on the racial hierarchy and managed to always find a way of supporting each other. Perhaps that was the case because Blacks of all social classes recognized the importance of interdependent relationships for their individual and collective survival. It was the Black physicians, funeral directors, farmers, merchants, teachers, and preachers who received what little respect given Blacks by Whites in the Delta.

Black sharecroppers, tractor drivers, day laborers, and farmhands in the apartheid South had the least amount of independence and economic security. Almost always, the shack they called home belonged to the plantation owner, and the cotton they planted, chopped, and harvested belonged to the plantation owner as well. From birth to death, they depended for all aspects of their livelihood on the plantation or landowner for whom they sharecropped or did day work. Often, if they did anything that did not meet the approval of the boss, they could be told on the spot to move or be fired without redress.

In many instances, they were even told with whom they could or could not associate. One of the plantation owners whose farm abutted ours had a tractor driver who was known to raise quite a ruckus during a Saturday night of heavy drinking, which would frequently turn into fights, shootings, and stabbings. The plantation owner is alleged to have told him, "Sammy, if you stay out of the ground, I'll keep you out of jail." Sure enough, he kept Sammy out of jail, because come Monday morning, Sammy would be back driving the tractor as though nothing had happened over the weekend.

By all objective measures, my neighbors, siblings, and I didn't just grow up poor; we were destitute. Except for those who have experienced firsthand the devastating effects of abject poverty worsened by political and racial oppression, it's nearly impossible to fully appreciate the triumph of the human spirit. The Delta-style apartheid we experienced was designed to break the human spirit, to rob us of hope and the belief that there was a place in the sun socially and economically for Blacks beyond the fields, which could easily soar to over 105 degrees.

Unless you have experienced the physiological and psychological effects of not eating for several days at a time, it's impossible to know the difference between needing to eat and wanting to eat. Unless you have experienced the humiliating effects of going to a White person's back door or hearing your daddy routinely called *boy* and your mama referred to as *gal* or having your fourteen-year-old friend gunned down by a White deputy sheriff because he allegedly made an inappropriate comment to a White girl, you have not experienced the racism of which I speak. The kind of apartheid I experienced growing up was nothing less than organized terrorism against Blacks.

* * *

Long before the phrase "It takes a village" was popularized, I was indelibly impacted by one. And that is how I got over. My village was headed by my parents and inhabited by members of my immediate and extended family, church members, teachers, and preachers, who all took collective responsibility for nurturing my personal, spiritual, and intellectual development. They offered food for my physical nourishment and encouragement for my emotional well-being. When the plantation owners and straw bosses told us that we were shiftless and lazy niggers who would never amount to anything, our barely literate pastor preached sermons that reassured us that God cared about each of us and that He would deliver us from all evil, including the evil of apartheid.

What our parents lacked in money, they compensated for with love. What our teachers lacked in instructional resources, they compensated for by improvising. When a member of the village hit rock bottom financially and health-wise, other villagers pitched in with a love offering of pennies, nickels, and dimes to buy food or medicine. Hog-slathering time meant that all members of the village ate well, not just the villager whose hog it was. The turnip-green patch belonged to the village, as did the wild honeycombs found in hollowed-out trees on a villager's little patch of land.

When it came time to turn raw sorghum into refined syrup or dry kernels of corn into cornmeal, everyone had access to the mill. When a member of the village died, all the village men and boys helped to dig the grave and lower the casket into the ground. A commercial service was neither available, affordable, nor required. When a village boy or girl excelled as a spelling bee contestant, in a 4-H Club event, or got a promotion in the army, the entire village celebrated.

In addition to my parents, the village in the Arkansas Delta responsible for nurturing my dreams and those of Black boys and girls across the spectrum of landowners, subsistence farmers, and sharecroppers included Mr. L. R. McNeil, principal of the all-Black K–12 school, and his multitalented wife, Mrs. Veola McNeil, who served as the home economics teacher, cafeteria director, counselor, social worker, basketball coach, choir director, drama teacher—all in the same semester!

This couple, like countless other Black educators across the South, approached their work as a calling, not a job. Whatever needed to be done, they did. They were our toughest critics and our fiercest defenders. They pushed us to be all that we could be without apology or compromise, and they refused to accept excuses. When the White superintendent refused to distribute the scarce dollars from the state of Arkansas in an equitable manner, they used their personal funds to purchase essential learning resources. *The Weekly Reader,* for example, a popular social studies series, was purchased by them and made available to those whose parents could not afford the fifteen-cent price.

Mr. McNeil stood little more than five feet tall, but he was nevertheless a giant of a man whose handshake told you he was on a mission to prove the plantation owners wrong about the intellectual capacity of his students and their potential for greatness. I never saw him without a smile, a word of encouragement, or a necktie—unless he was picking cotton along with us to buy curtains for the school auditorium.

Mr. McNeil was a mentor long before the word appeared in the literature of education or business. He always addressed us students as *Mister* or *Miss*, never by our first names. Likewise, he accorded our parents the utmost respect by referring to them as *Mr.* or *Mrs.* It was as though he knew they needed the respect the plantation owners and straw bosses would never give them. Amazingly, I never heard the man yell or saw him frown. He was as predictable as they come. Even when paddling us, he kept his composure and never gave any indication that he took pleasure in it. In fact, it was as though it pained him to do this part of the job.

Standing right next to Mr. McNeil, albeit a few inches shorter, was his spouse of many years and partner in education. They were equally committed to making productive and contributing citizens of us, no matter what our status in the racially constricted Arkansas Delta. Mrs. McNeil was a master teacher who both believed and expected that every student could learn. To her, if you didn't produce, it meant you hadn't tried hard enough. Of course, this wasn't necessarily the case, since the life circumstances confronting us varied considerably.

Mrs. McNeil carried herself with an air of dignity without appearing to be arrogant or to think herself above those whose status on the socio-economic continuum was below hers. Her form of discipline was not the paddle employed by Mr. McNeil. Instead, she deployed a terribly painful pinch on the fleshy part of the bicep. The pinch was always accompanied by a smile and a quiet lecture about where you went wrong.

Four of her lessons have served me well over the years. First, you are more than the sum of your possessions. Second, you must always endeavor to do the right thing, no matter how many friends it may cost you. Third, courtesy is not loud. And last but definitely not least, always be your best self.

I first met Mr. and Mrs. McNeil when I was a fourth grader in 1955, following construction of a consolidated K–12 school and the closure of more than a dozen rural Rosenwald School buildings. Mr. McNeil served as principal, and the school was named in his honor shortly after it opened. The McNeils recognized my academic potential long before I did, and Mrs. McNeil anointed me as her little speech maker. When I entered high school, she signed me up for the school's debate team, insisted that I join student government, and entered me in every local and regional oratorical contest possible.

Several times each week, I'd spend an hour or so with her practicing my public-speaking skills. Her investment paid off when I won the Eastern Star Statewide Oratorical Contest in 1965. The winning prize was a $150 scholarship, which was more than enough to buy books my freshman year of college. Thanks to Mrs. McNeil, I went on to perfect my speaking skills and have given literally thousands of speeches across the United States and around the world. Although she rarely had the chance to hear me speak after I graduated high school, her comforting spirit is with me every time I give a speech.

The word that best characterizes the nature of village that nurtured me in the Arkansas Delta is *philanthropy*, in its broadest sense. What the village elders lacked in money was more than compensated for in a giving spirit and the personal investment in our development. As poor as members of

Shiloh Missionary Baptist Church were, they took up a free-will offering and presented it to those of us in the congregation who were brave enough to venture off into the uncharted waters of college.

When we returned home for holidays or occasional visits, the congregation honored us by giving us a chance to say a word or two. Those smiles, complete with missing teeth, signaled pride and happiness over the fact that a member of the village was on the road to success. I can still feel the hugs, smell the sweat, and hear them say, "Don't you forget us now." I have never forgotten the village that provided safe harbor for me and set me on my journey of a lifetime of leadership and service.

Today, when my soul looks back and wonders how I made it over, I can answer unequivocally that it was the God of our weary years and the God of our silent tears who kept us in his sight.

3

TACKS AND SPLINTERS

THE COTTON HARVEST WAS BEHIND US, AND PAPA used the meager settlement from Ed Copeland to buy school clothes for each of us. For the boys, that meant new high-top shoes, long johns (underwear), a couple pairs of ill-fitting denim jeans, two cotton-flannel shirts, a corduroy cap with let-down flaps to keep ears warm, and a lined, waist-length denim jumper. For the girls, it meant black-and-white Oxford shoes, several pairs of bobby socks, at least one skirt-and-blouse ensemble, one or two dresses, undergarments, and a sweater. If Mama had saved enough Green Stamps, she'd redeem them for fabric to make dresses for herself and the younger girls. If the harvest was poor, only the older kids got one or two new items; the younger ones, me included, got hand-me-downs with patches on patches and a baggy fit.

Third grade was my last year of attending Smith Perkins, the preschool through sixth grade Rosenwald school that had no more than fifty to sixty kids enrolled at any given time. When they closed all of the Rosenwald schools, McNeil School, the "colored" high school, enrolled all kids in grades preprimer through twelfth grade—all on the same campus but in different buildings. The school was named for our beloved principal Mr. Leroy R. McNeil.

The year was 1961, my freshman year of high school, and I was fifteen. There I stood with my school-age siblings in front of Shiloh Missionary Baptist Church, a mile from where we lived, shivering and waiting for Mr. Cleo Dotson, our bus driver by day and a coon hunter by night, to pick us for the forty-minute ride, punctuated by numerous stops along the way.

Although my classmates and I felt considerable trepidation about entering high school, the anxiety was somewhat ameliorated by the fact that the physical distance between the elementary and high schools was less than fifty yards. The elementary school was on one end of the building, and the high school was on the other. The building itself was also a one-story, utilitarian, redbrick structure with essentially no redeeming architectural features. However, compared to the Rosenwald school, McNeil High School was what I would imagine dying and going to heaven to be like.

Why do I say that? Because the building still had that new look, smell, and feel, and it had lots of windows that prevented us from feeling like we were in a cage. The building even had a library, although it was less than two hundred square feet. By the time I graduated from high school, I had read many of those books several times over. *Up from Slavery* was among my favorites, and the tattered pages were a testament to that fact. I reasoned that if Booker T. Washington could overcome slavery and go on to establish a college, surely I could graduate from high school.

Make no mistake about it, going to high school was a big deal in my day, when so many rural kids dropped out of school in seventh or eighth grade to drive tractors or move up north with their family in search of better job opportunities. There were approximately ninety students in my ninth-grade class, enough to populate classrooms 9A and 9B, but only seventeen were still enrolled by the time we graduated. Furthermore, since members of the all-White school board did not consider us to be college material, they felt no commitment to ensuring the availability of a comprehensive high-school curriculum.

The most generous way to describe the curriculum is bare bones: English, general mathematics, algebra, geometry, physical education, American history, vocational agriculture, and general biology. Although foreign languages and advanced courses in social studies and mathematics were considered part of the curriculum for comprehensive high schools, which McNeil High was, such courses weren't offered. No matter how many or how few students there were, there was only one teacher per content area, and that person taught as many sections or classes necessary to serve students. All students took the same courses whether they were gifted learners, needed special education, or were visually or hearing impaired.

Mr. Roland Jefferson—a tall, skinny, cross-eyed man with a stern demeanor—was the homeroom teacher for all students in 9A. Whether Mr. Jefferson or Mr. Ozell Twillie, an affable man with a big smile, was your homeroom teacher depended on where your last name fell alphabetically. Since *N* fell smack in the middle of the alphabet, it was my luck to get Mr. Jefferson, a man not known for tolerating gum chewing or laughing, let alone talking.

He demanded and commanded complete silence and obedience. Without advance warning, he was known to throw erasers at students, thump them on the head, hit them repeatedly on their thigh with his leather strap, or make them stand in the corner of the room facing the wall. We jokingly referred to Mr. Jefferson as the "Undertaker," only to discover later that he was indeed a licensed mortician! I had Mr. Jefferson not only for homeroom but also for algebra and biology. I never once saw the man crack a smile or utter words of encouragement to students. It was fear that motivated me to do well, not the joy of learning for its own sake. I simply wanted not to suffer the ire of Mr. Jefferson—or the pain inflected by his strap, Big Ben.

* * *

Truth be told, I didn't have a favorite subject in high school, and it was often pure drudgery just getting through the day. However, I was fortunate to have a favorite teacher who did relate to his students in ways that made us want to learn. That teacher was Mr. Milton D. Mozell, who was not much older than his students. He taught us vocational agriculture, and so much more. McNeil High School was his first and only teaching assignment, eventually spanning more than three decades.

I remember the first time I met Mr. Mozell. It was a chilly but sunny January afternoon as all of us ninth-grade boys made our way, single file, to the newly constructed shop building, adjacent to the structure that housed middle and high school students. At that time, girls did not take Ag classes. Upon arrival, we were greeted by this nattily attired, articulate, warm, and newly minted teacher, who introduced himself simply as Milton D. Mozell. Before attempting to teach, he took time to tell us about himself, his family, and his expectations for us. He then had each of us stand up and tell him and our fellow classmates something about who we were and what we wanted to learn in his course, including the grade we expected to earn. As each student spoke, Mr. Mozell took meticulous notes, and those notes later served as the basis for individual and group conversations he had with us about our performance. Without hesitation, he would refer back to what we'd told him and our fellow students we wanted to learn.

Although corporal punishment was a commonly accepted disciplinary practice in the 1960s, I never saw Mr. Mozell paddle a student, send a student to the principal's office, or embarrass anyone in front of others. On the other hand, he'd ask you a series of questions, and by the time you finished answering them, you found yourself wishing he had paddled you!

Clearly, you knew exactly where you had erred and what you needed to do to avoid the same mistake. He was a master teacher who respected each student—from the most advanced and best-prepared learner to those who needed extra time or assistance.

One of the earliest lessons I learned from Mr. Mozell was the importance of self-discipline. When a student misbehaved, Mr. Mozell would ask these questions: Why did you do it? How did it make you feel? Do you know why your behavior was inappropriate? How do you think it made your fellow students feel? How do you think your parents would feel about your behavior? If you were to do things differently, what would you do and why? He would then have the offending student apologize to his fellow students for being a distraction and bringing disrepute to everyone.

In the years since having Mr. Mozell as a teacher and mentor, I have had a chance to reflect on what made him such an excellent, effective, and memorable teacher. First and foremost, he had a profound respect for every student and believed that we could all learn. Second, he recognized that teaching people took precedence over teaching content. Third, he understood that effective teaching required buy-in and commitment from each student. Fourth, he recognized the power of collective learning and peer influence. Finally, he accepted the challenge of teaching far more than just the content of his discipline.

If he needed to teach grammar, writing, speech, or math as prerequisites for mastery of vocational agriculture, he did so without complaining. So profound were the lessons I learned from Mr. Mozell that they became the foundation of my philosophy of teaching and leadership, spanning a career that lasted more than four decades. Perhaps the most important lesson I learned from Mr. Mozell was the recognition that education is the engine of opportunity, no matter a person's starting point in life.

* * *

With rare exceptions, the curriculum of most rural schools in the Arkansas Delta focused on the acquisition of basic literacy skills, not preparation for college or entry into apprenticeship programs. Since schools operated on a split session and the curriculum was not comprehensive, extracurricular activities were severely limited or nonexistent. There were no clubs like honor societies, language clubs, Future Teachers of America, Future Nurses of America, typing club, and so on. Basically, there were four clubs providing broad-based participation opportunities for Negroes: 4-H Club, for boys and girls; New Homemakers of America, for girls only; New Farmers of America, for boys only; and the school choir. There was basketball in winter and track and field in spring for boys and girls. Football was not an option, as the split session had us in the cotton field harvesting the crop during football season.

For farm kids, Black or White, 4-H Club was more than a social club. It complemented our school lessons by allowing us to test the ideals and theories that were an essential part of civic education and service learning, long before those concepts enjoyed the popularity they do today. My introduction to the Farmer's Home Administration (FHA) came through my participation in every 4-H Club activity imaginable, including gardening, showing animals at the county fair, mastering parliamentary procedures, hiking, and refining public-speaking skills, among other activities.

One summer day while I was still in high school, a well-dressed young man came to our house to speak with my parents. Mr. Thomas Vaughn was an FHA agent in his late twenties who wanted to enroll us in the 4-H Club. Although the membership fee was only twenty-five cents per month per child, for a family with eight eligible kids, that was a lot of money, and my parents struggled daily to make ends meet financially.

Papa had patches on patches on his overalls, yet Mr. Vaughn constantly referred to him as Mr. Nelms, never by his first name, Eddie. I was so impressed by Mr. Vaughn's authenticity, passion, and interpersonal communication skills that I decided this was the kind of job I'd like to have some day: meeting people on their turf and seeing how I could help them and their children enjoy a higher quality of life.

I felt strongly that as an FHA agent, I could help poor farm families like mine and could earn a good living for myself in the process. Obtaining a degree from Arkansas AM&N would be the first step in the process of achieving my dreams. The important role played by the teachers at McNeil High School notwithstanding, it was Mr. Vaughn who convinced my parents to enroll us in 4-H and convinced them that they could do without my older brother Willie and my sister Carrie on the farm. More than a decade later, my wife, Jeanetta, taught Mr. Vaughn's children as a first year math teacher in 1968. Mr. Vaughn and my dad remained good friends until Papa died in 1985.

As fate would have it, the Vietnam War came along, and I took a different path. I never worked for the FHA, but thanks to that entity, 4-H Club, and Mr. Vaughn, my career achievements exceeded anything I ever thought possible. Long retired and approaching one hundred years of age, Mr. Vaughn lives independently in Pine Bluff, Arkansas. When I last saw Mr. Vaughn in 2010, he was still wearing that big smile of his, and he reflected on his relationship with my dad. "Charlie," he said, "your father would be awfully proud of you and your sisters and brothers."

In retrospect, had it not been for my involvement in extracurricular activities like 4-H Club and a handful of teachers who took a personal interest in my personal, social, and intellectual development, I probably would have been among the Black migrants from Crittenden County who made their way to Flint to work for General Motors or AC Spark Plugs, or to Detroit to work for the Ford or Chrysler Corporations.

I might have ended up like those whose lives were explored by the Black journalist Isabel Wilkerson in her 2010 *New York Times* best seller, *The Warmth of Other Suns*. In her book, Wilkerson creates an intimate epic by focusing on the lives of three individuals to tell the broader story of the Great Migration. Former President Obama chose it for his summer reading in 2011, and in 2012, the *New York Times* named *The Warmth of Other Suns* to its list of the best nonfiction books of all time. Wilkerson is the first Black woman to win a Pulitzer Prize for journalism, in 1994, when she was Chicago bureau chief for the *New York Times*. Her book, which began as a labor of love inspired by her own parents' migration up north, required fifteen years of research and more than one thousand interviews. Their stories could also have been mine.

Reading Wilkerson's book made me more grounded in the historical and cultural context of the migration of many of my relatives and neighbors from the Arkansas Delta to places "Up North." And it reminded me why land and education were so entwined and important to my parents. Without land to call your own or knowledge to guide you, you were at risk, at the mercy of others. In too many cases, as we'd seen, those others in power could not be counted on to have your best interests at heart. Simply put, land and education could be the path to greater freedom, autonomy, and choice, some of the most precious gifts that slavery and its bitter legacy tried so hard to deny us.

* * *

When I was a kid in the racially segregated Arkansas Delta, besides 4-H and other clubs, there weren't many fun-filled activities for young people. Life revolved around farm work, school, and church. There were small cinemas—*picture shows*, as we called them—in Crawfordsville, the nearest town, and West Memphis, a few miles farther east, where you could see a movie if you had the fifteen cents for a ticket and were willing to bear the indignities of sitting in the balcony. I saw a total of three movies between the time I was born and graduated high school. I simply refused to bow down to segregation and sit in the balcony. Likewise, I refused to order food from the back or side doors of restaurants and never ate out as a high school student. It was my own way of protesting American-style apartheid.

* * *

On a cold day in January 1962, Principal McNeil paged me to report immediately to his office. Although I was less than a model student, I was known to be respectful of authority and a mediator in matters pertaining to student disagreements; I was a respected peacemaker. Mr. McNeil began the conversation by saying, "Nelms, I've been watching you, and I'm impressed with your deportment, temperament, and leadership skills. The boys' and girls' basketball teams need a scorekeeper, and I believe you're ideally suited for the job. Would you be interested?"

I was pleased beyond measure and responded affirmatively without adequately considering how I would get home following home and road games. After all, we lived more than five miles from school on a dirt road, and we didn't have a car. Being the basketball scorekeeper turned out to be one of the most important extracurricular activities in which I ever participated. I learned the importance of attention to details and being on time, every time.

From scorekeeper, I was promoted to clock operator, undoubtedly one of the most important jobs in the game of basketball. The respect and recognition accorded me by members of the home and visiting teams exceeded anything I had ever imagined. Mr. Twillie, the basketball coach, would often drop me off in front of Shiloh Missionary Baptist Church. Then I'd make the mile-long walk home on dark or moonlit nights, or I'd spend the night with Lonnie Beard, a classmate and McNeil High's star basketball player. It was during this stage of life that I learned to appreciate the true meaning of friendship and what it means to be your brother's keeper.

In addition to my unpaid jobs with the basketball team, I was named captain of McNeil High's debate team, where I quickly developed a reputation for being a fierce competitor and skilled rebuttalist, who instilled fear in the hearts of opposing team members. Because of my debate skills, I was soon tapped by our school's student government sponsor, Mrs. Mary Miller, to run for Student Government Association (SGA) president and to represent McNeil School at oratorical contests throughout eastern Arkansas.

Every few weeks I was being shuttled by Mrs. Miller, Mr. McNeil, or Mr. Mozell to an oratorical competition of one type or another in small communities adjoining my home county of Crittenden. Without fail, if my debate team didn't win, we always managed to finish in the top three. Back then, I had a near-photographic memory and could memorize nearly anything, no matter how long. Every day, sometimes twice a day, I found myself standing in front of one of the teachers and reciting a speech. They made sure that my pronunciation and enunciation were accurate and timed just right. The skills I perfected back in high school have served me well, as I have gone on to speak formally or impromptu without fear to audiences around the world.

Historically, school and church have had an enormous and irrefutable impact on the Black community. Before the days of economic, social, and political prosperity now enjoyed by many Blacks, the church was a refuge from the evils of racial segregation and White dominance that held sway over our lives from birth to death. The church was the *one* place where Blacks could be in charge, if only for a few hours of the week. The church was more than a place of worship; it instilled in many of us young people the idea that we didn't have to wait until we got to heaven to enjoy the fruits of our labor. I think it's safe to say that had it not been for the Black church, the civil rights movement would not have achieved the level of success it did, and I definitely would not have achieved the level of professional success that I did. Led in many instances by pastors who had been *called* to preach rather than trained to do so, both adult and youth protesters came from the pews of the Black church.

Although barely literate, Reverend George Mitchell, pastor of Shiloh Missionary Baptist Church, the place where my family and I worshipped, understood the importance of education. I don't recall ever hearing him preach a sermon without referencing the importance of education. A jet-black, impeccably dressed man with dyed, wavy hair held in place by a stocking cap during the week, Reverend Mitchell had a penchant for black suits, brightly polished shoes, and stiffly starched white shirts. He was steeped in the traditions of the Missionary Baptist Church movement.

He pastored two rural churches: Shiloh on first and third Sundays, and Philadelphia on second and fourth Sundays. The churches were less than ten miles apart and had a combined membership of fewer than one hundred parishioners. Where Reverend Mitchell acquired his organizing skills, I'll never know, because he never completed elementary school, let alone high school. Be that as it may, under his two decades of leadership, Shiloh had one of the most active Baptist Training Unions (BTUs) in the Tyronza Missionary Baptist Church District.

BTU was a platform for mastering parliamentary procedures, acquiring basic public-speaking skills, and becoming familiar with the church doctrine and history of the Black Baptist Church. I credit Reverend Mitchell for instilling in me an appreciation for public speaking, because he chose me to welcome visitors and make church announcements when I was in eighth grade. Those were the days before printed church bulletins filled with announcements and the names of those who needed prayer. I would later perfect those skills in college and throughout my forty-year career in the academy.

Although not deliberately planned, there was enormous overlap and reinforcement between high school extracurricular activities and church youth activities. An excellent example was the focus on public speaking and leadership development, both of which were priorities in 4-H Club and vocational agriculture. Rather than a favorite subject, extracurricular activities and a couple teachers were what made school an enjoyable experience for me. I was active 4-H Club, and with encouragement from the principal's wife, Mrs. Veola McNeil, and from Mr. Mozell, public speaking and oratory became my highest priority. I'd spend a couple of hours every day rehearsing a speech for an upcoming competition or honing my debate skills. At the risk of tooting my own horn, I've been commended many times for my ability to speak forcefully and extemporaneously.

* * *

On a hot humid morning in 1965, I stood before a jury of eight Black women who were all dressed in white dresses, gloves, and stockings to deliver my speech at the Masonic lodge on the corner of Fourth and Jefferson Streets in Pine Bluff, Arkansas. Neither Mrs. McNeil nor Mrs. Miller, my coaches, was there in person, but their spirits were right there next to me. Mr. Holiday, the farm manager at Arkansas AM&N for whom I worked milking Holstein cows, had given me the morning off to fulfill my last commitment from high school. Shoulders back and head high, just as I had been taught, I delivered a thirty-minute speech from memory about the importance of personal values and the way they determine who we are and what we become. I hit a home run and won the statewide Eastern Star Statewide Oratorical Contest. My prize was a $150 scholarship, enough to buy my college textbooks for a year.

This was well before the days of emails and texting, so I sat down and wrote letters to each of those teachers from McNeil High School who'd invested so much in me, thanking each of them for their support and confidence in me. That winning speech with the $150 prize gave me the confidence that I had the ability to lead and communicate with passion and in ways that captured the hearts of my listeners. Since we had no telephone, I could not call Mama and Papa to share my good news with them. So I did the next best thing; I wrote them a letter. In Mama's response, she said simply, "That's good, Charlie." I knew they were proud of me, but it was not their way to shower their children with fulsome praise or fawn over our accomplishments. Unlike today, when bluster and hyperbole have become the norm in some public discourse and on the Internet, my parents valued modesty and hard work. They, along with my teachers, pastor, and members of the community, all expected the best from me, as I did from myself.

*   *   *

"How many of y'all want to go to college? Raise your hands! Raise them high!"

Looking straight at me, the questioner asked, "Boy, you want to go to college? Don't be shy! Raise your hand high!"

Feeling a surge of energy, excitement, and uncertainty, four other high school students and I raised our hands high that day. And I continued to do so every time the question was asked thereafter. The person who asked the question of us was Mr. Jesse Mason Sr., an agent with the FHA. A college classmate of the McNeil's, Mr. Mason, a short, dark-skinned man, had an air of arrogance about him that often got in the way of his ability to connect with the poor Black farmers he was hired to help.

In addition to helping subsistence farmers improve crop practices for increased yields and less land erosion, Mr. Mason was also charged with helping them secure FHA loans to build or remodel their homes or purchase farm equipment, land, seeds, and fertilizer—whatever was needed to improve the quality of life. Despite their level of need or the willingness to put up their land as collateral, I don't ever recall a Black farmer receiving a loan. The farmers responded with a sense of resignation and helplessness, because they had no true advocates on their behalf. More often than not, because of the FHA's history of discrimination, Mr. Mason was perceived as an adversary rather than as an advocate.

* * *

Even though one of my older brothers, Willie, was a student at Mississippi Industrial College in Holy Springs, Mississippi, and my sister Carrie was enrolled at Arkansas AM&N in Pine Bluff, I did not consider college within my reach. After all, I reasoned, they were both so much smarter than me, and my parents could barely feed our family, let alone afford to lose yet a third field hand to college. One of the two times I saw my father moved to tears was when my sister Carrie told him and Mama that she wanted to go to college to study nursing. Although poorer than church mice, my parents borrowed $300 against their unharvested cotton crop in 1963, and Papa hired a friend to drive him and Carrie to Pine Bluff. With Carrie in tow and his hat in his hand, Papa went directly to see the college president, Dr. L. A. Davis Sr., in his office when they reached campus.

Recounting the story many years later, Carrie said that after introducing her and himself, Papa said, "My daughter wanna be a nurse. Here is three hundred dollars toward tuition and board. I'll pay you the rest when I finish picking my crop."

Unbeknown to Papa, his situation was quite similar to other Black families with children attending Arkansas AM&N. When I enrolled at the same college two years later and had the privilege of meeting President Davis at a reception for new students, he recalled having met my father, and he told me how impressed he was with my father's commitment to education and devotion to his family. When I became a college president and encountered parents who wanted their kids to go to college but didn't have the funds required to enroll, I never hesitated to call the Financial Aid Office and tell, not ask, the director to accommodate the family—and that I'd pay if they failed to do so. During my three college presidencies, only a handful of parents ever defaulted on these loans.

* * *

Any way you look at it, life in the Arkansas Delta was difficult, dangerous, and unforgiving. When we weren't trying to dodge the suffocating effects of American-style apartheid, my peers and I were dodging stray bullets fired by drunken or jealous husbands and boyfriends at the honky-tonks we frequented in search of a good time. Except for worship services, occasional church evening picnics also known as box suppers, or basketball games, teenagers had few social outlets. So we slipped off to forbidden places—the honky-tonks equipped with jukeboxes and occasionally live bands, where we could dance in a back room while adult men shot dice and women played blackjack or poker up front. The buildings did not have air conditioning, windows, or fire alarms, but that did not deter us from having a good time. The admissions fee was twenty-five cents for a night of necking, frivolity, and fun—except if a fight erupted when one woman said something to another woman's man, or a man said something to another man's woman. When bullets rang out, we would run for cover. Needless to say, our parents had no idea that we were at the honky-tonk. They thought we were visiting friends or at church.

Bullets weren't our only worry at honky-tonks; fire was an even greater threat. Many of the most popular places were located in rural communities with one door in and one door out, and that was the front door. There was no fire department or emergency medical technicians with ambulances to come to our rescue. Even so, we frequented these places to our own potential peril. Occasionally, one of the emerging stars—such as B. B. King, Johnny Taylor, Wilson Pickett, Al Green, or Bobby "Blue" Bland—would drop by the Top Hat at Black Fish Lake, Arkansas, a few miles from our house, for an unannounced jam session. Oh, what a session!

Johnny Taylor, a master vocalist in a wide range of music from blues, gospel, soul, doo-wop, rhythm and blues, and later disco, was born in the hamlet of Gregory, not far from Crawfordsville, Arkansas, the nearest town to where I grew up and in which McNeil High was located. B. B. King had a daughter who was in the class behind me. And his guitar, Lucille, got her name as a result of a fire that broke out at a honky-tonk in Heath, Arkansas, where King was performing. The woman who started the fire, Lucille, knocked over a kerosene stove when she got into a fight with her man—or so the legend goes. Music has remained an important part of my life ever since.

* * *

My classmates and I had to contend with every distraction imaginable from the time we were born until the time we dropped out of high school, graduated, or caught the Greyhound bus to some northern city in search of a better way of life. Although eighty-nine of us started high school, only seventeen graduated, while the other sixty-two went in numerous directions, including the military. Sammie Lou Johnson, Bobbie Jean Thornton, and I were the three who went directly to college, while several others would enroll later and graduate. The valedictorian of our class, the girl who stole my heart at an early age, decided against enrolling in college immediately after high school.

As fate would have it, a decade later our paths crossed when I was a graduate student at Teachers College, Columbia University in Manhattan. While waiting for the A train, someone sweetly called out, "Charlie Nelms, is that you?" The moment still resonates with me. It was the first and only time I'd seen her since graduating high school over fifty years ago. Except for Jeanetta, the woman to whom I have been married for nearly fifty years, the valedictorian of my class and my high school crush is the smartest person I've ever met. When I think back on what my classmates could have achieved had they received the encouragement and support I did, I am overwhelmed with gratitude. And I've made it my life's mission to offer that encouragement and support to others whenever I can.

* * *

There are moments from my youth that are still painful to remember. More than sixty years after my brother Willie's release from jail and five years following his death, I am still haunted by the pain his racist incarceration for a crime he never committed caused him and my family, especially my mother. On a cold, rainy January night in 1963, a Negro allegedly broke into an apartment in Crawfordsville, Arkansas, approximately five miles from where we lived, and sexually assaulted a White teacher. The next day, the local police chief, accompanied by the teacher, arrived at our high school, determined to identify the Negro boy who allegedly assaulted her. Looking at a crowd of teenage boys, the teacher pointed to my brother and said, "That's him." Just like that, my brother was transported to the Crittenden County Jail, a fortresslike, overcrowded antebellum facility in Marion, Arkansas. The next day he was marched before a county judge, where he was ordered held without bail pending trial.

My family and Negroes throughout the school and community were incredulous. Since it was a rainy night and we lived on a dirt road five miles from town—and we didn't have a car—we knew it was impossible for my brother to get out of bed in the middle of the night and walk that distance in the mud and rain, get back home before daybreak, and head to school.

I especially knew better because Willie and I slept in the same bed. But a White woman alleged that my brother was the perpetrator, and that was the end of the story. Clearly, White was always right back then, and sadly it remains so too often even today.

My parents, along with Black farmers in the areas, were so convinced of Willie's innocence that they attempted to put up their farms as collateral to secure his release. Not surprisingly, the local police chief, county judge, and White school superintendent would not consent. Thus Willie languished in jail for six months without shoes, belt, blanket, or any of the comforts normally accorded prisoners.

While Willie was awaiting trial, someone broke into an apartment complex occupied by two Black teachers in the same little town. The person was apprehended and jailed. He later confessed to assaulting the White teacher as well, and he was sentenced to life in prison. Following that person's conviction and sentencing, Willie was released from jail with neither apology nor compensation. The racist old police chief dropped him off a mile from our house, where he made the trek home barefoot on the dirt road on a chilly spring day. I can still see the tears streaming down Mama's face as she embraced him with such force that he thought she'd squeeze him to death. It's a homecoming I have never forgotten—and never will.

Perhaps the thing I found most surprising about Willie's jail experience was his reaction following his release. Amazingly, he did not show any anger or bitterness toward his accuser and jailors. It was as though he was able to tap into a personal reservoir of strength, valor, and resolve that prevented the segregationists from defeating his spirit. As a result of inadequate nutrition and caloric intake, Willie had lost more than twenty pounds while in jail. However, he emerged from his jail cell with inexplicable serenity, focus, fearlessness, and optimism.

Already a good student, Willie became an even better one. The Crawfordsville Public Library was off limits to Negroes, until Willie decided not long after his release from jail that it was time for this practice to end. He walked into the building and proceeded to pull books from the shelf to read while there and to check out upon leaving. From that point forward, Willie became a regular library patron without incident, and so did the less courageous among us. Of course, our parents feared for our safety every time we set foot in the facility. Willie once told me that his time in jail provided him an opportunity for deep reflection and introspection. He also said that while in prison, he developed a strategy for escaping the horrific and debilitating effects of racism. The centerpiece of Willie's strategy was to use education rather than anger to drive his actions.

* * *

I had a childhood playmate who was not as lucky as Willie. That person was Jerry, a carefree boy my age with an easy laugh and quick wit, known for his trash-talking and for making us teenagers laugh. For the most part, all Blacks in and around Crawfordsville knew each other, because we played and prayed together, picked and chopped cotton together, and attended the same school. There were no strangers or outcasts among us. We were all poor Blacks trying to navigate the throes of racial segregation and degradation while staying alive in the process. As such, we developed close relationships with each other whether we wanted to or not; it was all about mutual support and survival. When one person suffered a personal or family tragedy, we all grieved and came to each other's defense. We were a community, where no person was an island.

On this particular summer Sunday, farm families from miles and miles around gathered at Ephesian Missionary Baptist Church, situated on the banks of Buck Lake, approximately four miles from my house, for the funeral services of my childhood friend Jerry. He had been gunned down the week before by a Crittenden County sheriff's deputy for allegedly making inappropriate comments to a White girl. When the officer attempted to arrest him, Jerry panicked and started running, whereupon the officer shot him in the back and killed him.

Officer Billy Gladstone, the person who murdered Jerry, had a reputation for beating Negroes with his police blackjack and for arresting them because he considered himself the law rather than an agent charged with protecting people and property. If he said you were speeding or that you had been drinking, it didn't matter if it was true or not; his word carried the day, and the sheriff and the justice of the peace believed him.

The only ones who could rescue a Black person from the abuses of Billy Gladstone were the plantation owners, who promised their tractor drivers and cotton choppers that if they stayed out of the grave, they would keep them out of jail. The only exception to this pledge was if a Black person allegedly "got out of place" with a White girl or woman. The best known example of getting out of place is that of Emmett Till, a fourteen-year-old Black boy from Chicago who was beaten, mutilated, shot, and dumped into the Tallahatchie River by a group of White men while visiting his family in Money, Mississippi, for allegedly flirting with a White girl. When Till's body was returned to Chicago, his mother insisted on a public funeral service with an open casket to make the world witness the brutality of the killing.

Whether or not my friend Jerry said anything inappropriate to the young White girl, we will never know, because dead people can't talk. But Billy Gladstone said he did, and that was all that mattered. As we gathered at Ephesian Missionary Baptist Church that hot July day in 1960, we mourners were shrouded in fear, sadness, and hopelessness. There was talk of the local chapter of the NAACP filing a lawsuit against Gladstone and the sheriff's department. No one knew what punishment would be inflicted on the Black community if a lawsuit was indeed filed. There was even talk that Gladstone was a member of the Ku Klux Klan, and they would take retribution if one of their members in a position of authority was challenged publicly.

If I listen hard enough, I can still hear Jerry's mother screaming uncontrollably as the undertaker and the Black grave diggers lowered his body into the ground. She kept asking, "Why, God? Why?"

I had never felt more helpless or sad than I did that day. Like everyone around me, I was confused, and I was angry at White people and at God for allowing Billy Gladstone to take my friend's life. During the brief funeral services, I remember hearing the preacher say, "God is a just God, and he will equip us with everything we need to bear our burdens." Although I was only fourteen years of age, I asked myself, "Why must we bear this burden, and where is this just God when we need him?"

Two weeks after Jerry's funeral, we got our answer when Billy Gladstone fell dead of a massive heart attack. We were convinced that this was the just God of whom the preacher was speaking!

* * *

Despite the profound personal impact racism had on me while growing up in the Arkansas Delta, I made three very important decisions that would influence me for the entirety of my life. First, I decided that I would never treat others the way I was treated because of their race, gender, or any other physical characteristic. Before I knew there was no biological basis for race, I knew intuitively that it was an irrational and indefensible reason to hate others. Of course, I would later learn through courses I took in college that race is a social construct designed to create a rationale for dominance, power, and control on the part of White oppressors.

Second, I decided that I would not allow myself to be blinded by hate and have it distract me from my efforts to dismantle racism, bigotry, intolerance, and injustice. During the days of my youth, how Black people expressed their anger, disagreement, or disapproval of the actions of White people could get them killed. While I was often very angry working in the fields from sunup to sundown, I learned to deflect my anger by dreaming and plotting a way out of those conditions. I knew that hating White people meant giving them control over my thoughts, body, and soul—which I was unwilling to do.

Third, I promised myself, "When I get grown, I'm going to change this shit." I knew that to change this shit, I had to equip myself with the knowledge, skills, and experiences required to do so. I knew I that I had to learn to express myself in clear, passionate, and professional ways. I had to be able to forge effective working relationships with people of goodwill, no matter their color. In the words of my favorite Langston Hughes poem, "Mother to Son," life for me "ain't been no crystal stair." I had already seen life's splinters and hard tacks, its "boards torn up" with "no carpet on the floor— / Bare."[1] I'd seen the dark corners where there was no light. Yet I also knew I could use my voice for those who'd been silenced. Life for us was clearly no crystal stair, but I would keep climbing. I had already decided that nothing could stop me from trying to make those changes I knew needed to be made.

4

COLLEGE BOUND

O<small>N MAY 9, 1965, JUST THREE DAYS AFTER</small> my high school graduation, Mr. Mozell picked me up in his white, four-door, 1963 Biscayne Chevrolet. It was around nine o'clock in the morning, and we were embarking on the four-hour drive to Pine Bluff, with our destination Arkansas AM&N. Never having taken an overnight or extended trip in my life, I didn't own a suitcase, nor did anyone in my family. Miss Jane, our farm neighbor about a mile east of us, was kind enough to loan me one of the nice suitcases she used for her trips to and from Chicago to visit her sister. Miss Jane had no children but took a liking to me and let me perform odd jobs around her house and yard, for which she'd pay me twenty-five to fifty cents, depending on how long it took. I know that doesn't sound like a lot of money, but when you're truly poor, a little money can make a big difference. Fifty cents was enough money to buy several pounds of neck bones or ham hocks, which Mama would use to season the turnip greens or pinto beans we'd have for dinner the next day.

Every item of clothing I owned (worth taking to college) fit in Miss Jane's suitcase—and there was room to spare. I had used the little money people had given me as graduation gifts, along with a few dollars I'd managed to save from my shoe-shining job at Mr. Leroy's barber shop, to buy underwear, a couple of shirts, jeans, a straw hat, and a pair of used high-top shoes, which Mr. A. T., the Negro shoe cobbler who worked at Miss Rose's shoe shop in Crawfordsville, had managed to give a new lease on life. Following all my purchases, I had a whopping sum of $10.25 to my name.

All Mama and Papa could offer me were their prayers, love, and best wishes for success. On that hot, humid summer Sunday, I gave Mama a quick hug and Papa a handshake. I left the house without looking back, for fear that I would break down and cry or, worse still, change my mind. That day when I left my parents' house on my way to a little Negro college in Pine Bluff, I had in mind my favorite poem by Robert Frost. I, too, was taking "the road less traveled," filled with hope that it would make all the difference.

The only thing that exceeded my fear was the determination not to disappoint Mama and Papa or those teachers who had invested so much time in my development. Although I didn't have any money to speak of, I had everything I needed to be successful; I had hope. Little did I know at the time that this thing called *hope* would sustain me during the good times and the bad times for the rest of my life.

* * *

My decision to attend AM&N had less to do with a personal choice and more to do with which of the total of three bachelor-degree-granting Negro colleges in my state—Arkansas Baptist, Philander Smith, or AM&N—offered me admission and provided the best opportunity for actually earning a degree. Also foremost in my mind was cost. At AM&N, I knew that I could get a job working on the college farm to help cover college costs. I couldn't do this at the other Black colleges, which were liberal arts institutions without as many chances for work study—and without college farms.

In 1965, only a handful of Arkansas's predominately White colleges would admit a Black student. For those lucky enough to be admitted, paying for the college tuition and fees, room and board, and books was a monumental task. This was well before the days of federal and state grants and loans to help cover the cost for college. During that era, working one's way through college was possible, and some students worked as many as three jobs to make college attendance possible.

The route to Pine Bluff wasn't completely foreign to me, since my older brother Eddie had let me ride with him once when he went to pick up my sister Carrie from college for the Christmas break. As Mr. Mozell maneuvered his Biscayne along Highways 70 and 79 East, past and through small hamlets like Black Fish Lake, Heth, Stump City, Horse Shoe Lake, Hughes, Haynes, Cotton Plant, Mariana, Brinkley, Altheimer, and Clarendon, he dispensed words of encouragement and wisdom to my friend Tommy Pounders and me about college life and what we needed to do to be successful.

While I wanted to think positively about college, I could not help but entertain the possibility that Mr. Holiday, the college farm manager, would not be willing to hire us as student workers. If that were the case, I'd have no choice but to make my way to Chicago to look for work or to face the high probability of being drafted and sent to Vietnam, like many of my friends and acquaintances. My spirits lifted as we passed through Stuttgart, the home of the Riceland Rice Company and the duck capital of America, where I spotted the sign "Pine Bluff: 38 Miles." While rice was an inexpensive dietary staple during the days of my youth, until that drive on May 9, 1965, I had no idea that so much of it was grown in Arkansas.

As my little Timex watch signaled 2:00 p.m., Mr. Mozell slowed the Biscayne down, just to make sure he was below the speed limit and wouldn't attract the attention of a White cop and end up getting a speeding ticket, or worse. Just inside the city limits stood the college, surrounded by a magnificent grove of mature white pine trees on our right and the athletic complex consisting of the football stadium, a track, and Hazzard Gymnasium on our left.

In his polite, optimistic, and energetic voice, Mr. Mozell said, "Gentlemen, welcome to my alma mater, AM&N College. I'm confident you'll love it here."

Just beyond the campus stood rows of white clapboard houses, whose owners rented room to students. Intermingled among the houses were several churches, along with the infamous Duck Inn Cafe and Black-owned restaurants that sold fried chicken, hamburgers, and hot dogs. There were also auto shops and Mr. Alexander's grocery store, which catered to the needs of college students. Mr. Mozell's prediction was spot on. The three years I spent at AM&N were some of the happiest years of my life.

Approximately fifteen minutes after reaching Pine Bluff, we arrived at the home of Mr. O. R. Holiday, chair of the Department of Agriculture and farm manager, and his wife, Mrs. Irma Holiday, a teacher in the Pine Bluff School District. Given to southern hospitality, the Holidays welcomed us with the kind of warmth I had never experienced from strangers before or since. After a restroom break, we settled into overstuffed chairs.

"Honey, these boys must be starving!" said Mrs. Holiday. With those words, she served us the most delicious bologna sandwich I'd ever eaten, with plenty of mayo, and the sweetest ice tea I'd ever drunk, topped off with big, chunky, chocolate chip cookies.

After sizing us up, Mr. Holiday, a handsome, olive-skinned man in his mid-fifties, finally decided to speak. "Mozell tells me that y'all are smart boys, well behaved and hardworking. Mozell worked for me when he was in college, and I trust his judgment. Based on his recommendation, I'm willing to give you fellows a chance if you're serious about going to college. My only request is that you keep your word. Let's head over to the campus, and get you settled in the dorm. I'll see you at seven tomorrow morning at the college farm."

And so began my affiliation with Arkansas AM&N, a love affair that has lasted more than fifty years and shows no sign of abating.

* * *

On this particular May Monday in 1965, two weeks after commencing my job on the college farm, I joined several hundred anxious and sweaty-faced freshmen in Caldwell Hall's auditorium, which, needless to say, was not air conditioned. Caldwell Hall was one of the most utilized buildings at Arkansas AM&N. It was home to offices that housed the president, vice presidents, deans, and a wide range of units that provided support services to students. The centerpiece of the building was a simple yet elegant auditorium, which served as the venue for mandatory Sunday afternoon vesper services. It was also the venue where visiting dignitaries like Dr. Martin Luther King Jr., Dr. Benjamin Mays, and Dr. Mary McLeod Bethune addressed the student body, where Marian Anderson performed, and where the college choir performed Handel's *Messiah* to overflow audiences. It was where the Student Government Association showed doubleheader suspense or romance movies nearly every Sunday night for a token fee of twenty-five cents. Later, Caldwell Hall Auditorium would be the place for a much sadder occasion. It was where my fellow students and I came together upon learning that Dr. Martin Luther King Jr. had been assassinated.

We were all waiting to learn how we had performed on the American College Testing (ACT) and what classes we would be taking our first year of college. While all students were required to take the ACT before having their admissions finalized, I never met a student denied admissions because of his or her test score. If applicants had indeed been required to achieve a certain score, I'm sure my composite score of four would have left me out in the cold.

An unknowing passerby looking at all of those Black faces gathered in the auditorium that day may have erroneously concluded that the place was chaotic and dysfunctional, but it wasn't. Within the crowd were four Freshmen Studies instructors who doubled as academic advisors. Surrounded by a group of students waiting their turn to be advised was the most beautiful and elegantly dressed lady I'd ever seen in my life.

A chocolate-complexioned woman in her late sixties, with every strand of her salt-and-pepper hair in place, Mrs. Gladys Smith, my advisor-to-be, flashed a reassuring smile that only the angels could have arranged for a frightened freshman like me. As I reflect on it now, Mrs. Smith looked a lot like the color photos in *Ebony* magazine, except the women in those photos were lighter skinned. Before the days when James Brown proclaimed, "I'm Black, and I'm proud," or Steve Biko and other Black-consciousness movement leaders proudly declared that "Black is beautiful," women of Mrs. Smith or my mother's color almost never appeared in magazines, whether Black or White owned.

It's a little-known fact that *Black is beautiful* were words spoken well before the 1960s. John S. Rock, an African American abolitionist who was the first Black person to be admitted to the bar of the Supreme Court of the United States, paraphrased them in a speech in 1858.[1] Of course, seeing Black women and men like my parents, pastor, and my favorite mentor, Mrs. McNeil, on a frequent basis, I already knew that Black was beautiful, whether or not light-skinned women were featured over darker-skinned women in magazines.

After what seemed like an eternal wait, I found myself being invited to have a seat by the woman with the angelic smile and patient disposition. Upon hearing my name, she searched through the files of what looked like a cardboard box, until she came up with a file bearing my name. After studying my transcript, ACT scores, and profile for a few minutes, Mrs. Smith looked up and said to me, "Mr. Nelms, your scores are sort of low, but if you follow this program, you'll be all right."

The ACT was a standardized college-admissions test introduced in 1959 as a competitor to the College Board's Scholastic Aptitude Test (SAT). The ACT consisted of four tests: English, math, social studies, and natural sciences. Since I had never taken a standardized test before or heard of statistics, I had no idea what it meant to have a low score. All I knew for sure was that while taking the ACT, I got off a line or two when circling those little bubbles associated with my responses. I grew increasingly frustrated and never got back on track. I ended up with one of the lowest scores ever recorded in the history of the test. The schedule Mrs. Smith handed me that day included all remedial classes; they're called *developmental courses* these days. No matter what they were called, those courses signaled that the apartheid system of K–12 schooling had not adequately prepared me for college. How could it, when we never attended school more than four or five months out of the school year?

There was neither shame nor stigma associated with taking remedial classes when I registered for classes at AM&N. There were several reasons why this was the case. First, well over 60 percent of my freshmen classmates were required to take these classes. This meant that we weren't isolated. Second, we knew that we were more than the sum of our test scores and could achieve our educational goals if we were given an opportunity to do so and worked hard enough. As for me, Mama had already told me I could be anything I wanted to be, and I was naive or trusting enough to believe her. Of course, Mrs. Smith confirmed it all when she handed me my schedule and said I'd be all right if I followed it. Third, as the children of sharecroppers and subsistence farmers, we had learned to have faith in ourselves, to work collaboratively, and to not squander our time or engage in superfluous activities.

Like the overwhelming majority of my classmates, I made it through those remedial classes with relative ease. We needed the classes not because we were dumb or had failed on previous tries. Rather, we had never been exposed to the materials needed to establish a solid foundation for future learning. What my classmates and I lacked in preparation was more than offset by our motivation, determination, focus, and work ethic. We went on to become teachers, principals, physicians, leaders in corporate America, military officers, elected officials, and attorneys. The faculty at AM&N College cared so much about our well-being and the role we would play in advancing the hopes and aspirations of other Blacks that they refused to accept excuses or subpar performances from us. The excellence they demanded of us was color and gender neutral, and no excuse was defensible or acceptable.

* * *

To make sure that I got to class early enough to get a front-row seat in Professor Albert Baxter's remedial math class, my milking buddies helped me out by agreeing to feed the calves and wash down the barn after we'd finished our milking chores so that I could get back to campus in time to take a quick shower and eat a bite of breakfast. They had already frightened the daylights out of me by telling stories about how demanding and difficult Baxter was as a teacher.

They were right about Baxter being a demanding professor, but they left out the part about him being a caring professor who understood the relationship between cognitive and affective development and the importance of a faculty member removing as much ambiguity as possible about expectations.

Baxter understood better than any professor I've ever had the difference between teaching students and teaching content, even if he demonstrated this understanding in sometimes unorthodox ways. Needless to say, Baxter, who had a degree in agriculture, and I quickly developed a respectful relationship. He appreciated my inquisitiveness and desire to learn, and I respected his expectation that anything less than our best was unacceptable. The relationship that we forged in his summer-school remedial class would last a lifetime.

I knew college would be different, but being in an introductory chemistry class with over one hundred other students wasn't an experience for which I was fully prepared. After all, there were fewer than three hundred students in grades nine through twelve at McNeil High School, and chemistry wasn't even offered. Although my chemistry class took place in an auditorium-style classroom, there weren't enough front-row seats for me to claim one. It seems that many of my classmates had the same idea and arrived early to class that first day. The classroom was inadequately lit with poor acoustics, and the instructor was a soft-spoken person you had to strain to hear. Even so, one-on-one interactions with Professor William Willingham revealed his passion for his subject matter and his undeniable patience with students. If he needed to go over the same concept a dozen times to ensure your understanding, he would hang in there with you, until he sensed your mastery of it.

I quickly discovered that grasping chemistry required the capacity to think critically, analytically, and abstractly, along with mastery of mathematics. I learned that reading science textbooks wasn't the same as reading social science materials and that virtually all chemistry concepts built on each other. I worked hard to earn a C from Professor Willingham, but I fell in love with the discipline in the process. I would go on to graduate in three years with a double major in agronomy and chemistry. Chemistry II was the only other course I took from Professor Willingham, but we became lifelong friends. I credit him for instilling in me the importance of being patient with myself. This lesson would take on added significance as I tackled advanced chemistry classes, microbiology, and statistics in graduate school.

* * *

During the apartheid period in the Arkansas Delta, schools were completely segregated by race. There were no Black teachers at White schools, and there were no White teachers at Black schools. The only staffing exception was the

White superintendent of schools, who served as the chief school executive for both races. I had my first non-Black teachers when I arrived at AM&N, but none was White. Instead, they were persons of Asian or Indian ancestry who could not get jobs at predominantly White institutions (PWIs).

Many held terminal degrees from their country of origin and were hired at HBCUs in large measure because regional accrediting agencies required that college-level instruction be delivered by persons with terminal degrees. In addition to a poor command of English, many of these individuals appeared culturally incompetent or insensitive and showed little interest in learning about or embracing the culture of the institution, their colleagues, or the students they were charged with teaching.

Imagine a professor distributing the midterm or final exam and then jumping on the top of his desk and loudly announcing, "Now, I can see all of you and know who is copying!" The day that happened in my political science class, I realized that this political science professor from South Korea neither respected nor cared about the intellectual or personal development of his Black students. When he said that, it took everything within me to refrain from confronting him and literally trying to beat the prejudice and racism out of him. I felt insulted, betrayed, and disrespected in one fell swoop. I felt betrayed because the department head, the dean, and the vice president of academic affairs were all aware of the disrespectful antics of this instructor, yet they still allowed him to remain on the faculty.

Several years later, when I encountered that instructor at Indiana University where we were both pursuing graduate studies, he greeted me as though he were seeing a long-lost friend for the first time in ages. More than forty years later, when I was chancellor of an HBCU, I encountered a number of international faculty who exhibited attitudes of disrespect and indifference toward Black students. In an effort to explain why there were so few students in some science, technology, engineering, and mathematics (STEM) disciplines, several faculty members, including a department chair, attributed it to a lack of academic ability and work ethic. When I confronted one department chair and several of his faculty in a public meeting, they attempted to walk back their assertions and alleged miscommunication. Of course, the damage had been done by that time.

The attitude of this particular group of people notwithstanding, there were international faculty who embraced the mission of the institution and served as great teachers and mentors. It would therefore be a mistake for anyone to conclude that the attitudes of a small subset of culturally incompetent or insensitive faculty, whether domestic or international, defined or dictated the student experience at AM&N.

Quite the contrary, the culture of caring that defined the college and many other HBCUs was nurtured and sustained by a cadre of first-generation faculty and staff who viewed their work as a calling rather than a job. They approached every teaching, mentoring, counseling, and advising encounter from the perspective of students' assets, not their deficits. As such, they established authentic and trusting relationships that withstood the test of time. Respect and a feeling of obligation to nurture the dreams of others just as their dreams had been nurtured—not personal recognition or aggrandizement—motivated their efforts.

* * *

Although my dorm room was nothing to write home about, it was a monumental improvement over the little shack without electricity or running water that we'd called home. Hunt Hall, named for Silas Hunt, the first Negro to attend the University of Arkansas (UA) Law School, was poorly constructed and without air-conditioning. It was an austere, two-story, redbrick building designed to accommodate approximately 120 male students. However, depending on the college's enrollment, as many as 4 guys would be placed in a single room during the academic year, bringing total occupancy to more than 200 residents. Since the majority of AM&N's students worked on their family's farms during the summer or went up north to secure a job, summer enrollment was much lower, and only 2 students would be assigned per room.

More often than not, we ended up taking cold showers, either because the hot-water heater couldn't produce enough hot water to accommodate all residents or because it was often not working. When it rained heavily, the dorm director placed buckets throughout the building to catch the water, or we used the trash container in our rooms to do so. The dorm lounge contained an old black-and-white television set, several badly worn chairs, a couple sofas with broken legs, and an upright stereo that no longer worked. So much for the entertainment that was never there!

Settling into Hunt Hall included meeting my roommate, a student by the name of Hazell Reed, from Stump City, which was not far from Heth, Arkansas, which wasn't far from Hughes, Arkansas, where he attended high school. Although Stump City was less than ten miles from the Buck

Lake Road where I grew up, the fact that I'd never heard of it is a reflection of just how insular my life was as a farm kid in the Arkansas Delta. A very friendly fellow, Hazell's energy level was off the charts. He was anxious to orient me, the new kid on the block, to the intricacies of herding and milking nearly one hundred heads of Holstein and Jersey cows twice a day, rain, shine, sleet or snow.

The cows had to be milked, and Reed, as we affectionately called him, had mastered the art of doing so and was anxious to show off his skills. The college farm was about a twenty-minute walk from the dorm along Spruce Street in the center of a middle-income Negro neighborhood. It was as hot as hell, or the temperature I would envision prevailed in hell. As we made our way to the farm, Reed spoke nonstop and authoritatively about the art of milking cows and ways to not get kicked in the head by one of those big Holstein cows, which could easily reach five feet tall and weigh as much as 1,500 pounds. He told me he'd let me watch the first day, and the serious work would get underway first thing Monday morning.

Reed's milking buddy was A. O. Biles, an articulate, trash-talking ag major who kept us laughing from the time we commenced our daily milking duties until we finished. He and Reed played classical music to the cows, based on the supposition that it relaxed them, resulting in them giving more milk. While I never saw any research to sustain or refute their theory, I can confirm that when we played music, the cows seemed less restless or agitated by our use of the electric vacuum-milking machines. After milking the herd of Holsteins and Jerseys, we had to wash down the barn of what seemed like endless piles of manure and then bottle feed the calves, who were kept away from their moms. Otherwise, there'd be no milk for the college cafeteria or the labs in animal husbandry.

It was as though the cows knew exactly what time we'd be arriving! All one hundred of the herd of Holsteins and Jerseys huddled around the gate leading from the barnyard to the milking shed and greeted us with a moo upon our arrival. They seemed happy to see us, even though the feeling was seldom mutual. No matter how late our milk crew stayed up the night before, whether studying or goofing off, the cows had to be milked, and there was no such thing as taking a holiday recess, spring break, or vacation from performing this essential task. That's exactly what Mr. Holiday was trying to convey to us when he said, "I expect you boys to keep your word." This meant that we'd milk the cows every day, twice a day, 365 days of the year and that we wouldn't try to trick Mr. Holiday into believing all of them had been milked by washing down the milk shed and giving each cow more than her share of feed to show that all allocated feed had been used.

As dairy hands, we rose each morning between 5:00 a.m. and 5:30 a.m., ensuring that we'd be at the milk shed no later than 6:00 a.m. to greet the cows and commence the milking ritual. There was an old, beat-up 1956 Dodge truck available to transport student workers to and from the farm, but we never knew whether it would start or not and couldn't risk being late or missing an 8:00 a.m. class.

The walk to and from the farm was about twenty minutes each way, and we had to be prepared for the trip, no matter the mode of transportation. A student work crew was assigned to each specialty area within the college's Department of Agriculture: agronomy, beef and dairy cattle, poultry, and horticulture, among others. By far, dairy was the most responsible and challenging assignment, because the season of the year was irrelevant. The cows had to be milked.

Milking cows is not a job for the faint of heart, even if you are listening to classical music! During the summer, temperatures inside the milk shed could reach upwards of one hundred degrees Fahrenheit, and the smell from the cow manure could be so nauseating that you wanted to throw up. During the winter months, the smell wasn't as overwhelming, but the pain your hands and fingers endured while attaching the vacuum milking machines to the cows' teats served as constant reminder of the importance of completing your degree—and getting the hell out of dodge! When I told my high school classmates, many of whom headed to Chicago, Detroit, Cleveland, or Flint, that I was headed off to college and would be working on the college farm, they were incredulous and would say, "Why in the hell would you go to college to major in agriculture and work on a college farm? Brother, you can do better than that!"

Even though my high school classmates had reservations about working on a college farm, my college classmates had enormous respect for the work ethic, intellectual acumen, and the leadership role played by ag majors throughout the university. Many of these students worked on the college farm and had a reputation for going on to graduate school at some of the best universities in the country.

About twenty students worked on the college farm in any given semester. Although we didn't see each other every day, we shared a bond that has lasted a lifetime. My milking buddy Hazell Reed and I have remained friends for over fifty years, and we talk weekly by phone. When I was named chancellor of North Carolina Central University (NCCU), another HBCU, Reed joined me as vice chancellor for graduate studies and research and later became vice chancellor for research and economic development. Together, we worked to transform the university into the number one HBCU in the country for two consecutive years. We also initiated the institution's first PhD program in more than forty years. We'd come a long way from milking cows.

Between milking cows in the morning and the evenings, our four-person team of farmhands tended the hogs, sheep, and beef cattle; bailed hay to feed the cows during the winter months; made fence repairs; and assisted Mr. Holiday with the artificial insemination of the cows. For these endless, various, and sundry farm tasks, I earned seventy-five cents per hour. I would later learn that there were two types of work-study programs: one funded by the state of Arkansas and the other by the federal government.

Since there were not enough federal funds to finance all students who qualified on the basis of need, the college used a person's ACT scores to determine who would be placed on which program. In order to be on the federal work-study program, the ACT cutoff was a composite score of eight. Those on the federal program earned $1.25 per hour, while those on the state program earned $0.75 per hour. So for shoveling all that manure and milking cows alongside my colleagues Hazell Reed and A. O. Biles, I was paid $0.50 less per hour than they were—all because of a damn test score.

Until taking the ACT, I had never taken a standardized test in my life and had no idea what the experience was like or how the results could be used to discriminate against people. I had low test scores on all standardized tests: the ACT, GRE, MAT, and others. The only time they impacted me was when I was paid less than my fellow milking buddies and when I enrolled in remedial classes. Thank goodness that was the only time my test scores would be used against me. Low scores on the Graduate Record Exam (GRE) or the Miller Analogy Test could have prevented me from being admitted to graduate school at Indiana University, Columbia University's Teachers College, the University of Illinois, or the University of Florida. Except for the knowledge and compassion of faculty who served on the Graduate School Admissions Committee who understood that standardized test scores alone are not the predictors of academic success, I would not have been admitted to these national universities.

Peeved that I was working as hard as—if not harder than—my milking buddies and worried about not being able to save enough money to pay tuition, fees, room, and board for the fall semester, I made an appointment to speak with Mr. Holiday. He started the meeting by saying how pleased he was with my work and asking what was on my mind.

Nervously, I said, "Mr. Holiday, I'm working as hard as these other guys, but I'm being paid considerably less. At the rate I'm going, it's impossible for me to save enough money to take classes this fall. I'm considering leaving so I can take join my uncle on a construction job, which pays ten dollars per hour. That way, I can save some up some money."

Holiday looked me dead in the eye and said, "Son, if you maintain your positive attitude and work ethic, when it's time for you to register for classes in college, I'll make sure you're able to do so."

With that assurance and tears in my eyes, I stood up, thanked Mr. Holiday, put on my straw hat, and returned to the farm for the evening milking chores. Before heading for vacation the last Friday of July 1965, Mr. Holiday gave his secretary, Miss Elnora Lee, a blank check bearing only his signature. He instructed her to make out the check for whatever amount I needed for books, tuition, and fees for the second summer session and the fall. To this day, I have no idea what amount she wrote on that check. Neither Miss Lee nor Mr. Holiday ever told me, and Mr. Holiday resisted every effort I made to repay him. I aced those remedial classes and went on to graduate from college three years later.

Lest one mistakenly conclude that I believe I was adequately prepared for college, I want to be crystal clear. The K–12 education represented by the split session and the Rosenwald school structure, of which I was a product and a victim, was never designed to produce college-ready students. The primary goal of that system was to provide White plantation owners and planters with a ready source of workers who could read and write. That was all. How Black farmworkers of my generation got over is a testament to our will, ingenuity, work ethic, and resolve—nothing more and nothing less.

Of course I never forgot Mr. Holiday's generosity, but the things I remember most were his warmth, authenticity, mentorship, and willingness to use his voice to give witness to the power of human potential. Taking a page from Mr. Holiday's playbook, for more than forty years, I have paid tuition and fees and have bought books, clothes, and food for students in need, without any expectation of repayment. When they tried to pay me back, I replied, "This is a gift from Mr. Holiday. It's a long story with details you don't need to be bothered with. When you're able, pass along a favor to someone else in need."

Many years later, on May 16, 2002, to be exact, the University of Arkansas at Pine Bluff (UAPB) awarded me an honorary doctorate in humane letters. Except for the honorees, their family, and their nominator, the award of such a degree is little more than another event on a lengthy commencement program. On that day, my nominator, Mr. Holiday, who had retired as chairperson of the university's Department of Agriculture, and members of my family who had come from around the country were seated on the front row of the commencement venue.

As I introduced Mr. and Mrs. Holiday to my son, wife, and other family members, Mr. Holiday beamed with pride. When I thanked him for the umpteenth time, he simply said, "Nelms, I knew you were destined for success from the very first day I met you nearly forty years ago. I'm just happy that you are the recipient of an earned honorary doctorate and not just another political type who's seeking recognition and the opportunity to be called *Doctor*."

Continuing, he said, "I respect you and admire your accomplishments. Stay humble, and you'll continue to prosper." Mr. and Mrs. Holiday had no children, and they left the majority of their estate to their beloved alma mater, UAPB. The estate included a large swath of timber and farmland near Brinkley, Arkansas.

In a recent conversation with Dr. Hazell Reed, my milking buddy of more than fifty years ago, we reflected on the success we achieved as faculty members and administrators in higher education. We concluded that four factors accounted for our success. First and foremost, our parents instilled in us the belief that we could be anything we wanted to be if we were willing to work hard. Second, we were blessed to have teachers at the K–12 level who had an unswerving commitment to our success and did whatever was required to ensure it. Our parents, teachers, and mentors instilled in us the commitment to pursue our goals with the confidence we could and would achieve them. Third, we assumed personal responsibility for our success and refused to confuse what we didn't have with what we did. Last, we chose to take the road less traveled, even when we didn't know where it would take us—and that did indeed, as poet Robert Frost wrote, make all the difference.

5

FROM DAIRY HAND TO
BOOKSTORE CLERK

O N THE WAY TO MY 10:00 A.M. CLASS, I made a quick stop by the college bookstore to buy a package of peanut butter crackers to quiet the rumbling noises made by my empty stomach. I'd overslept by half an hour that morning, which meant I got to the farm a bit late and had to miss breakfast in order to make it to my 8:00 a.m. class on time. Depending on the instructor and the course, arriving to class late by as little as five minutes could have a negative impact on your final grade.

As I reached into my pocket to pay for my ten-cent purchase, I heard a man's voice from behind mountains of boxes filled with books. "Young man, young man! Do you have a minute?" Since there were several male patrons in line waiting to pay, I had no reason to conclude I was the target of the reference coming from the unseen face. After glancing around, I heard the voice say, "Yes, I'm talking to you. I need to speak with you for a moment."

Although time wasn't exactly on my side, I replied, "Yes, sir," paid for my snacks, and waited for him to signal for me to follow him to his office. The desk seemed to have a little of everything on it, including an overflowing ashtray that gave off the smell of stale tobacco.

Plopping down in his seat, he said, "I'm Booker Williams, bookstore manager, and I've been observing you for a while now. Where are you from? What's your major and grade point average?"

When I finished responding to his queries, he surprised me by letting me know how much he already knew about me with this observation: "You work on the college farm milking cows for Mr. Holiday, don't you?" Then he said, "You seem to be a serious and trustworthy young man with your head on straight. I'd like for you to come to work for me. The pay is one dollar and twenty-five cents per hour, and I want you to start immediately."

As I raced across campus to my poultry science class, I was both ecstatic and in a state of shock. While I was tired of the backbreaking work milking cows and performing other farm chores in all types of weather, I felt I wouldn't be keeping my word to Mr. Holiday if I accepted the job offer from the bookstore manager, even if the pay was fifty cents more per hour and I'd be off weekends, spring break, and holidays. One thing I knew; I wouldn't leave my job as a member of the milking crew until they'd found a replacement for me. There was nothing the bookstore manager could say or do to cause me to renege on my word to Mr. Holiday or my commitment to my milking buddies. We were more than colleagues and fellow ag students; we were family!

When I shared the news of my job offer with my milking buddies, they were excited for me and let it be known that I was always welcome to return if I missed them and the cows or simply couldn't stomach ringing up the high price of textbooks. As for Mr. Holiday, I scheduled an appointment to talk with him. After inquiring about how my classes were going, in his epic Holiday manner, he asked, "What's on your mind, Mr. Nelms?"

When I shared with him my offer from the bookstore, which I suspect he already knew about, his response relieved and surprised me. He responded, "Mr. Nelms, it's great having you as a member of our milking crew and work-study team. I understand why you want to leave. Just know we'll always have a job for you. Best wishes in the years ahead."

Relieved, I thanked Mr. Holiday profusely and stopped by the bookstore to tell Mr. Williams that I would accept his offer with one condition: I couldn't start until a replacement farmworker for me had been identified and was in place. Three months later, I joined the bookstore staff but remained lifelong friends with Mr. Holiday and the milking crew at Arkansas AM&N.

During my tenure on the college farm's milking crew, I learned a tremendous amount about cows and calves, milk and butterfat, artificial insemination and gestation periods, responsibility and accountability, and the importance of keeping your word. For sure, the additional fifty cents per hour the bookstore paid enabled me to afford more fast food and to enjoy an occasional dinner with my girlfriend. More importantly, I learned what it meant to trust and respect those with whom you work. Booker Williams taught me the difference between management and leadership, and the importance of both. Long before I had ever heard of the management guru Warren Bennis, Booker Williams taught me that people, not processes, were the basis of effective leadership. Although Booker Williams is long deceased, he lives in me and the lives of those he touched.

* * *

"What do you want to major in?" asked my advisor, Ms. Gladys Smith, before rummaging through her cardboard box of advisee academic files.

Without hesitation, I answered, "Agriculture." To be honest, I answered without even knowing there were numerous fields of study within the broad discipline of agriculture, ranging from agronomy to weed science and many in between. By the end of my first semester of college, I had decided to specialize in agronomy, the science of soil management and crop production, because I felt it gave me the greatest opportunity for employment after graduation.

Equally important, the program chair, Dr. D. J. Albritton, had an easygoing style and was known to get internships and jobs for his "boys" with the US Soil Conservation Service, which is now called the Natural Resources Conservation Service. I mean *boys* literally because there were no females majoring in any field of agriculture during my days at AM&N. Like many of my classmates, I had a completely unsophisticated understanding about the relationship between college majors and careers. I had never, for example, taken a career awareness inventory, such as the Kuder Preference Record, the Princeton Review Career Aptitude Test, or the Complete Aptitude Test. In fact, I'd never heard of such tests or inventories! Since I had grown up on the farm and been mentored by Mr. Mozell, farming was a topic about which I knew the most.

When choosing agriculture as my field of study and agronomy as my area of specialization, I had no idea just how many science courses I'd be required to take. They included chemistry, physics, microbiology, quantitative chemical analysis, biochemistry, soil science, and astronomy, among others. So much for those who think farming is simple! In a span of three short years, I went from an entering freshman with literally no math or science background to a senior graduating early with a double major in agronomy and chemistry. The courses I enjoyed most were calculus, biochemistry, and microbiology. The courses I found most difficult and least enjoyable included physics and quantitative chemical analysis, both of which were taught by instructors who were brighter than a light but who had not mastered the art of teaching or interpersonal communications.

Biochemistry was taught by a gifted young AM&N alumnus just a few years my senior who earned his PhD in plant science and biochemistry at Purdue University but who chose to return to his alma mater to teach rather than teach at a White university for significantly higher pay. Dr. Paul Smith, a native of Crossett, Arkansas, was by far the most enthusiastic and effective teacher I have ever had, period. He loved people, he loved his discipline, and he was a superb communicator who was never too busy to teach. If you saw him in the cafeteria and asked him a question, he took time to answer it. If you asked a question and paper was not immediately available, Professor Smith would grab a napkin and commence writing while talking, even writing in the palm of his hand or on his arm. As I prepared to head to Indiana University (IU) for graduate school, he took me to lunch to tell me about what life was like in Indiana and to convey his confidence in my ability to succeed academically. After several years of teaching, Professor Smith resigned his teaching post and earned his medical degree. He went on to serve children from Pine Bluff and southeast Arkansas as a successful pediatrician.

* * *

I would be lying if I said my initial interest in student leadership while in college was driven by my desire to address many of the challenges associated with discrimination in the Black community at large. My interests were closer to home. I was tired of the repressive rules associated with in loco parentis, the living conditions in the dormitories, the poor quality of services throughout the campus, the disrespectful treatment of students by some faculty, and the disrepair of many campus facilities.

Like many of my fellow students, I thought the solution to these problems resided with the administration ensconced in Caldwell Hall. Later, I would learn that the problems were far more complex and nuanced. In my roles as vice president of the freshman class, officer in my dorm, and clerk in the college bookstore, I became acquainted with students across a broad spectrum of majors, sorority and fraternity affiliations, athletics, choir, marching band, and honor societies, just to name a few. I developed a reputation for being friendly, approachable, and unafraid of bringing student concerns to the attention of the college administration. So I ran for vice president of the Student Government Association and planned to run for president during my senior year of college. Of course, the best-laid plans sometimes take a different turn.

As a candidate for vice president of SGA, I was supported by a posse of young men and women who, like me, wanted to see demonstrable changes in the way the college administration interacted with students. We were tired of administrators treating us like children, incapable of making decisions for ourselves. Yes, we were tired of weekly room inspections, mandatory vesper service, 9:00 p.m. curfew, and rules restricting women from leaving the campus without written parental permission, among other such regulations. Simply put, we wanted to be treated as the young, responsible adults we considered ourselves to be.

I ran and was elected in part because of my ability to serve as a messenger for students without upending the administration or threatening them. My diplomacy skills were embraced by all parties, students and administrators alike. In the interest of full disclosure, I must admit that not all of my fellow students agreed with my more measured and diplomatic approach. Some of my more militant colleagues wanted to stage a sit-in at the president's office and demand immediate changes consistent with our demands. Had we taken that approach, I suspect that those of us leading the protest would have been summarily suspended without recourse. Filing a lawsuit would have been out of the question, since we didn't have the money to retain legal counsel. Thus, my suggestion that we take a more measured approach was embraced and pursued.

Everett Davis, a brash, overconfident fellow from Chicago, was elected president of SGA at the time I was elected vice president. Immediately following his election, Everett announced that he was going to "set us free"— his words, not mine! Feeling invincible and empowered by his election, Everett went on a spending spree over the summer. Among his purchases were expensive office furniture, custom-made draperies, a new wardrobe, and an off-campus apartment for himself—all from the SGA fees paid by students.

When the other officers and I protested, Everett called the SGA cabinet together the first week of fall classes to make sure there was no mistake about who was in charge. Addressing us in an arrogant, disrespectful, and condescending manner, Everett began his remarks by stating, "You cotton-picking, chittlin'-eating Negroes are more frightened than jackrabbits, and you take any and everything dished out by the administration. Hell, I'm president of student government, and the proverbial shit is about to hit the fan. I'm in charge and will run over anyone who gets in my way, including you, Mr. Charlie Nelms, with your slow-ass Uncle Tom self. The only authority you have is whatever I decide to give you, and for the record, I don't plan to give you any damn authority! Now, all you little snotty-nosed niggers, get up and get the hell out of my face." He declared the office off-limits to all duly elected SGA officers except himself and proceeded to have the locks to all of the doors changed that very same day.

Everett's erratic and irrational behavior, along with his inappropriate purchases, had already attracted the attention of the college administration, especially Vice President of Student Affairs Dr. L. A. Torrence, who had a reputation for being fair but not tolerating any foolishness from students. Torrence was known to send home those students who violated college rules and regulations. It was his way of maintaining order and keeping students safe. Although I didn't always agree with him, we had a mutually respectful relationship, and he became my greatest advocate and mentor.

Everett's outburst was the last straw. I had a choice of challenging him to a fistfight or walking away and letting Dr. Torrence or the student judicial system handle matters. Following a lengthy discussion with the other SGA officers, we decided to head over to Dr. Torrence's house, just two blocks from the campus, to apprise him of what we interpreted as a serious situation requiring his intervention. After hearing what we had to say, Dr. Torrence noted that we had done the right thing by not becoming embroiled in a physical confrontation. He advised us to return to campus and abstain from any interaction with Everett, and he'd look into the matter the next day.

True to his word, Dr. Torrence looked into the matter, and he discovered that Everett had not registered for fall classes and was thus ineligible to hold an SGA office. Dr. Torrence denied Everett's demand (not request) to register late and told him to pack his bags and head home to Chicago. To my knowledge, not a single student protested Everett's departure. With Everett out, as the duly elected vice president, I assumed the SGA presidency three weeks into the fall semester in 1967.

While I found Everett's behavior abhorrent, egregious, and unacceptable, I had mixed feelings about Dr. Torrence's refusal to allow him to register late. At the same time, I realized that if Dr. Torrence allowed him to register three weeks into the semester, he not only would have set a bad precedent but also would have given Everett an additional reason to believe that he was exempt from following campus rules. Everett threatened to sue Dr. Torrence and the entire college administration, SGA officers, and me personally. His czar-like behavior and tendencies aside, he was a bright, charismatic, and creative fellow with enormous potential, if only he could have found a way to control his sense of power, entitlement, and exceptionalism.

While I didn't like the circumstances that led to my becoming SGA president, I poured myself into the role and darn near flunked out of college in the process of pursuing an aggressive agenda related to student rights in an era defined by in loco parentis. There were always meetings on and off campus to attend and issues to be addressed. They included matters related to the quality of campus life on the one hand and racism in the broader Pine Bluff community on the other.

On numerous occasions, I seriously considered resigning the position but was persuaded not to do so by Mr. Holiday and Mr. Booker Williams, two people for whom I had enormous respect. They helped me see the value of working through the challenges of leadership rather than simply walking away. When things got out of balance between my academic work and campus politics, it was Mr. Holiday who helped me keep things in perspective. He never let me forget why I had come to college and challenged me keep my priorities straight.

I remember Mr. Holiday telling me during one of our many talks, "Nelms, you can't do everything. The problems you're trying to address are systemic and aren't likely to be resolved for many years to come, let alone during your time as SGA president. Do what you can and leave the rest for someone else." It wasn't just what Mr. Holiday said, but it was the passion with which he said it and the concern he had for me. With that conversation, I found the energy and the focus to do what I came to college to do— earn my degree.

* * *

One pleasant April morning in 1967, as I approached the college library, I noticed a group of students, mostly males, milling around the back of a pickup truck occupied by a handsome, comedic man who had everyone clapping and laughing. To my amazement and delight, it was Muhammad Ali, the heavyweight boxing champion of the world! Formerly known as Cassius Clay, Ali was touring Black colleges around the country during the period of his suspension from boxing for refusing to be drafted into the army. Ali's induction refusal was predicated on his conscientious objection claim. The US Supreme Court eventually ruled in Ali's favor, and he went on to reclaim his title by beating Joe Frazier.

When I was within a few feet of the truck, he yelled out, "Boy, where you goin' looking all important? I oughta get down from the back of this truck and knock you out. You wanna box me, boy?" Ali held up his big fist and swung it through the air, and the crowd exploded with laughter at my expense. I, of course, at that precise moment, wished I could have escaped the embarrassment and humiliation without being noticed, but that wasn't even a remote possibility.

Once the group quieted down, our unannounced visiting dignitary proceeded to give one of the most poignant and stirring lectures I'd ever heard on Black history and legalized segregation. Ali pointed aptly to the existence of Black colleges like ours and the disparate funding levels between our school and overwhelmingly White state-supported colleges in Arkansas. He challenged us to stop being scared and acting like Uncle Toms.

"Why," he asked, "should Black males go halfway around the world to fight a White man's war, killing people whose name you can't even pronounce?"

Ali was right. We were all afraid, including me, but we had neither his notoriety nor his money to challenge the establishment as he was doing. Up until that day, everything I'd ever heard about the Vietnam War was from the perspective of politicians and talking heads delivering sound bites on the national evening news. I decided that day that Blacks did indeed have choices. We did not have to kowtow to the whims of White politicians, many of whom put their needs and interests above all others. I disagreed with Ali's braggadocio, but his message still resonates with me to this very day.

In 2003, nearly forty years to the day that I met Muhammad Ali for the first time, I had the pleasure of a private audience with him and the Dalai Lama during their joint appearance in Bloomington, Indiana. It was the first meeting of these two living legends, who were in town for the dedication of an interfaith temple in support of world peace. The event was sponsored by the Tibetan Mongolian Buddhist Cultural Center, founded by IU professor emeritus Thubten J. Norbu, the eldest brother of the Dalai Lama.

Ali was visibly slowed by Parkinson's disease. Yet he was still intellectually sharp, and his eyes twinkled as I recounted the story of our meeting during a tumultuous time in our country and in his life. Although he did not remember me personally, he remembered his visit to my little HBCU alma mater, and that was good enough for me!

* * *

Despite the high-profile civil rights demonstrations led by students at North Carolina Agricultural & Technical State College, North Carolina College, Fisk College, and South Carolina State College (which are now all universities), student protests were not universally embraced at HBCUs for several reasons. First, Black presidents were expected by White governors, legislators, and businessmen to "keep students in line." Many presidents feared that failure to do so would result in a loss of state funds, thereby placing the continued existence of their college in great peril. Second, fearing the consequences that could occur from "out-of-control protestors," Black college presidents and deans did everything within their power to discourage student demonstrations, even if it meant suspending the students from school without the most basic due process hearing. Of course, since none of us wanted to be sent home, we towed the line. Third, many Black males in my friendship circle at Arkansas AM&N and other HBCUs in Arkansas feared the possibility of languishing in jail (or worse) should we be arrested, because our families did not have the necessary funds to bail us out of jail. The confluence of these three factors served as powerful incentives to keep many students in line.

Rather than engage in protests, my SGA colleagues and I chose to sponsor periodic teach-ins. We also accepted an invitation from the mayor of Pine Bluff to join forces with the Pine Bluff Biracial Commission, a cross section of business, civic, religious, media, and elected officials to find solutions to the city's challenges related to the full inclusion of Blacks in all aspects of city governance, employment and workforce development, protective services, K–12 education, and health care.

As SGA president, the task of representing the concerns of students fell to me. Given the economic impact that the college's workforce had on the city's tax base and the impact student purchases had on its retail and commercial health, it was apparent that elected and business leaders were prepared to make a concerted effort to address the concerns that Black representatives among us brought to the table. The publisher of the *Pine Bluff Commercial* newspaper and the representative from Simmons National Bank had little difficulty grasping the magnitude of the challenges. They seemed not only receptive but also eager to avoid the racial strife besetting many other college communities around the nation. Those two representatives often found themselves serving as interpreters of reality for their White colleagues. In addition to serving as effective interpreters, they seemed to possess a sense of fairness and respect for Pine Bluff's historically disenfranchised Black citizens.

Prior to serving on the Pine Bluff Biracial Commission, I had never had the opportunity to engage in substantive discourse with White people. Any trepidation I may have had about whether or not I could hold my own as a member of the commission quickly subsided. I found myself speaking truth to power and not taking a back seat to anyone, all the while doing so with passion, confidence, firmness, and focus. I concluded my service on the Pine Bluff Biracial Commission feeling that my communication skills were effective and reflective of the values I believe are crucial to effective leadership.

*   *   *

"Boy, you can do it!"

That's how my mentor, Dr. Lawrence A. Davis Sr., also known as Prexy, responded when I told him I wanted to be an HBCU president. My interest in becoming a college president was fueled by the belief that leaders can and must take a more active role in advocating for increased funding for facilities and academic programs that lead to greater employment opportunities for students. I believed then and still do now that elected officials and philanthropists are unresponsive to the cumulative effects of underfunding on Black colleges, in part because the leaders of these institutions and their alumni have been reluctant to challenge the system legally.

Equally important, my aspirations to become a Black college president were driven by the desire to make the institution that I would someday lead the centerpiece of community uplift envisioned by its founders. Prexy's words of encouragement were enough to get me started on preparing for a leadership journey that would include serving as president of three universities, two PWIs and an HBCU. Once on my leadership journey, I quickly discovered that HBCUs weren't the only institutions in need of strong, effective leadership.

*   *   *

"Betty, what's your friend's name, and where is she from? She's very attractive, even if she is a bit skinny."

"Boy, you're so crazy! Would you like to meet her? Confidentially, she asked me about you too."

This exchange with my dear friend Betty during my freshman year in fall 1965 led to my meeting Jeanetta Sherrod, a petite, smart, serious, warm, and soft-spoken coed from Turrell, Arkansas. Like me, she was a person of the soil, a farmworker seeking a better life through education. Since I was in the cafeteria line early every day, she assumed I was a football player. Little did she know that at the time I'd already been up for two hours, had milked a herd a cows on the college farm, and was waiting in the breakfast line before heading to an 8:00 a.m. class. After nearly fifty years of marriage, we still laugh about her wanting to meet a football player but instead meeting and marrying an ag major with a job milking cows for seventy-five cents an hour!

It didn't take me long to fall head over heels in love with this lovely girl from Turrell, and our courtship has continued after over fifty years of marriage. Jeanetta and I quickly discovered that our values were compatible and that we both had an unswerving commitment to serving humanity and being a source of inspiration for young people from backgrounds like ours. During long, moonlit campus walks, we plotted our future together, including the type of house we wanted, complete with its location and layout. Since both of us were from families of low wealth (my euphemism for *poor*), our courtship was not defined by materialism. We both lived in single-sex residence halls on campus, took our meals in the college cafeteria, and walked everywhere we went. Or we rode the city bus, since neither of us had a car. Except for seeing an SGA-sponsored movie in Caldwell Hall Auditorium, we never saw a movie in Pine Bluff while we were dating. The reasons were twofold: we didn't have any money, and even if we had, city buses didn't run in the evening.

Consistent with its in loco parentis culture, the college strictly enforced rules governing curfew and what it considered appropriate student behavior. Quiet hours (study hours) were in effect from 6:00 p.m. to 9:00 p.m., Monday through Friday, and the hour from 10:00 p.m. to 11:00 p.m. was set aside for males to visit females in their residence hall, but only in the lounge. Otherwise, we could sign out of the residence hall to stroll around campus or to head to one of the small home-based restaurants near campus or to the Chicken Shack to purchase a sandwich and a soda. Perhaps it was our low-wealth status that led us to share most things, including laundry detergent, food, books, and even our meager funds. In 1967, my junior year of college, Jeanetta and I became engaged and got married in 1968 when we both graduated college. We were married in a small wedding ceremony coordinated by our friend Betty, the same friend who introduced us. More than forty years later, Betty would also serve as my executive assistant during my tenure as chancellor at North Carolina Central University (NCCU).

Jeanetta was a teacher long before earning her bachelor's degree in mathematics with honors from AM&N and her master's degree in the same discipline from Indiana University. The only thing that exceeds her intellect is her patience, buttressed by the consistency of her caring. I'm the number one beneficiary of the many lessons this master teacher has sought to instill during her illustrious career. Humility, honesty, compassion, commitment, thrift, loyalty, generosity, and teamwork are just a few of the lessons I'm still learning from her. When I reflect on what my life might have been had I not met Jeanetta all those years ago, I can say without a doubt that it would not have been complete.

When we joined forces through marriage, we became genuine partners. Soon after we were married, our dream of having a particular house gave way to chasing dreams of making the world a better place, not just for rural Black kids like us but also for those from urban or suburban backgrounds, as well as those of all ethnic groups. The return on our commitment to each other and to our careers has produced thousands of high school and college graduates who've gone on to become vital members of their communities. They include teachers, lawyers, physicians, accountants, entrepreneurs, ministers, and elected officials.

Our most important joint production is an intelligent, sensitive, and caring global citizen, Rashad Zakee Nelms, who has an unswerving commitment to changing the world by working for the UN World Food Programme (WFP). It's fair to say that I got more than a smart, attractive, and sensitive girl from Turrell, and she got more than a guy milking cows on the college farm!

* * *

It was May 12, 1968, three years following my arrival at AM&N. Hazzard Gymnasium had been magically transformed into a place of beauty, and the faculty in their regalia looked resplendent as they processed into the building for commencement ceremonies. President Lawrence A. Davis Sr. led the faculty procession, while faculty marshals led the graduates by discipline. Within smiling distance, I spotted Mr. Holiday, who, as chair of agriculture, was marshal for my group of graduates. For a moment, I was nearly overwhelmed with gratitude. After all, I was officially in the class of 1969, and here I was graduating a year early, despite my inadequate academic preparation and low ACT score.

I thought about the words of Mrs. Gladys Smith, the woman with the angelic smile, who had said that if I followed the schedule she gave me, I'd be all right. I don't remember who our commencement speaker was, but I do remember the charge Prexy gave to the class. Quoting Langston Hughes, he reminded us that the plight of Black people in America demanded that we commit ourselves to the struggle for justice, equality, and the dignity of all humankind.

"It's not enough," he noted, "for you to walk across this stage to receive your degree and not be concerned about those who will come after you. Remember how you got here, and invest in your alma mater so it'll be here for others."

In appreciation of the support we received from the college, Jeanetta and I started investing in the institution within a short time of graduating. Over thirty years ago, we established our first endowment, and a few years later, we established a second one. In 2016, ten students received scholarships from the Charlie and Jeanetta Scholarship Endowment at UAPB. We also established scholarship endowments at Indiana University East (IU East), University of Michigan–Flint, and North Carolina Central University. Each year, thirty students are assisted from the earnings accrued by these endowments. With all the generosity I'd experienced, philanthropy was one way of paying it forward.

* * *

As I prepared to begin a new chapter in my life following graduation, there was a great deal of uncertainty about how that chapter would unfold. The thought of being drafted and sent to Vietnam to fight a "White man's war" when there were places in this country that would not rent me a room or hire me was concerning and unsettling, to say the least. As an agronomy major, I had received my federal service rating, which allowed me to compete for jobs within the US Department of Agriculture and other federal agencies. My rating of ninety-three all but assured me that I would be hired to work for the US Soil Conservation Service or the Farmer's Home Administration.

However, the probability of being drafted was even higher, since I had already received three deferments to remain in college and Secretary of Defense Robert McNamara needed a fresh set of troops as replacements for those who had either completed their military obligation or been killed. While the idea of heading to Canada crossed my mind on multiple occasions, the reality of not having the necessary funds to sustain me until—or even if—I could find a job was upmost in mind. And I couldn't think of anyone from whom I could secure a loan to wait it out in Canada. I wasn't even sure that even Mr. Holiday would be receptive to becoming entangled in the legal affairs of a draft dodger.

It turned out that an escape plan to Canada wouldn't be necessary. Two days before commencement, President Davis invited me to his office, where he was joined by Dr. Torrence. Prexy began the meeting by telling me how impressed he was with my maturity, commitment, and leadership as president of SGA. He wanted to know if I still wanted to be a college president, to which I responded with an enthusiastic yes!

I could have fallen out of my chair when he said, "After conferring with Dr. Torrence, I'd like to offer you the position of ombudsman for student affairs, reporting to Dr. Torrence. If you decide to accept the position, I will formally request that your draft board in West Memphis grant you a deferment. While I can't promise they'll give you one, they have worked successfully with me on a few other occasions."

There was nothing more to discuss. I accepted the position on the spot with a twelve-month salary of $6,500. After working with Dr. Torrence for just six months, I knew I wanted to pursue my dream of becoming a Black college president. There were no vacancies in the National Guard because all the White boys had claimed those. So I joined an infantry US Marine Corps Reserve unit in Little Rock, Arkansas, and requested a leave without pay to complete the required six months of active duty. Following completion of active duty, I worked a year for Dr. Torrence before heading north to Indiana University to pursue graduate studies.

I have been asked repeatedly by aspiring university leaders to share with them what accounts for my success as a college student and a three-time college president. The common denominator of the support I've received over the years was the mentorship of people who saw potential in me and who refused to allow me to take the easy way. They established high expectations and would not accept any excuses for not meeting them.

They pushed or pulled me when they needed to and advocated for me even without my requesting it. Above all, they treated me with respect, all the while instilling in me the confidence to persevere. The takeaway from all of these encounters is to repay those who invested in me by being the best leader I could be and by investing in those in whom I see potential, ir-respective of the person's gender, race, or ethnicity.

In the gospel classic "If I Can Help Somebody," Mahalia Jackson sings,

> *If I can help somebody, as I pass along,*
> *If I can cheer somebody, with a word or song,*
> *If I can show somebody, how they're traveling wrong,*
> *Then my living shall not be in vain.*

I am the sum total of the teachers, mentors, and classmates who've been placed in my life to teach me the lessons I needed to master and to grow personally, intellectually, and spiritually for a life of service through leader-ship. I am the beneficiary of the kind of help Mahalia Jackson exults. Most of all, I am an ardent believer that each and every one of us can, in our own lives and in our own way, help somebody.

6

EVERYTHING BEFORE US

THE OLD ADAGE "YOU CAN'T JUDGE A BOOK by its cover," is generally true, but it is especially so in the case of Dr. L. A. Torrence, who would become my mentor, friend, and leadership coach for more than four decades. Impeccably dressed in what appeared to be a Hickey Freeman suit from Henry Marx Men's Store in Pine Bluff and standing a little over six feet tall, Dean Torrence, as we called him, looked like he'd spent a lifetime working out. I caught a glimpse of this dignified but stern-looking man as I made my way to President Davis's office in Caldwell Hall on a hot and humid June day in 1967.

Having been elected vice president of the Student Government Association in May of that year, I was eager to share with Prexy my aspirations for the SGA and for the college during my tenure as a student leader. Little did I know at the time that in less than twelve weeks, I would be catapulted into the role of SGA president, because of the elected president's failure to register for classes—and Dean Torrence's resolve to let students know that *he*, not the SGA president, was in charge.

Dean Torrence hailed from Stephens, Arkansas, a farming hamlet of fewer than five hundred inhabitants, near Camden, a town of ten thousand in southern Arkansas. His subsistence farmer parents were determined that at least one of their children would graduate from college. The youngest of eight children, Dean Torrence was the chosen one and did his part to fulfill his parents' dreams. He excelled academically and athletically, earning a football scholarship to Arkansas AM&N, where he graduated magna cum laude. Legend has it that in the heat of battle in a football game between AM&N and Jackson State College, another HBCU, Dean Torrence played with a broken leg, yet he still managed to catapult his team to victory. It was this same determination and grit that resulted in Dean Torrence becoming the first African American to earn a doctorate in counseling and higher education administration from the University of Kentucky in 1967.

Prior to graduating from college, I had never met an ag major who'd gone on to pursue graduate studies in agriculture, except for Dr. Paul Smith, my biochemistry professor. Most AM&N grads in my field took jobs teaching vocational agriculture in rural communities throughout the South, or they were among the first wave of HBCU graduates to secure jobs with the Farmers Home Administration or the US Soil Conservation Service. Since almost all of my classmates and I were from poverty-stricken backgrounds, our highest priority was to obtain a "good job" in order to enjoy the fruits of our labor, assist our families financially, and improve the quality of life for our neighbors who were not fortunate enough to attend college.

The first mention of graduate school came from Prexy, who responded enthusiastically when I apprised him of my desire to be a college president. In retrospect, I suspect Prexy's support of my presidential aspirations, rather than a covert willingness to help me avoid the draft or to help AM&N work through an array of challenges it faced, was the driving force behind his willingness to ask my local draft board to grant me a military deferment. Since I had no idea what graduate school entailed, I had not prepared for it in any significant or intentional way. It was only after graduating college and working as ombudsman for student affairs under the tutelage of Dean Torrence that I gained a clearer sense of what graduate school was all about, including the application process and the universities to consider. I had never even heard of the GRE. Most importantly, I had absolutely no idea of how to go about paying for graduate school, let alone which universities to consider.

The difficulty of these issues notwithstanding, I had a far more serious and immediate challenge: informing my new bride that I wanted to go to graduate school and convincing her to quit her job and do the same. We had been married on August 3, 1968, in Pine Bluff, Arkansas. Our first year of marriage involved alternating weekend visits between West Memphis, Arkansas, where she worked as a middle school math teacher, and Pine Bluff, where I worked as ombudsman for student affairs at AM&N. We began our second year of marriage with me on six months of active duty with the US Marine Corps Reserves in San Diego and with her serving as a lecturer in mathematics at AM&N. A truly outstanding math student and teacher, Jeanetta was hired with only a bachelor's degree to teach math on a full-time basis to first- and second-year college students only a few years younger than her. As she was warmly embraced by the college's math faculty and her students alike, graduate school was the farthest thing from

Jeanetta's mind. We were finally in a position to assist our parents financially, and here I was talking about grad school!

The decision to pursue graduate studies was made even harder by the fact that Jeanetta was her mother's only child and leaving Arkansas for graduate school meant infrequent visits. Being the warm, kind, and optimistic person she was, my mother-in-law, Julia Sherrod, gave us her blessing, although it was clearly a painful decision. She realized that her little girl was an adult now. She did not want stand in the way of her daughter supporting her husband, nor did she wish to discourage her from pursuing a graduate degree in mathematics at a nationally recognized university.

Four months after we began our studies at Indiana University, my beloved mother-in-law died at age forty-seven from a massive stroke. I've never felt more helpless than seeing her in a coma for twenty-four hours and wondering if our being closer to home and seeing her on a regular basis might have enabled us to detect any changes in her physical conditions leading up to that devastating stroke. Neither Jeanetta nor I have ever fully gotten over my mother-in-law's death, and I doubt seriously that we ever will. Even so, we have the comfort of knowing that her spirit is always with us. She would be proud of our career accomplishments, and she would have enjoyed spoiling her only grandchild. In honor of our parents, we established the Nelms-Sherrod Scholarship Endowment at the University of Arkansas at Pine Bluff in 1998.

* * *

Despite my inadequate academic preparation, I had followed the schedule Mrs. Gladys McKindra-Smith handed me on that hot July day in 1965, and I had managed to graduate a full year *ahead* of schedule. Although I was in the class of 1969, by attending summer school every year, I graduated with the class of 1968. Holding down jobs as a diary hand milking Holstein cows on the college farm, a clerk in the college bookstore, and later president of SGA required a level of discipline that actually facilitated my early college graduation. That's why in many respects I have difficulty understanding why the majority of today's college students graduate in five or six years—with many requiring as long as seven years! It's no wonder that college borrowing exceeds a trillion dollars and many undergraduates leave college with loan indebtedness that far exceeds their starting salaries.

* * *

The 1960s was a decade marked by protests and demands for an end to racial discrimination in education, employment, and social accommodations on the one hand and an end to the Vietnam War on the other. Depending on one's political views or social status, racial inequality and the war were among the most unifying or the most polarizing issues of the twentieth century. Families, churches, and communities were divided in ways not seen since the Civil War and the signing of the Emancipation Proclamation by President Abraham Lincoln on January 1, 1863.

Tired of waiting for the ruling class of White power brokers and conservative Black civil rights leaders to strike a deal, Black college students took matters in their own hands, in Greensboro, North Carolina; Nashville, Tennessee; Orangeburg, South Carolina; Atlanta, Georgia; Jackson, Mississippi; Washington, DC; and West Virginia, among other locations. Undeterred by the threat of being kicked out of school, arrested, and sentenced to jail or prison—or even being killed—student protestors demanded justice immediately, not when the power brokers saw fit to concede it. At the same time, White war protestors at Kent State and other universities around the country seized control of campus buildings, engaged in hunger strikes, and staged sit-ins to underscore the seriousness of their demands for an end to the war. The protests reached a tipping point May 4, 1970, when members of the Ohio National Guard shot and killed four Kent State University students.

Looking back to fifty years ago, I seriously doubt I would have sought the position of SGA vice president if I'd had a thorough understanding of the evolving social and political tenor of the times and expectations of me as a student leader. Moreover, I had no idea that I would be pressed into service as SGA president. Thanks to a close circle of stalwart supporters, friends, and faculty-staff mentors, I accepted the reins of leadership while seeking to avoid the jagged edges of discord that often defined the relationship between idealistic and impatient students and college administrators who felt they had an obligation to keep the peace on campus and to protect us students from ourselves. We reasoned, and rightfully so, that if we were old enough to be drafted into military service and die in a war halfway around the world, we were old enough to make decisions about mundane rules related to curfew and room inspections!

* * *

"Shut it down! Shut it down! Shut it down, now!"

As I entered the main lounge of the L. A. Davis Student Union Build-ing in November 1967, I was greeted by a vociferous group of my peers demanding an end to in loco parentis, improvements in living conditions in the dormitories, improvements in the quality of food served in the col-lege cafeteria, and an end to racial discrimination in Pine Bluff. There was absolutely nothing in my life up to that point, nor since, that prepared me to deal with the demands of leadership in the context of constituent expectations.

Once the group had quieted down, I took the handheld microphone, composed myself, and said, "You are not the only ones frustrated. I am too. But frustration alone won't get us the results we seek; we have to be stra-tegic, focused, and willing to prioritize our demands. For example, while ending discrimination in Pine Bluff is a laudable goal, the probability of our doing so is practically nil."

This comment, of course, resulted in a litany of disagreements and comments about student protests around the country and the importance of students at AM&N taking a stand and demanding our rights. One of the more vocal organizers of the meeting proceeded to passionately quote from Frederick Douglass's 1857 speech on the struggle for freedom of West Indian slaves: "If there is no struggle there is no progress. Those who profess to favor justice and yet depreciate agitation, are men who want crops with-out plowing up the ground. They want rain without thunder and lightning. They want the ocean without the awful roar of its many waters."

For a moment, the eloquence of the speaker held the audience spell-bound. When it was my turn to speak, I outlined a three-point plan for how I felt we should proceed. First, we had to reach consensus on our agenda and establish priorities. Second, we had to commit to meeting with appropriate college administrators, beginning with the president. Third, we needed to be prepared to negotiate rather than insist that we wanted everything on our list of demands or nothing at all. Although I was a political novice, I knew enough to recognize that our refusal to negotiate with the college administration and elected city officials was a path to nowhere.

And so we began the slow and arduous task of negotiations, with me leading an eight-person team of students who met with President Davis and members of his cabinet on a weekly basis. After meeting with us three or four times, President Davis turned the convening task over to his vice president for student affairs and dean of students, Dr. Torrence. President Davis was one of the most charismatic and authentic leaders I have ever known. To demonstrate his sincerity and to convince us that he was on our side, he went to great lengths to explain the college's budget, even sharing a copy with us.

Prexy effectively presented a master class on how the historic and cumulative effects of structural racism and inadequate state funding negatively impacted the administration's ability to make repairs to residence halls and academic buildings, upgrade essential laboratory equipment, purchase instructional materials, build a new library, meet monthly payroll, or to even pay the food service vendor. President Davis used his persuasive communication skills and charisma to convince utility companies, businesses, and service providers to whom the college was indebted to accept partial payments, on the promise that they'd be paid in full at a specified date. Needless to say, when the agreed-on date arrived, the college's financial status had not improved, and in many instances, it had deteriorated.

Given Prexy's level of candor and transparency, our team of student negotiators quickly realized that the Arkansas state legislature was our nemesis, not President Davis and his cabinet in Caldwell Hall. While demonstrating against the administration may have grabbed a few headlines in newspapers around the state and nationally, it probably would have done little if anything to motivate legislators to appropriate more funds for AM&N. Instead, it would have certainly created a highly publicized distraction for President Davis to try and manage.

Despite the realities of the college's budget and the racist foundation on which it was based, my negotiating team and I held firm to our demand that the administration reduce the rules governing student life. Weekly dorm-room inspections, strict and unreasonable curfew hours that discriminated against female students, dress codes for students who dined in the college cafeteria on Sundays, and mandatory vesper services gave way to rules that respected our ability to make decisions for ourselves—decisions consistent with the values instilled in us by our parents and reinforced by the communities that nurtured our early development. As products of Black villages and towns across Arkansas, we would never knowingly do anything to bring disrepute on those on whose shoulders we stood.

Beyond the boundaries of the campus of AM&N, as SGA president, I had the opportunity to be part of a national gathering of student leaders committed to the pursuit of diversity long before the term enjoyed the acceptance it does today. In 1967, I joined a group of student leaders from mostly predominately White colleges and universities for a leadership conference at Principia College, an institution in Elisha, Illinois, affiliated with the Christian Science Church. For four days, we wrestled with what we could do individually and collectively as student leaders to create a more just and racially integrated country. This marked the first time I had ever attended a meeting where the overwhelming majority of the student leaders in attendance were White. It was also the first time I found myself in the position of being expected to speak for all Black people.

I was just as curious about White people as my fellow student leaders were about Blacks. They repeatedly asked me what Blacks wanted, and I always responded, "We want respect, equal treatment, and the opportunity to enjoy the fruits of the labor of our foreparents." Without fail, I always asked them, "Why are White folks so resistant to embracing the humanity of all people irrespective of race or gender?" Those conversations with my fellow student leaders were filled with candor, curiosity, and civility. It was in that tranquil setting at Principia College that I had the chance to ask my fellow student leaders and myself some pointed and poignant questions about what really matters in life—and our collective responsibility for changing the world.

The trip to Principia via St. Louis was the first time I'd ever been on an airplane. Words cannot convey the fear, excitement, and trepidation I felt as we sped down the runway at Little Rock Airport. As a country boy, I was surprised when I learned that there weren't parachutes for passengers in the event of a crash. That was perhaps the first and only flight I ever took where I didn't fall asleep before takeoff!

While many of today's millennials may erroneously believe that diversity in higher education began with them, they would do well to study the history of higher education within the context of the student protest movement. They would quickly discover that the mass student protest for equity in higher education can be traced to the 1960s and 1970s.

Several months following the Principia leadership summit, by virtue of my SGA presidency at an HBCU, I was invited to attend the annual conference of the National Student Association at Chicago's McCormick Place convention center. Never in my life had I been at a place with so many people—and White people at that. In addition to meeting new colleagues from around the country, I had the opportunity to reconnect with acquaintances I'd made earlier in the academic year at Principia. Student and faculty exchanges between PWIs and HBCUs were among the most discussed topics on the agenda of the Chicago meeting. It resulted in the establishment of short-term student-faculty exchanges between my school AM&N and Grinnell College in Iowa.

In addition to week-long reciprocal visits by students, a White political science professor from Grinnell actually spent a year teaching at my school. Unable to attract funding from private foundations, the program only lasted a couple of years. Interestingly, three decades after participating in what was at the time a bold experiment in diversity, I had the privilege of returning to Grinnell College to speak at a precommencement ceremony sponsored by the Black Student Association. I doubt seriously whether my Generation X audience had any inkling of Grinnell College's forays into diversity long before they were born. For me, however, the invitation was an affirmation of the positive outcomes of the determination of a group of idealistic student leaders who believed that the world could be different from the one in which we lived. In 2010, Grinnell College installed its thirteenth president, a gay Black male with a husband and children.

Although it's been over fifty years since I served as SGA president at AM&N, my definition of a good leader has not changed, nor have the people I would characterize as good leaders and have sought to emulate. I am more convinced than ever that a good leader possesses integrity, humility, clarity of vision, commitment to causes that transcend themselves, courage, focus, and follow-through. No matter the sector of their work, effective leaders seize every opportunity to nurture the dreams of others without expecting to be publicly acknowledged or rewarded financially. Leroy and Veola McNeil, Milton Mozell, O. R. Holiday, Gladys McKindra-Smith, L. A. Davis Jr., Robert Shaffer, Betty Greenleaf, L. A. Torrence, Glenn Nygreen, Marion Mochon, and John Ryan were among the great leaders who nurtured me but whose names may not be well known by many. All save one, Milton Mozell, are now deceased, but they are very alive through me and the thousands of others they mentored during their leadership journey and life.

Nationally, no leader impacted my views with respect to the confluence between leadership and service more than Dr. Martin Luther King Jr. Although I never had the privilege of meeting Dr. King, his assassination on April 4, 1968, forever changed my life and those of my generation. When I, my fellow SGA officers, and our classmates got the news that Dr. King had been gunned down by James Earl Ray, we experienced a range of emotions. We were devastated, disappointed, disillusioned, and downright angry.

As we gathered in Caldwell Hall Auditorium the morning of April 5, 1968, all of us felt the need to make our voices heard, but the strategy for doing so was not as clear. There were those among us who wanted to march on city hall, while others simply wanted to take time to reflect on the consequences of Dr. King's death, what it meant for America in general and for us in particular. Rather than march on city hall or burn down campus buildings, we chose a nonviolent way of honoring Dr. King. We spent the better part of two hours sharing with each other our pain, fear, and trepidation about the future. We concluded our assembly by taking a pledge I'd hastily drafted, recommitting ourselves to nonviolent social and political change. Six weeks later, I graduated college with a job and empowered by the belief espoused by Gandhi that I could be the change I wished to see in the world.

* * *

The date was August 5, 1968, and I was determined not to be a minute late to my first meeting as member of Dr. Torrence's staff. As I exited our little two-bedroom rented bungalow at 61 Watson Boulevard, two blocks west of AM&N, where I was about to commence my first-ever full-time job, there was an extra spring in my step. Although my duties weren't exactly clear, I felt extraordinarily fortunate to have both a job and a military deferment that would stave off the draft for a couple of years. If I were lucky, I might even get a low lottery number in the upcoming draft.

In the weeks leading up to my first day of work, I had timed the walk from home to the office and knew exactly how long it took—exactly thirteen minutes. The hum of the window air conditioner in the office provided a distraction for my nervousness as I waited for Dean Torrence to finish his meeting with his secretary, Miss Dewberry, a warm, dimpled-cheeked woman who would become one of my best advocates and supporters. A perfectionist, she took her work seriously but not herself. In typing my weekly reports for Dean Torrence, Miss Dewberry didn't just type what I had written; she made sure there were no incomplete sentences or misspelled words and that my word choices were accurate. Without ever articulating it out loud, she taught me the importance of loyalty, professionalism, punctuality, teamwork, and kindness. Those lessons would serve me well for the entirety of my leadership journey.

The most persistent question asked by a handful of students opposed to negotiating with the administration was, "Charlie, what do you do as ombudsman for student affairs? Is that simply a sophisticated way of saying that you spy on students for the administration?" I would reply, "I am the chief advocate for students and a thorn in the side of the administration with respect to holding them accountable for addressing student concerns within the realm of their control. If you have problems with that, let's talk over a cup of coffee or glass of wine." Following just two such conversations, word quickly spread throughout the more radical elements of the student body that I was my own person with the courage to speak truth to power.

My primary duties as ombudsman were twofold: first, documenting areas of student life that needed improvement and, second, working with administrators to resolve student concerns. The ombudsman title and my reporting relationship gave me access to administrators across academic, student, and fiscal boundaries. President Davis and Dean Torrence let it be known to all college constituents that they had empowered me to solve problems and speak on their behalf. My work as ombudsman prepared me well for success in graduate school and ultimately in my forty-year leadership role in the academy.

Left to my own devices, I would have pursued graduate studies at a PWI in Arkansas, since they were gradually extending admissions to Black students. Without apology, Dean Torrence let it be known that he felt strongly that I should leave the South if I was serious about becoming a college president. He opined that if I stayed in the South, I would be relegated to working at HBCUs. Not that this was a bad thing, but I would be pigeonholed and have limited opportunities for promotion. He spoke warmly about his relationship with Dr. Robert Shaffer, IU dean of students and professor of education, with whom he had teamed up to lead a national effort to expand the participation of Blacks in the college student personnel profession.

Furthermore, he spoke proudly about one of his former high school and college football players, Jimmy Ross, who was pursuing his doctorate in higher education administration while working as an administrator in Student Financial Aid at Indiana University. Coincidentally, Jimmy was just completing his tenure as SGA president as I arrived at AM&N in 1965.

Following numerous conversations over lunch and drives to and from Little Rock Airport, Dean Torrence became convinced of my genuine desire to pursue a career in higher education. He proceeded to do what all good mentors do; he reached out to his network at Indiana University and made arrangements for me to speak with the department chair, while also nominating me for assistantships and fellowships and helping me prepare for the GRE. Dean Torrence even let me read his letter recommending me for the master's degree program in college student personnel administration.

In his letter, he wrote that my low GRE scores were not an accurate reflection of my intellect, work ethic, or ability to solve problems. On the strength of letters of support from President Davis and Dean Torrence, Indiana University granted me conditional admission to its Graduate School of Education, while the Department of Residential Life awarded me an assistantship as a resident assistant in a residence hall where all of the residents except two were White. I was required to maintain a 3.33 cumulative grade point average (GPA), which I surpassed with ease.

Although I was admitted to several major universities, including the University of Florida, the University of Illinois, and Southern Illinois University, the decision to attend Indiana University was a no-brainer. Thanks to IU, Jeanetta and I were both armed with the financial support needed to sacrifice for a year or two to earn graduate degrees. It's one thing to be admitted to a particular university but quite another to have access to the necessary financial resources for successful matriculation.

The conditions surrounding the opportunity for me to attend Indiana University came together quickly and smoothly. The only details remaining were when—and convincing Jeanetta of the wisdom of quitting our jobs to chase my dream. She had one key question for which I did not have an acceptable answer: "Charlie, how will we pay our bills?" She agreed to accompany me on my campus visit, while making it clear that she wasn't about to quit a good job and try to secure employment as a secretary at Indiana University. Jeanetta encouraged me to request a leave from my job, and she'd keep hers while I pursued my master's. As a madly-in-love newlywed, I knew I'd be a miserable creature at IU without my soul mate. After all, having been in a commuter marriage for a year and on active duty with the Marine Corps for six months, I had a personal relationship with loneliness, and I didn't like the feeling.

* * *

In February 1969, I made two of the most important telephone calls of my life. One call was to Dr. Robert Shaffer, professor of education at IU, and the other was to Jimmy Ross, a fellow native Arkansan and associate director of financial aid at IU. Each of them readily agreed to meet us and rolled out the red carpet. After getting lost several times and caught in one of the worst thunderstorms of our lives, we arrived in Bloomington more than sixteen hours after what should have been a twelve-hour drive.

This was not an auspicious beginning to a trip designed to convince a reluctant spouse that going to Indiana for graduate school made sense.

Following a delicious dinner meal prepared by our host and a sound night's sleep that Saturday night, Jimmy gave us a driving tour of the campus that following Sunday. The campus looked like a small city with limestone buildings everywhere. The cobblestone streets gave a glimpse of the past, although their roughness made you wonder whether your car would break an axle any minute.

On Sunday afternoon, I met with Dr. Shaffer, and he gave me a personal tour of the building where his office was located, as well as departmental offices in the School of Education. A short, bespectacled man, Bob, as he requested I call him, made me feel like IU was the greatest place on earth. Dean Torrence had made Bob aware of Jeanetta's reluctance to quit her job, and Bob had arranged for her to meet with the chair of the Mathematics Department to discuss participating in a National Science Foundation (NSF)–funded project designed to increase the number of HBCU faculty with graduate degrees in math. The project paid tuition, fees, books, and supplies, as well as a $500 monthly stipend.

After sharing her GPA and work experience but before formally applying for the program, she was offered an NSF fellowship. My assistantship covered the full cost of attendance and also an efficiency apartment for the two of us. Jeanetta's stipend was enough to cover our bills and to purchase a meal ticket and bus pass for her. Since on Sundays the cafeteria only offered breakfast, we subsisted those days on Hormel chili, saltine crackers, and a Coke each. We lived that way for the one year we were in graduate school. By attending summer school, we both completed our master's degrees in twelve months. It was one of the most challenging years of our life and marriage. Many times I found myself wishing I'd followed Jeanetta's advice about deferring graduate school until we could afford to cover the true cost of attendance, but in retrospect, we agreed it had been the right decision.

* * *

The faculty in the college student personnel administration master's degree program at Indiana University were and still are some of higher education's most accomplished scholars. I had the privilege of studying under three of the field's pioneers: Dr. Kate Hevner Mueller, Dr. Elizabeth Greenleaf, and Dr. Robert Shaffer. Dr. George Kuh, who is a leading scholar in the field, joined the faculty as a tenure-track assistant professor during my first year of matriculation and would go on to retire as a chancellor's distinguished professor of higher education. The program's foundation was based on social and behavioral theory and research, and students were required to complete several practicums and internships in various student affairs offices, such as residential life, student activities, academic advising, financial aid, and admissions, among other areas. By the time we earned our master's degree, we were expected to have an understanding of the confluence between cognitive and affective development in college students and to serve as facilitators of that development.

My greatest challenge as an IU graduate student was keeping up with the massive amount of required reading and with writing what seemed like an endless number of reaction and book reports, research papers, and case notes related to our practicums and internships. We practiced the art of teamwork and group problem solving. As an undergraduate science major, I was accustomed to having only a couple of textbooks per class, working alone, and writing an occasional research paper in my non-science classes. A lab report for my chemistry classes required far less narrative and analysis than we were expected to produce in college student personnel administration. I soon adapted to the cadence of the graduate school workload while mastering the art of time management.

Counting me, there were three Black students in my cohort of approximately thirty students. Except for one or two students who thought rather highly of themselves and constantly vied for the professor's attention, members of the cohort enjoyed collegial and cooperative relationships. The faculty and students alike exhibited a high level of cultural competence and seamlessly made sure my Black classmates and I were part of all class discussions, not just those which centered on "Black issues." With the passage of time, I have lost contact with most of the students in my class, but from reading alumni updates over the years, I see that many of us became chief student affairs officers, college presidents, and faculty members.

* * *

Having grown up in the Arkansas Delta attending racially segregated schools from preschool through university, I'd had limited opportunities to work with White students. The exceptions were the brief stints spent with student leaders at Principia College, participation in the National Student Association Leadership Conference, and the student exchange program between AM&N and Grinnell. As limited as those experiences were, they provided me with a glimpse into what life would be like as a resident assistant in an overwhelmingly White residence hall at IU.

The head counselor, my boss, was a liberal New Yorker who proved to be a great advocate, wonderful mentor, and loyal friend. Like me, Ron had been SGA president, he at Lehman College, formerly Hunter College in the Bronx. When I graduated from IU, it was Ron who called his mentor, Lehman College's dean of students Glenn Nygreen, and convinced him that he should make a concerted effort to hire me as a member of his staff. So responsive and persuasive were the two of them that I reneged on a job offer at an upstate New York college to join the staff at Lehman. At IU, Ron was assisted by Nancy, a White woman with Indiana roots whose DNA appeared to be infused with warmth, fairness, and ethnic and cultural sensitivity. Ron and Nancy did more than anyone I have ever known to create, nurture, and sustain a culture of caring and support for all students, long before *student retention* and *graduation* became buzzwords in academia.

As a resident assistant living in my little efficiency apartment on the ground floor of Shea Hall in Foster Quad, my primary role was to ensure the adjustment and well-being of approximately sixty male freshman. For me, the key to success entailed establishing rapport with each resident rather than assuming they were all alike. Although the overwhelming majority were from Indiana, I quickly discovered that the culture of southern Indiana, for example, is significantly different from that of northwest Indiana. Similarly, students from suburban Indianapolis were different from those from eastern Indiana.

Being from the racially segregated South, I had readied myself for nearly every racist response imaginable from Shea Hall residents. I was elated when my worries and concerns proved baseless. While I'd never been around Whites to any significant degree, they had not been around Blacks either. So we each used our curiosity about the other to become acquainted. Even the marijuana growers, smokers, and I enjoyed a positive working relationship. Color and cultural backgrounds aside, the students were respectful, responsive, and understanding of my need to do my job. They also came to appreciate my fairness and rejection of a one-size-fits-all approach to working with residents whose backgrounds differed vastly from each other, as well as from mine.

Prior to arriving at Indiana University at the age of twenty-four, I'd never developed a friendship with any White person. I left with several friends who shared my passion for creating a more just and equitable America. Chief among them were my supervisors, Ron and Nancy. Rick, a Californian and a member of my cohort, was another. Rick and his spouse, Sue, a nurse, joined me and Jeanetta for picnics, fishing trips to Lake Monroe, and an occasional movie together. Upon graduation, we vowed to keep in touch, though that didn't end up being the case. Rick and Sue made their way back to California, and Jeanetta and I headed to New York City. It was there that the cultural shock we experienced as a young couple just a few years after leaving the farm came to occupy a definitive meaning in my life.

Because I entered the college student personnel administration program with two years of work experience, I was not required to complete as many practicum experiences as most members of my cohort. Thus, I completed the program in twelve months instead of the customary two years. With a graduate degree and work experience under my belt, I left IU ready to change the world, or so I thought. I had several solid offers in hand, including one from Dean Torrence inviting me to return to my alma mater, Arkansas AM&N, along with tendered offers from Earlham College, Rensselaer Polytechnic Institute (RPI), and Lehman College of the City University of New York (CUNY). Eventually, I accepted a position that proved to be far more interesting and challenging than I ever imagined.

* * *

Except for the trip to New York City for my interview, I'd never been there before and was nearly overwhelmed by the number of people, cultures, and languages; the size of the buildings; the honking of horns; the speed people drove; and even the number of cars. I easily saw more cars during my one-day stay in New York City than I'd seen in the entirety of my life in Arkansas!

When I returned home from New York, I excitedly told Jeanetta about my offers from RPI and Lehman College. However, she found neither one of interest and wondered out loud why we couldn't just go someplace without the hustle and the bustle of New York City or the snow in upstate New York. I knew she was right, but I just had to tell her about the opportunity to pursue my doctorate, which was a requirement if I really wanted to be a college president. Against Jeanetta's better judgement, we headed to NYC to join Glenn Nygreen at Lehman.

It turns out that Glenn and Bob Shaffer were close friends, and they were both friends with the chair of the Department of Higher Education and Student Affairs at Teachers College, Columbia University (TC). A sociologist, Glenn Nygreen believed strongly that anyone wishing to pursue a career in the academy should possess a terminal degree. He hired me with the written stipulation that I would enroll in a PhD program within a year of being hired. The CUNY faculty-staff union contract covered tuition reimbursement, and I was admitted and enrolled at TC my first year at Lehman. A year later, I was awarded a Ford Foundation Graduate Fellowship and enrolled full-time at TC. Meanwhile, Jeanetta took a job teaching math at a middle school in Mamaroneck, New York. It was the job from hell, as Jeanetta sought to contend with the whims of wealthy White parents accustomed to their children getting good grades, whether they earned them or not. One student's attempt to jump out of a second-floor window was enough to convince Jeanetta and me that New York wasn't a good fit for either of us. So we returned to Indiana, where I accepted a position at Earlham College, an excellent Quaker-affiliated institution.

Clearly, I earned more than a master's degree at Indiana University. I came to appreciate the assets I'd accumulated in the Arkansas Delta and expanded on as a student and leader at AM&N. I learned that not all White people are evil, any more than all Black people are good. I came to appreciate the importance of having supportive people in my life, both family members and professionals. The power and importance of networking, mentoring, self-confidence, focus, hard work, and the willingness to take risks manifested themselves in ways I'd not experienced so far.

I learned not to confuse detours with dead ends and to trust my gut. At Indiana University, I honed my leadership and communication skills, along with my ability to forge sustainable relationships based on mutual respect and a commitment to serve the commonweal. I left Indiana knowing that I could and would change the world because of my willingness to change myself. More importantly, I formed friendships with countless like-minded people that have withstood the test of time. Six years after earning my master's degree at Indiana University, I was awarded a doctorate degree in higher education administration and student affairs.

When I first arrived at Indiana University, I had hope and a network of people committed to my success. It was the "best of times and the worst of times," to quote Charles Dickens's *A Tale of Two Cities*. It was indeed the spring of hope, and the winter of despair. I had everything I needed for success—and everything before me.

Mama and Papa headed on their first-ever vacation, 1955.

Brother Eddie standing in front of our little country shack with cousins from Chicago, circa 1960.

College sophomore, AM&N College, 1966.

Jeanetta and me on our wedding day, August 3, 1968.

US Marine Corps, 1969.

Mama and Papa
visiting Jeanetta
and me in Pine
Bluff, Arkansas,
1977.

Celebrating with family and friends after finishing the Chicago Marathon, 1982.

Photo courtesy of Indiana University. Indiana University president Tom Ehrlich (in yellow shirt) with members of his university-wide leadership team, circa 1993.

Mama and me on Inauguration Day, University of Michigan–Flint, 1994.

IU East colleagues who joined Jeanetta and me at my inauguration as chancellor at the University of Michigan–Flint, 1994.

Photo courtesy of University of Michigan–Flint. University of Michigan–Flint chancellor's inauguration speech, 1994.

Photo courtesy of University of Michigan–Flint. Chancellor's 5K Run. Theme: setting pace, 1994.

Photo courtesy of University of Michigan–Flint. Jeanetta and me welcoming President Bill Clinton, "our homie," to UM–Flint, 1994.

My siblings and me celebrating Mama's eightieth birthday, 1995.

Standing in the cotton field near Mama's little house, off the Buck Lake Road, 1995.

Photo courtesy of University of Michigan–Flint. My University of Michigan–Flint executive leadership team in 1998.

Rashad seated with my AM&N College mentors, Dr. L. A. Torrence *(front row)* and Mr. and Mrs. O. R. Holiday at UAPB commencement, where I was awarded a doctor of humane letters, 2001.

The loves of my life, Jeanetta and Rashad, at the 2001 University of Michigan commencement. Rashad graduated with honors.

Jimmy Ross, Arkansas native, friend, and mentor, who served as director of scholarships and financial aid at Indiana University, 2002. Jimmy was the first black person to serve in a major leadership position at Indiana University.

Photo courtesy of North Carolina Central University. NCCU football players helping me move students into a residence hall, 2007.

Photo courtesy of North Carolina Central University. Being congratulated by the NCCU board chair following my inauguration as chancellor, 2008.

Photo courtesy of North Carolina Central University. Speaking at my inauguration as the tenth chief executive of NCCU, 2008.

Photo courtesy of North Carolina Central University. Posing with my friend and mentor Vic Jose from Richmond, Indiana, after being inaugurated as the tenth chancellor of NCCU, 2008.

Photo courtesy of North Carolina Central University. Talking with students in the NCCU campus cafeteria, 2008.

Photo courtesy of North Carolina Central University. Visiting with NCCU students in the chancellor's office, 2008.

Photo courtesy of North Carolina Central University. US Supreme Court Chief Justice John Roberts, NCCU Law School dean Raymond Pierce, and me at the NCCU Moot Court Competition, 2009.

Photo courtesy of North Carolina Central University. Presenting Muhammad Yunus, founder of microlending, with a copy of my book *Start Where You Find Yourself*, 2010.

Photo courtesy of North Carolina Central University. Ground-breaking ceremony for the third NCCU Habitat for Humanity house, 2010.

Photo courtesy of North Carolina Central University. Welcoming Donna Brazile, CNN political commentator and Democratic strategist, to NCCU, 2011.

Photo courtesy of North Carolina Central University. Congressman John Lewis with Jeanetta and me following his stirring 2011 commencement speech at NCCU.

Photo courtesy of North Carolina Central University. Hooding Reverend Dr. William Barber II at the 2012 NCCU commencement after awarding him the honorary doctor of humane letters degree. He earned his undergraduate degree from NCCU.

Photo courtesy of North Carolina Central University. Presenting an NCCU student with his degree at the 2012 commencement ceremony.

Photo courtesy of North Carolina Central University. Presenting an NCCU student with her degree at the 2012 commencement ceremony.

Two of my most loyal NCCU team members, Susan Hester, vice chancellor and chief of staff *(standing)*, and Betty Willingham, assistant to the chancellor, 2012.

Jeanetta and me preparing to celebrate Christmas, 2016.

Photo courtesy of Howard University. Posing with HBCU presidents following a dinner hosted by Howard University president Dr. Wayne Frederick, 2016. I continue to serve as mentor to the group.

Visiting the UAPB college farm in 2017 with Dr. Hazell Reed, my cow-milking buddy from 1965 to 1966.

Photo courtesy of Indiana University. In recognition of lifetime giving, Jeanetta and I were inducted into the Indiana University Presidents Circle, 2017.

7

BOOT CAMP

"WHY IN THE HELL ARE YOU LOOKING AT me, boy? Do you like me or something? Are you a damn faggot? If you keep staring at me, I'll come over there and kick your ass all the way back to where ever you came from! Is that clear? Listen up, girls, I'm going to make men out of you. I'm going to make a marine out of you that'll make your mama cry tears of joy and your daddy wonder if you are really his punk-looking son, the little snooty-nosed boy who joined the Marine Corps. For the next one hundred thirty-five days, I'm gonna be your mammy, your pappy, and your boss!

"I'm Gunnery Sergeant Tommy Rucker, your chief drill instructor, twenty-four-seven. I'm the last person you'll see before going to sleep at night and the first one you'll see when you get up the next morning. I'm like a damn ghost; I'm always there whether you see me or not! You will do everything I tell you to do without giving me any back talk or bullshit. Is that clear? Is that clear? I can't hear you! You will neither sneeze nor take a piss without my permission. Do I make myself clear? I can't hear you, girls! Louder! Louder! Louder, dammit! You sound like a bunch of damn sissies, but when I get through with you punks, you're going to sound like marines with some *balls*."

After I was sworn into the US Marine Corps at the Little Rock Armed Services Recruitment Office in June 1969 by the commander of the Marine Corps Reserve unit at Camp Robinson, a young White recruiter who was full of himself, Corporal Swinton, drove the other marine recruit, a White fellow from Monticello, Arkansas, and me to Little Rock Airport for our flight to San Diego. With a lengthy layover in Dallas, it was well after 9:00 p.m. in California and midnight in Arkansas, when we arrived. We were met at the airport by Gunnery Sergeant Rucker and his staff of two drill instructors, who accompanied us to the Marine Corps Recruiting Depot Reception Center.

Before proceeding inside, where our hair was cut to the lowest level possible by the barber's clippers, we were required to stand at attention on yellow footprints painted onto black asphalt and listen to what seemed to be an endless stream of well-rehearsed insults hurled at us by the chief drill instructor and his staff. I felt like I was about to pass out from a confluence of sleep deprivation, jet lag, anger, and hunger. At the same time, I had to urinate so badly that it seemed my bladder would explode any second. Yet none of us dared ask for permission to go to the "head." How any of us managed to go so long without urinating was nothing short of miraculous!

Following our identical haircuts—bald—we were issued skivvies (or underwear), shaving kits, socks, boots, dress shoes, field jackets, dress uniforms and hats, training caps, canteens, field uniforms, knapsacks, and sea bags, in addition to other gear. Afterward, we recruits were required to write home to inform our loved ones that we were being treated with respect and dignity and to give them our mailing address, all of which made us feel that we would be killed in the ensuing hours. In addition, we were required to change into our military-issued clothing and to bundle our civilian attire for shipping home. As I made my way through this denigrating process, I found myself asking, "What in the hell have I gotten myself into?"

It was well past midnight by the time we arrived at the Quonset huts that would serve as home during basic training. These World War II military barracks had no windows, air conditioning, electric fans, or indoor plumbing. With light bulbs extending from the ceiling, each of these austere Quonset huts accommodated around twenty-five recruits in double-bunk beds. There were two sets of bunk beds: four people in one room. At 5:00 a.m. sharp, Gunny Rucker or one of his loyal assistants would flick on the lights and start yelling, "Get up, dammit! Get up, you sissies!" After shaving, brushing our teeth, washing our faces, and making our beds, we'd be marched off to breakfast, followed by a day of classes filled with Marine Corps history, first aid, firearms safety and practice, swimming and calisthenics, and precision drill and survival training, among other activities. To be sure, there was never a dull moment.

* * *

Prior to joining the Marine Corps, I was not acquainted with anyone who'd served, and I had no inherent or patriotic interest in doing so. With a low draft-lottery number, I knew the possibility of being drafted and shipped off to Vietnam was high if I gave up my deferment to attend graduate school at Indiana University. Since the White fellows had snapped up all of the National Guard vacancies in Arkansas, the Marine Corps Reserves was my only option. Once we settled into our boot-camp training routine, I discovered that I was the only reservist in the platoon and just one of two college graduates. As a college graduate and reservist, I was dubbed by drill instructors a communist who didn't care enough about America to defend it against the Vietcong or other foreign enemies. Needless to say, the drill instructors made my life pure hell and did everything within their power to ensure my failure.

While many of the Marine Corps general training practices were physically and psychologically abusive, I am convinced that I was treated differently because I was a Black man with a college degree, and my Southern drill instructors sought to prove that I was just another nigger who got lucky and earned a college degree. In their view, it was their job to teach me a bit of humility and respect for America. They seemed to never tire of trying to belittle me and even seemed to relish singling me out for maltreatment. It quickly became a test of wills, and I wasn't about to wince or cry out aloud.

The more they abused me, the harder I worked to prove I was a survivor. Mama had convinced me that I could be anything I wanted to be, and this lesson had been reinforced by the faculty and staff at McNeil High School and AM&N College. Simply put, failure was not an option, and I found a way to deal with everything thrown at me without, to paraphrase Kipling, losing my head when all about me were losing theirs and blaming it on me.

I still have the physical and psychological scars from being forced to do knuckle push-ups on hot asphalt on the drill field. If I listen hard enough, I can still hear the taunts from one drill instructor in particular, a White racist from Louisiana, who made it his job to try to get under my skin. Thankfully, I never took the bait. When he pushed me off a fifty-foot diving platform, knowing full well that I couldn't swim, I managed to tread water long enough to be rescued by a lifeguard. I vividly recall an incident on the firing range when I might have put a bullet through his skull if he'd pushed me harder. I think even he realized he'd pushed me too far and I was prepared teach him a lesson, even to my own detriment.

Despite the painful antics of the drill instructors, I was treated with a great deal of respect by my fellow marines. They admired the fact that I had graduated from college and was headed to graduate school upon completing the six months of required boot camp and advanced infantry training.

They readily turned to me for advice about family matters and problems they were having with girlfriends or recently entered marriages.

Even with the impoverished conditions of my life in the Arkansas Delta, I discovered that I had something many of my fellow recruits did not. I had the love and support of family and the mentorship of faculty and administrators at what many considered a little, nondescript Black college. I was part of a village that claimed me as their own and took the necessary measures to ensure my success. Equally as important, I was married to my college sweetheart, and she partially deflected my attention from the horrors of my boot camp experience by making sure there was always a letter for me during mail call, which occurred two to three times each week. Occasionally, she'd have our friend Betty Willingham, who coordinated our wedding, use our little Kodak Polaroid camera to take a photo of her and enclose it in her letter. Words cannot capture the pride and comfort I felt upon receiving Jeanetta's weekly letters and sharing her photos with several close Marine Corps associates.

No matter how I look at it, I simply wasn't prepared for the personal insults, psychological assaults, and denigration heaped on me and my fellow Marine Corps recruits in boot camp. If the objective was to tear down recruits and to rob them of their individuality, clearly that objective was accomplished with the overwhelming majority of the recruits. I was among a handful of recruits who refused to accept the corps's tactics of humiliation. Despite having grown up in an environment where racism permeated all aspects of a Black person's life, I must admit that I was not prepared for the dehumanization I experienced for what felt like ten endless weeks in 1969. Maybe it was this experience that caused me to reject ever using Marine Corps training tactics. The words of Eleanor Roosevelt spoke volumes to me then, and they still do now: "No one can make you feel inferior without your permission." I can say unequivocally that I never gave the Marine Corps permission to treat me with disrespect. And I have never meted out that kind of disrespect to others.

* * *

Upon completing my obligatory active duty, I was welcomed back to my job at AM&N College, while most of my fellow marines were sent off to Vietnam. Regrettably, I never saw or heard directly from a single one of them again. However, hardly a year has passed since 1969 when I haven't wondered what happened to the members of Platoon 3322. Did they suffer the devastating effects of Agent Orange? How many of them were ambushed by the Vietcong and died thousands of miles away from home, fighting in a thankless war? How many of their names are inscribed on the Vietnam Memorial Wall in Washington, DC? Did they, like me, live long enough to father and parent a son or a daughter? Are those who are still alive financially secure, or are they struggling to survive from day to day, month to month? Are they served effectively, respectfully, and promptly by the veterans administration health system? Are they homeless, or are they sufficiently housed? Are they suffering from post-traumatic stress disorder (PTSD) or substance abuse?

While I have more questions than I have answers, I have reconciled myself to the fact that these are questions to which I'll probably never know the answers. However, what I *do* know is the absolute necessity of treating those who have served our country with the dignity and respect they deserve. Like issues of diversity, the treatment of our veterans often attracts more political rhetoric than effective policy. This must change. How we treat our veterans, many of whom confront life-altering injuries and PTSD, should be a national priority for us all.

* * *

When I returned home from a combined six months of boot camp in San Diego and advanced infantry training in the California desert, the most persistent questions I got were these: What was it like? Did they treat you well? What was the hardest part of the training? Were you fearful of being sent to Vietnam, or is that your next stop? The most important question for me, as one who experienced the rigors of what is arguably the toughest training regime to which military recruits are subjected, was, what did you learn? This last question was posed by my mentor Dean Torrence. My reply was candid and straightforward, absent any inclination or need to be politically correct.

I told Dean Torrence that I learned far more about myself than I did about the Marine Corps. Despite many of the negative and demeaning training tactics used by the Marine Corps, I learned three critical lessons that I believe will serve me for a lifetime. First and foremost, I learned the importance of working collaboratively with your fellow marines to stay alive. Marines in a foxhole together are totally dependent on each other for survival. Loyalty is more than a seven-letter word, and it's nonnegotiable.

Second, being in optimal physical condition may not save your life, but it will enable you to compete on a level superior to that of an out-of-shape fighter. Third, knowing who you are and what you value will sustain you well beyond the insults hurled at you by insecure people who, in their minds, would like to bring you down a notch.

Thankfully, before completing my six-year obligation to the US Marine Corps, I had the opportunity to meet and work with some of the most professional officers and enlisted men to serve in the corps. For the most part, they valued education and did not have an ax to grind when it came to race. By the time I completed my commitment, I'd served with reserve units in Indianapolis, Indiana; Bronx, New York; and Dayton, Ohio. In April 1975, I was honorably discharged with the rank of sergeant. Since I was plagued by a skin disorder aggravated by shaving that disproportionately affects Black men but was not recognized by the Marine Corps at the time, when I was discharged, I vowed never to shave again. That was forty-four years ago, and even today, I'm physically defined by my bald head and fully gray beard. Despite the racism and discrimination I experienced as a Marine Corps recruit, to avoid being drafted and sent to Vietnam, I'd volunteer all over again.

* * *

Two years after being discharged from the Marine Corps, I was awarded a doctoral degree by Indiana University. After all, my primary reason for joining the Marine Corps Reserve was to have the opportunity to pursue graduate studies without the fear of being drafted. Although earning a doctorate in higher education administration was a personal objective, I never viewed myself as owning my degree.

I was simply its steward. The rightful owners were members of my family and community, the mentors and university faculty who'd mentored me throughout my undergraduate and graduate days at AM&N, Indiana, and Columbia universities. When I was presented with my degree on Mother's Day, May 8, 1977, I was joined by my mom, my spouse, and several of my siblings, all of whom had encouraged me not to let anything get in the way of completing my degree. My only regret was that Papa, who had a brief illness, wasn't there in person to celebrate with me. Although neither he nor Mama had a clear sense of what it meant to earn a doctoral degree, they knew it was the highest credential in my field of study and that it had value in the world of education. I was always a bit put off by those who refer to themselves as *Doctor*, but that didn't seem to stop my parents from quietly telling relatives and friends that their son Charlie had his doctorate degree!

* * *

Over my professional career of four decades, several forces have been constants. Most importantly, I have had extraordinarily supportive mentors from all walks of life. Second, I was willing to take professional risks, and I was blessed to have a spouse who shared my desire to change the world. Third, my entry into the field of higher education coincided with passage of a bevy of federal legislation designed to increase college access for low-income ethnic minorities and other historically disenfranchised groups. As these federal barrier-breaking pieces of legislation were passed, the nation was confronted by a dearth of Black faculty, staff, and administrators to fill the positions created at predominately White colleges and universities. Key legislation that fueled the career of baby boomers like myself included the following:

- Higher Education Act of 1965 and authorization of TRIO programs, which are federally funded programs included in the 1964 Equal Opportunity Act. They include Talent Search for middle school students, Upward Bound for high school students, and Special Services for college students. These programs were created to increase college enrollment, persistence, and graduation. They serve the needs of low-income and first-generation students and other individuals from disadvantaged backgrounds.
- 1968 Reauthorization of the 1965 Higher Education Act
- 1972 Reauthorization of the 1968 Higher Education Act
- 1976 Reauthorization of the 1972 HEA

On an icy-cold February day in 1971, decked out in new clothes purchased from Kahn's men's clothing store in Bloomington with proceeds from a student loan arranged by my homeboy Jimmy Ross, I boarded a plane in Indianapolis for the long trip to Rensselaer, New York, via Chicago and Buffalo. This marked the first time I'd ever purchased a wool winter overcoat or wool pants, because the weather seldom got cold enough in the Arkansas Delta to wear heavy winter clothes. The purpose of my visit to New York was to interview as assistant admissions director at America's oldest engineering college, Rensselaer Polytechnic Institute.

For the better part of the 1970–71 academic year, RPI had been faced with a rash of racial incidents, and the administration had made a commitment to increase the number of minority students; in those days, *minority* was a euphemism for Black. At the end of my interview, I was given a campus tour by a Black-White student duo from New York City. To their great dismay and chagrin and to my surprise, we were greeted by a message on a hallway chalkboard in a major academic building that read, "It's time for all niggers to go home." As a Southerner, I had mistakenly thought that such language was unique to the South and that New Englanders were somewhat more racially sensitive and enlightened. Upon seeing that message, I was delighted that I had accepted an invitation from the Lehman College's dean of students, Dr. Glenn Nygreen, to visit with him while in New York.

I took the train from Schenectady to Grand Central Station in Manhattan and walked a couple of blocks to board the D train that would take me north to the Bronx, where I had been advised to get off at Bedford Park Boulevard stop, two blocks from Lehman College and the Bronx High School of Science. Having never been on a city train before, I found myself growing increasingly anxious as the engineer, whom I could not understand, announced stop after stop. Finally, I asked the passenger standing next to me about my stop, whereupon she looked at me like I was a madman. She said enough for me to know that her command of English was only a tad bit better than my Spanish.

This was the first time that it really dawned on me that not all American citizens speak English. It was a lesson that served me well during my stay in New York. Carrying my luggage, long before the days of rolling suitcases, I made my way to Lehman College. I was greeted by Dean Nygreen and his wonderful administrative assistant, Agnes, as if I were a long-lost son who'd found his way home. Little did I know at the time that these two individuals were god-sent angels who would help me navigate the steep mountain of culture shock I would experience as a country boy from Arkansas. Although I thanked them constantly while I was at Lehman College, I look forward to thanking them in the afterlife, because I know there is a VIP reservation for the two of them!

Insisting that I call him Glenn, Dean Nygreen gave me a personal tour of the Student Services Division, stopping along the way to introduce me to members of his staff. He referred to all of them by their first names and inquired about the well-being of their children, grandchildren, spouses, or significant others. My whirlwind tour was followed by an interview with Glenn's executive leadership team, which was followed by him personally driving me to the airport in his little convertible Dodge Dart. As he drove speedily toward LaGuardia Airport, darting in and out of traffic, Glenn talked with unbounded enthusiasm about the recent decision by the board of trustees of the City University of New York to endorse open admissions. He made it clear that he was committed to hiring a more diverse staff and that he'd canvassed his leadership team, who had encouraged him to offer me a job as a counselor and instructor in education. After Glenn promised that he'd follow up with a written offer in a few days, I hurried out of his car, running as fast as I could to catch my flight to Indianapolis. En route to Indianapolis, sleep never visited me, as I thought about how fortunate I was and how best to break the news to Jeanetta about my interest in taking a job in New York.

Like clockwork, Glenn's letter arrived three days after my visit. He of-fered me a salary of $13,900, tuition remission for a doctoral program of my choice, a small moving allowance, and the opportunity to live rent-free with him and his wife, Beverly, until I found an apartment. As an apartheid-era baby boomer, I never imagined living in the same house as a White person. I would later discover that Glenn and Beverly, liberal Scars-dale residents, had a deep and abiding commitment to integration. They treated me as though I was their son and devoted countless hours to helping me find an apartment before the era of open housing in Yonkers, Scarsdale, and White Plains. The Fair Housing Act was part of the Civil Rights Act of 1968. Housing discrimination was a very serious issue in New York City and surrounding areas during the 1960s and 1970s. Beverly had an eye for discriminatory practices and never hesitated to challenge landlords if she felt something was awry.

Once Jeanetta finished her degree and joined me in New York, Beverly and Glenn made a concerted effort to make sure we were okay. We never spent a major holiday or birthday alone. If we failed to check in with them, they checked in with us. Some of my fondest and most hilarious times in New York were the times we spent with Glenn and Beverly Nygreen. Clearly, they were cut from similar fabric as Bob Shaffer, Betty Greenleaf, and Bob Kinker, Indiana University faculty members who also embraced me.

* * *

The sign on 125th Street read, "No Standing or Parking." I must have circled the blocks around Columbia University a half-dozen times before realizing what *no standing* meant. After an unsuccessful search, I gave up and parked illegally in a no-parking-or-standing zone, and I hurried to the Teacher's

College admissions office. My request for an admissions application was responded to immediately, and fortunately I did not incur the wrath of the police, who seemed to take pleasure in giving parking tickets to drivers near the campus.

It was the fall of 1971, several months after moving to New York. Jeanetta had accompanied me on my drive from Yonkers to Manhattan to pick up graduate school information from Teachers College of Columbia University. As I jumped in the car, tears were streaming down her face. Concerned, I asked, "What's the matter?" to which she replied, "Nothing." It only took a nanosecond for me to realize that she was completely stressed out and feeling the overwhelming effects of culture shock. That was over forty-five years ago, and I still haven't forgotten the adverse effects our move to New York had on Jeanetta. Although I worked full-time at Lehman College and attended Columbia's Teachers College full-time while Jeanetta taught middle school math in suburban Mamaroneck, our lives were without the joy and the laughter we'd shared as newlyweds only a couple of years earlier.

One late afternoon while recording notes from my last advisee, I was visited by Leon, a colleague of Pakistani descent who'd spent stints as a Peace Corps volunteer and an employee with the Ford Foundation before joining Glenn's staff. Leon began the conversation by asking how my work was going and whether I was receiving the support I needed to be successful. After I replied affirmatively, Leon surprised me by confessing he'd nominated me for a Ford Foundation Minority Doctoral Fellowship. If granted a fellowship, I could study full-time at a university of my choice. Needless to say, I was elated beyond measure, accepted the nomination, and was later awarded a fellowship. Glenn was equally pleased and readily agreed to let me work part-time while pursuing my doctorate full-time at Teachers College.

At TC, I had the opportunity to study under a combination of senior and emerging scholars who embraced diversity in its infancy. In fact, more than one-third of the members of my cohort of thirty students were people of color; the most notable was Donald Byrd, an internationally acclaimed jazz musician and chair of jazz studies at Howard University at the time. I suspect that few TC faculty members, or those in my cohort, would have predicted that I would become a three-time college president. In all candor, there were a couple of faculty members who discouraged my interest in HBCUs because they were convinced that such institutions would no longer be relevant or needed. Nevertheless, I persisted in my unswerving belief in the significance of the HBCU sector and concluded my career in higher education as chief executive officer of America's oldest public liberal arts HBCU, North Carolina Central University.

* * *

There is an often repeated adage in many quarters of the Black community that "we're all standing on the shoulders of others." I'm living proof of this truth, because I am standing on the shoulders of men and women of all races who went out their way to nurture my dreams and aspirations, beginning with my wise but uneducated parents, Eddie and Carrie Nelms. To make sure that I remain connected to those who gave me hope in the Arkansas Delta more than seventy years ago, I joined forces with three of my siblings and bought our parents' farm, and a few years later, several cousins and I purchased our paternal grandmother's farm. To honor the legacy of my parents and grandparents, my portion of their land will be placed in a land trust never to be sold or occupied by an individual but instead to be enjoyed freely by generations to come.

Among the strong shoulders on which I stand are a supportive group of administrators, faculty, and staff at Earlham College, a small, Quaker liberal arts college founded in 1847 in Richmond, Indiana. When I accepted the position at Lehman College, I had offers in hand from Earlham, RPI, and my alma mater AM&N College. Little did I know that two years later I'd find my way back to Earlham College and begin to forge important relationships that have lasted until this very day.

After two years of stressful teaching in Mamaroneck, Jeanetta made it clear that she was leaving New York with or without me. Of course, love trumps misery, so I called Earlham's director of admissions John Owen to inquire about a recently posted position that sounded much like the one I had turned down earlier. John informed me that it was indeed the same position. He went on to say that the person they'd hired had accepted a faculty position at another institution and that Earlham would be delighted to have me join the administrative faculty as assistant director of admissions without going through the search process again.

Asked what it would take for me to entertain an offer, I noted that Earlham needed to match my Lehman College salary, pay my relocation expenses, provide me with tuition reimbursement for at least one graduate course each semester and during the summer at Indiana University. When I reached candidacy level for my doctorate, I wanted to be able to take a minisabbatical to complete my dissertation. John shared my requirements with the provost and the president, and to my amazement, they said yes to all of my requirements, except matching my Lehman salary. Because the cost of living was significantly lower in Richmond than New York, we agreed on a salary of approximately $1,500 less than I requested. I joined the Earlham College family July 1, 1973, and thus began a relationship that still lasts today.

* * *

In my role as Earlham's assistant director of admissions, I led a national effort to increase the recruitment and enrollment of African American students. From mid-August through mid-December, I crisscrossed the country searching for students anywhere they could be found—public and private high schools, churches, community centers, public housing projects, barber shops, boarding schools, and sorority- and fraternity-sponsored college fairs, among other places.

My approach to recruitment was unorthodox and uncomfortable for some of my colleagues. I knew that convincing a prospective student and his or her parents to seriously consider Earlham would require more than glossy brochures and completed contact cards. I knew that successful recruitment efforts depended first and foremost on establishing authentic relationships with families. The starting point had to focus on the interests and aspirations of prospective students, not on a missionary zeal on the part of the institution. I was just as comfortable visiting the Ada S. McKinley Educational Services Center in the Cabrini Green Public Housing Project in Chicago as I was in visiting a high school in upscale Evanston, Illinois. My unorthodox recruitment strategies and Earlham's commitment to providing students with competitive financial aid packages resulted in record numbers of African American students choosing to enroll.

The positive aspects of my Earlham tenure notwithstanding, I dare not inadvertently convey the view that Earlham was free of racism or that all my faculty and staff colleagues possessed a basic level of cultural competence. While there were some truly wonderful people at Earlham, the passive-resistant tendencies of many were well represented. Sadly, some of my colleagues were racists without even recognizing their racism or microaggressions—the everyday slights and insults made by those with White privilege who remain unaware of what that means.

Such colleagues included two senior administrators, the president and the dean of students, who used their "Quaker heritage and values" as a cover for some of the most egregious forms of racism with a smile. They relegated Blacks to junior-level faculty and administrative positions under the guise of not being able to attract and retain faculty and administrators. Although Earlham was founded in 1847, not a single Black person, to my knowledge, had ever been tenured as a faculty member when I was appointed to a mid-level administrative position in 1973. The racism that many of my colleagues and I experienced was a confluence of acts and attitudes reflected in many of Earlham's board members and faculty.

Having grown up in America's apartheid era, I had mastered the art of dealing with White people long before my arrival at Earlham. I had also gained a level of confidence in myself that allowed me to speak up and to speak out without fear of retribution. After two years of success leading Earlham's diversity efforts in admissions, I was invited to serve as associate dean of student development and assistant professor of education. In this role, I directed the college's Living and Learning Program and served in an advisory capacity on a $150,000 Ford Foundation–funded organic-farming grant. With my degrees in agronomy and chemistry, I was the only person at Earlham with both practical and academic training in agriculture. In connection with the grant, Earlham provided the students I advised with a house and a ten-acre parcel of farmland. In addition to the organic-farming project, I team taught a nutrition course with a student, Sharita Bell, and a professor of botany, Bill Stephenson.

As a result of those experiences, I became a vegetarian and joined forces with Oxfam in their efforts to increase awareness of world hunger on a local level. For me, it wasn't enough to simply change my eating habits and to participate in local marches. I felt that it was my calling to do more. In 1975, after reading a disturbing article in *Time* magazine about the devastating impact of drought in the Sahel region of Africa, I wrote a letter and sent it by airmail to C. Payne Lucas, a former Peace Corps administrator and founder of Africare. I asked how I could be of service to his organization.

To my surprise, within a few days of mailing my letter, I received a call from Mr. Lucas explaining that Africare had just been awarded a major grant from the Lilly Endowment for a comprehensive hydroagriculture project focused on irrigation, crop production, and health education. The project was located in Niamey, the capital of Niger in West Africa. Mr. Lucas informed me that he was looking for a person with a background in agriculture who could manage a large-scale initiative. He proceeded to invite me to get myself a passport and visa so I could accompany him on a trip to Niger for a field interview in six weeks.

Having never been to Africa, I felt a range of emotions, including excitement, apprehension, and fear. I knew it was time for me to put up or shut with respect to aligning my activist philosophy with my actions. Not knowing exactly what reaction to expect, I reluctantly shared the news with my wife of only five years. Incredulous, she made it clear that she wasn't about to go that far away from home, family, and friends. What would happen if one of us became ill while there? What would she do while I was away trying to change the world? Where would we live? There were numerous needs right here in America; why did I need to go all the way to Africa to help people?

While I knew that all of Jeanetta's questions were reasonable and I couldn't provide the reassurance she sought, I felt the need to at least go to Africa myself to see what the situation was. She consented to my making the trip with the full understanding that if I took the job, she would not be accompanying me. With the assistance of officials at Africare, I secured my passport and visa for my first intercontinental flight—a flight to the cradle of civilization.

Charles Johnson from the Lilly Endowment, whom I had never met, linked up with me at the Indianapolis International Airport for our flight to John F. Kennedy International Airport, where we rendezvoused with Mr. Lucas for our flight to Africa by way of a two-day stop in Paris. I will never forget the fear that I felt upon landing at the airport in Niger and making my way through customs. There were soldiers with guns everywhere, and neither I nor Charles could speak a word of French!

A world traveler who'd directed all Peace Corps activities for the continent of Africa before founding Africare, Mr. Lucas made it clear to the soldiers that our papers were in order and that we would not be paying any bribes to get through customs. Even if his French wasn't impeccable, Mr. Lucas spoke with a level of authority, arrogance, and passion that resulted in our being waived through customs while being stared down. I experienced none of the warmth and love that I'd expected to be greeted with when arriving for the first time in the home of my ancestors.

Having grown up in the apartheid South, I knew firsthand the face of poverty. But I was not prepared for the heartbreaking levels of malnutrition, poverty, and starvation I observed in Niger's towns and cities, as well as its countryside. I felt guilty eating while those around me were starving. Over a period of two weeks, we made our way to villages small and large, but they all had one thing in common: starving people who made my childhood poverty seem like wealth.

Deep in the woods, situated on the banks of the Niger River, was the Africare house where Jeanetta would have lived with me had she chosen to accompany me to Africa. Except for a wood-burning stove for cooking, beds with mosquito nets, a chest of drawers, and two or three broken cane chairs, there was no furniture. Nothing in my background or training had prepared me for my first African experience. Even so, I was still committed to putting my money where my mouth was with respect to trying to improve the lives of those less fortunate than I had been. At the core of my being, I knew that Jeanetta and I could arrive at an arrangement that would enable me to undertake a two-year assignment with Africare while she retained her job as a social worker in Richmond, Indiana.

Jeanetta was right. I could see that the isolation and living conditions would prove difficult for me individually but especially for the two of us. During my second week in Niger, a military coup toppled the government, and I had to leave the country in a hurry. Africare delayed implementing the project for a year, and by the time they were ready to proceed, I had decided to take a leave from my job at Earlham and pursue my doctorate in higher education on a full-time basis. The political instability in Niger prevented me from undertaking the mission for Africare.

Nearly thirty years after my job offer in the Sahel, my only child, Rashad, who wasn't even born at the time of my offer, joined the staff of the UN World Food Programme, where he has held an array of positions over a fourteen-year period. Today he's based in WFP's headquarters in Rome, serving as Human Resources officer. WFP feeds nearly one hundred million people worldwide who are affected by natural or man-made disasters. As you can imagine, I'm very proud that he has chosen this path for service.

* * *

I would describe my time at Earlham as a period of searching, self-discovery, and enormous personal and professional growth. Without a doubt, Earlham was more than just a college. It was an imperfect community of teachers and learners unified in their pursuit of a world where people were defined by their commonalities rather than their differences. It was a community of Friends willing to engage in self-examination, to ask the tough questions, and to search for answers that could only be found within. Consensus was the modus operandi, not counting how many people were in favor of an idea or initiative and how many were opposed.

The Quaker approach to decision making had a profoundly positive and significant impact on my leadership style as well as my interactions with students, faculty and staff, and administrative colleagues throughout my forty-year leadership journey. Consensus making was tiring, clumsy, and messy. It required patience, openness, candor, and a willingness to consider the views of those with whom you didn't necessarily agree. Similarly, it required acknowledgment of what you didn't know as well as an openness to the discovery of truth.

At Earlham, every faculty gathering or formal event began with a moment of silence. I shall never forget how long that moment of silence felt the first time I attended a faculty meeting. I was more fidgety and uncomfortable than I imagined possible. What was only five or so minutes long felt like half an hour! As I had grown up in a southern culture dominated by talking, singing, and dancing, being quiet felt more like a punishment than a period of reflection.

By the time I left Earlham, I had come to appreciate the value of moments of silence and to feel comfortable with myself during the hour-long periods of worship at the Friends Meeting House on campus. When dealing with challenging personal and professional issues, I often gravitated to the meetinghouse, just to reflect on how best to succeed. During my three chancellorships, I sought to incorporate aspects of consensus building into the decision-making process. Invariably I would be asked, "When are we going to vote?"

Feeling the need to not delay completing my doctorate any longer, in April 1976, I requested and was granted a leave of absence from Earlham to complete my dissertation. I spent the 1976–77 academic year as a Lilly Endowment Fellow in the Dean of Faculties Office at Indiana University–Purdue University Indianapolis (IUPUI). Jack Buhner, the founding chief administrator at Indiana University Northwest (IU Northwest), was one of the best mentors anyone could hope to have. Jack considered me a full member of his staff and involved me in all aspects of his office, including faculty promotion and tenure dossiers, faculty search committees, budget conferences with deans, Strategic Planning Committee deliberations, and meetings of the Indiana Higher Education Commission. Supportive of my aspirations to serve one day as president of an HBCU, Jack took it on himself to create for me a year-long fellowship modeled after the national ACE Fellows program, in which I would later have the opportunity to participate.

The end of my internship with Jack coincided with the completion and defense of my dissertation. Then I had to decide whether to return to Earlham as associate dean of students or to seek a dean's position. As chance would have it, the dean of student development at Earlham resigned unexpectedly, and when a search was launched, I applied for the position. Needless to say, I was highly disappointed and insulted that I was not offered the position. Instead, a unilateral decision was made to rehire the White man who had previously held the associate dean's position and had left to take a dean's position at another college. Recognizing that the position was not a good fit, he sought to return to Earlham, and there were several key advocates on his behalf.

When I called Earlham's president to inquire about the status of the position, he gave me a long story about how much he valued my contributions and had created a position just for me as director of affirmative action. When I replied that such positions were roads leading to nowhere and that I had no interest in the job, he replied that he did not think that students or alumni would accept a Black dean and that he had to do what he felt was in the best interest of the college. I let him know in no uncertain terms how disappointed I was in his spineless decision and that I had no interest in returning to Earlham.

My anger, hurt, and disappointment exceeded anything I'd experienced since leaving the Arkansas Delta. I felt the need to share my outrage with the president, and I drafted a letter to him to that effect. Fortunately, I had the good sense to share the letter with a colleague, who asked me a simple but important question: "What do you wish to accomplish?" When I replied, "I just want to give this racist a piece of my mind!" she suggested that I sleep on it a few days because I didn't know when I might need to cross that bridge again. I followed her advice and never sent the letter. This simple but important lesson served me well for more than four decades.

As a young African American male with a doctorate in higher education and professional experience, finding a job was the least of my problems. Convincing Jeanetta to leave a job she enjoyed and a house she loved was the challenge I had to confront. I had several offers but gravitated toward two in particular: the director of the University Division at IU Northwest and the associate director of the Center for Educational Development at my alma mater the University of Arkansas at Pine Bluff, previously named AM&N. Each appointment included a tenure-track teaching position.

Excited about the prospect of returning to an urban campus, I accepted the position at IU Northwest and set about the business of looking for housing, but to no avail. I had no idea of just how racially segregated communities were in northwest Indiana and the southern suburbs of Chicago until I went looking for housing. I quickly discovered that Blacks were restricted to overwhelmingly Black neighborhoods dominated by substandard housing. Having lived in communities of our choosing in New York and in Richmond, Indiana, a Quaker community, we were not prepared for the blatant racism we encountered in our housing search. Upon finding something we liked, we'd telephone, only to be told that it had been rented earlier that day.

After countless unsuccessful attempts, I called Dean Torrence in Arkansas to let him know I'd changed my mind and would be returning to my alma mater after all. Needless to say, Bob Morris, the IU Northwest dean of students, was disappointed and did his best to persuade me not to go to Arkansas. Appreciative of all the unswerving support I'd received from Jeanetta, I was determined not to put her through a stressful move to an area dominated by northern-style segregation, accompanied, no less, by ice and snow. So we headed home to a region of the country with which we were acquainted, where the racial barriers that separated Blacks from Whites were beginning to be dismantled.

* * *

When I entered the world of academia in the early 1970s, you could easily count the number of Black administrators at PWIs, and those who were there were concentrated in student affairs. It didn't take much research to discover that there was more rhetoric than action regarding integration in higher education. Glenn Nygreen at CUNY, Bob Shaffer at IU, William Max Wise at Teacher's College, John Owen and Paul Lacy at Earlham, and Bob Morris at IU Northwest, were exceptions when it came to the Whites I knew who supported hiring talented people without regard to race, ethnicity, or gender.

Early in my leadership journey, I learned to be comfortable with myself and mastered the art of communicating with people from all walks of life. I didn't communicate with Whites one way and with Blacks another, which is now commonly referred to as *code switching*. As a Black professional with credentials from some of the best schools and programs in the nation, I refused to take a back seat to anyone. In meetings and at professional conferences, I always took a seat in the front of the room. If there were no seats up front, I squeezed past others to get a seat in the middle of the room. The back of the room was never my choice. When it came to speaking up and speaking out on important issues, I always did so in a calm, articulate, and passionate manner, never attacking others. I knew better than most that I wasn't just representing myself but all Black people, whether I wanted to or not. I also never forgot that the eyes of the village that had supported me were on me and that failure was not an option.

My life and career have been defined by the presence of mentors who've helped me navigate my leadership journey. They have been my GPS! My mentors made sure that I was prepared to compete on all levels, in all settings, and in all circumstances. They asked me more questions than they offered me answers, and in doing so, they helped me to become my best self. My mentors instilled in me the importance of keeping my head, never losing the common touch, and taking informed risks. Among the lessons I've never forgotten are these: there is nothing sacred about structure, as it only exists to facilitate goal achievement; the most important role of a leader is nurturing the dreams of others; be sure to keep some "go to heck" money; and never put your degree on your business card, because although you're a doctor, you can't heal anyone! Many of my mentors are dead now, but they live in me and in those for whom I serve as mentor and as a GPS for those who have embarked on the journey of leadership in higher education.

8

"IF I HAD A HAMMER"

THE SUN WAS JUST SETTING AS JEANETTA AND I arrived in Pine Bluff on June 12, 1977. I was driving a twenty-six-foot U-Haul truck containing all our worldly possessions, and Jeanetta was trailing me in her little apple-green hatchback Chevy Vega, which contained our collection of live plants, several boxes of books, and enough clothes to tide us over for a couple days as we settled into our temporary living quarters at the home of our mentors, Dr. and Mrs. Torrence. They lived in a lovely three-bedroom, brick, ranch-style home, in an all-Black subdivision, a couple blocks east of the UAPB campus.

During the height of housing segregation in America, Black neighborhoods like the Torrences' were prevalent in most cities in which HBCUs were located. Of course, a limited number of on-campus houses were available to senior members of the college administration. The Torrences, however, had chosen to build a home near the campus rather than live in a college-owned house.

Not wanting to park a large truck in a residential area yet wanting to make sure that our belongings were safe, we decided to park on a lot adjacent to the campus police department, thinking that it would surely be safe there. Oh, how mistaken we were! When we arrived on campus the following morning to transport our belongings to a storage facility, our hearts sank as we discovered that people had broken into the truck and helped themselves to items of their choosing. Since the truck was parked so close to the police department, we concluded it was an inside job. We filed a complaint with both the campus and city police departments, to no avail. Although the ordeal left a bitter taste in our mouths, we persisted in maintaining a positive attitude. Needless to say, this was just the beginning of several early negative experiences that colored what we had hoped would be a happy homecoming.

Within two weeks of arriving in Pine Bluff, we found a house and took occupancy a couple weeks later. In fact, Dr. Torrence was part owner of a rather-successful Black-owned real-estate firm and actually sold us the house. It was a residence of not more than five years old, but it had not been particularly well cared for. Jeanetta and I poured ourselves into landscaping and interior decorating, while I commenced my duties as the associate director of the Center for Student Development and prepared to teach two large sections of Psychology 101. By the start of the fall semester, Jeanetta had landed a good position with the Social Security Administration, and we were happily settling into our new home. Although Papa was not known to venture far from home, he and Mama came for a long weekend visit, which gave Papa the opportunity to reconnect after many years with the FHA home demonstration agent Thomas Vaughn, who had encouraged him to allow my siblings and me to participate in 4-H Club activities many years earlier.

Within weeks of taking up my duties at UAPB, there were murmurings about the lack of effectiveness on the part of the chancellor, Dr. Herman B. Smith, an intelligent, articulate, and dapperly dressed man with a doctorate from the University of Wisconsin. In 1972, AM&N College had been merged with the University of Arkansas and renamed the University of Arkansas at Pine Bluff. Smith was not reluctant to tell you how great he was and to share his desire to turn the school into a "real" university, much to the consternation of key alums, faculty, and staff opposed to the merger and Smith's decision to reassign or fire several popular long-serving administrators.

Unfortunately, he made the mistake of thinking that he could use me to upend my mentor and longtime friend Dr. Torrence as vice chancellor of student services. The chancellor indicated that Torrence's position was mine if I wanted it and pledged my loyalty to him. I made it crystal clear that I was not interested in the position and would never do anything to undermine the person who was like a father to me and had been unswerving in his support of my personal and professional development. In addition to such cracks within the internal UAPB administrative-faculty armor, there were also disagreements between senior UAPB leaders and those in charge of the University of Arkansas system in Fayetteville. UA system administrators exhibited little real interest in transforming UAPB into a more competitive and responsive institution of higher learning.

The creation of the University of Arkansas system and the merger of AM&N into that system was the result of a lawsuit known as *Adams v. Richardson*. In 1972, the National Association for the Advancement of Colored People (NAACP) sued the federal Department of Health, Education, and Welfare for allowing states to continue receiving financial support in violation of the 1964 Civil Rights Act.[1] The consent decree emanating from that lawsuit paved the way for creation of the UA system and the ensuing merger. Except for several new residence halls and academic buildings, when I returned in 1977, the campus looked a lot like it did when I had graduated nearly a decade earlier. A handful of new degree offerings had been introduced, including baccalaureate programs in nursing, social work, criminal justice, special education, and computer science, along with a few graduate programs in education.

With the desegregation of higher education in Arkansas, many of the top Black students chose to enroll at PWIs, while a growing number of White students, especially those with jobs and families, chose to stay close to home and enroll at UAPB. Arkansas State University, the University of Arkansas at Little Rock, the University of Central Arkansas, and Henderson State University experienced an influx of Black students. With its endowment prowess, the flagship campus in Fayetteville succeeded in attracting the cream of the crop, the best prepared Arkansans, irrespective of race or ethnicity. Thus, this reality left UAPB to serve the educational needs of some of the state's poorest and least prepared students, while confronted with the cumulative effects of historic underfunding, which many politicians and the UA system chose to ignore when it came to enforcing performance expectations and accountability metrics.

By October 1977, just four months after my return, I had reached the conclusion that there were significant limitations to the amount of positive change I could effect as an untenured assistant professor and a relatively junior-level administrator. After much reflection and discussion with Jeanetta and others whose judgment I valued, I concluded I was in the right place but not at the right time.

Having never before burned any bridges during my leadership journey, I picked up the phone and called Bob Morris, dean of students at IU Northwest, to tell him that my return to my alma mater had not proven to be the haven I had envisioned. Dealing with the internal and external political currents bearing down on the university required more energy than

I was willing to expend. Due to the lateness of my notice to Bob that I was not joining his team at IU Northwest, he had chosen to make an interim appointment, with the idea of reopening the search in spring 1978. Bob was happy to hear from me and told me that he welcomed my interest and would have a conversation about foregoing a search and sending me an offer letter. His only request was that I put my interest in writing. I did so right away.

True to his word, Bob talked with the chancellor, and by December 1, 1977, the trustees of Indiana University had approved my appointment. I resigned my UAPB position effective June 30, 1978. Needless to say, my decision left Dr. Torrence disappointed, but he understood my concerns and wished me well. Fortunately, I had a wonderful 1978 spring semester at UAPB. We sold our house without a realtor to the first person who looked at it, and two months before making our move from UAPB to IU Northwest, Jeanetta and I announced to family and friends that after a decade of marriage, we would be parents. What a happy ending to our short-lived tenure at UAPB!

* * *

Amid streams of tears, hugs, well-wishes, and goodbyes, on June 16, 1978, I handed the keys to the new owners of our house at 4211 Scott Avenue in Pine Bluff, and we headed north to Gary, Indiana. This time, I was driving the little Chevy Vega that Jeanetta had trailed me in just a year earlier. Thanks to IU Northwest, our belongings were being shipped via American Van Lines. With the assistance and advocacy of one of my IU graduate-school classmates, Dr. Lavell Wilson, we leased an apartment at the Mansards, a relatively new and overwhelmingly White tennis community in Griffith, Indiana, approximately a fifteen-minute drive from the university that would serve as my employer for the next six years.

A decade later, I would become friends with the developer-owner Jim Dye, an IU graduate and trustee who was one of my strongest supporters during my tenure as chancellor at IU East. Except for my friend Lavelle Wilson, there were only three or four Black families who lived at the Mansards, but we never had a moment of trouble. While training for the Chicago Marathon, I became a familiar Black face on the streets of all-White towns, hamlets, and villages of northwest Indiana. My fellow runners and I had one thing in common: we loved to run!

* * *

"Wow, what's that smell? Why is it so smoky? Where are all of the particulates getting in my eyes coming from?"

These were persistent questions I posed to my colleagues shortly after commencing my duties at IU Northwest. But there was only one person who knew enough to break it down to me, Dr. F. C. Richardson, a biologist and chair of the Division of Arts and Sciences. A Tennessean by birth; a graduate of Rust College, a Mississippi HBCU; and a holder of a PhD from the University of California, Santa Barbara, Dr. Richardson served on the Gary Board of Health.

"The smell, smoke, and particulates," he said, "are coming from the steel mills in Gary, East Chicago, and Burns Harbor, and the oil refineries in Whiting are emitting the smell to which you are referring. If you think it's bad now, you should have been here five years ago!" He went on to say, "The combination of these emissions is creating an environmental halo effect that not only wreaks havoc on the environment but also negatively impacts the quality of the air we breathe."

Thanks to the professional and persistent work of Dr. Richardson and his colleagues on the Gary Board of Health, they held the Environmental Protection Agency (EPA)'s feet to the fire and significantly reduced the harmful emissions that greeted the residents of northwest Indiana and Chicago's south suburban communities every single day. By the time Jeanetta and I left Gary in 1984, I suspect area steel mills met or exceeded most EPA air-quality standards.

Gary was a cultural mosaic of citizens from more than fifty countries who moved there to work in the steel industry. At the time of our arrival in 1978, the city had a population of approximately one hundred fifty thousand inhabitants, nearly half of whom were Black. Unlike the Arkansas Delta, where I was born, lived, and nurtured, there were no signs in Gary that read, *Colored Only* or *White Only*. However, housing, employment, and socializing patterns reflected a strict adherence to norms that favored nearly all ethnic groups over Blacks.

Gary was a gritty, working-class city that elected its first Black mayor, Richard Gordon Hatcher, in 1967. Hatcher was one of the first Blacks elected mayor of a major American city, and upon his election, many Whites fled to overwhelmingly White suburban communities throughout Lake County. This White-flight pattern persisted well into the 2000s, until there were few Whites left to flee. By 2017, more than 84 percent of Gary's population was African American.[2]

From 1968 to 2015, Merrillville, Indiana, Gary's nearest neighbor to the south, blossomed from a very small town to the most populated town in Indiana with over thirty thousand inhabitants. The majority of its growth was due to White flight from Gary.[3] Ethnic social clubs dotted the regional landscape of Gary and northwest Indiana. White flight, aided by redlining practices on the part of local real-estate firms, led to Whites selling their homes to Blacks at greatly inflated prices. Eventually, the Gary Housing Authority sued, and the injunctive relief granted by the courts prohibited real estate agents from placing for-sale signs on the lawns of properties up for sale. By that time of course, the damage had been done, and the adverse impact was irreversible. The city remains a ghost of its previous self, with factories closed and shops boarded up. US census figures have shown that northwest Indiana, including Gary, is the most segregated metropolitan area in the country.[4]

As with Mayor Hatcher, when Carl Stokes, a Black man, was elected mayor of Cleveland in 1967, that city experienced the flight of Whites to the suburbs. In fact, it was in one of those communities, Parma Heights, Ohio, in which I was called a nigger by a group of teenagers while recruiting students for Earlham College in 1973. When I mentioned the incident to the head guidance counselor at Valley Forge High School, she sought to play it down by saying, "It was just a group of kids acting out." Similar White-flight patterns would play out with the election of Black mayors in Newark, Los Angeles, Houston, and Chicago, among other cities. This legacy of racism and discrimination has done untold damage not only to the specific cities in question but also to the very fabric of our nation at large.

* * *

As the director of the University Division and associate dean of students, I reported to Bob Morris, dean of students. I had responsibility for a wide array of student services, including placement testing, new student orientation, academic advising, major certifications, tutorial support, and academic dismissals and reinstatements, among other responsibilities. More than one-third of the university's 4,800 students were served by a core staff of three full-time professional counselors, a recorder (certification officer), and a cadre of five part-time faculty advisors. We were aided by a small clerical support staff and three or four talented work-study students. Already woefully understaffed and trying to deal with long lines of students who waited until the last minute to register for classes, within two months of assuming my duties, I was told that I needed to cut my budget by 20 percent.

Bob Morris was a consummate student-services professional with an unyielding commitment to students who had joined the IU Northwest senior leadership team just two years prior to my arrival. Before that, he was on the student services staff at the State University of New York (SUNY) at Albany. As a thoughtful and politically liberal man, fairness seemed to be a part of Bob's DNA! I could not have asked for a more passionate, authentic, and caring supervisor than Bob.

Like Drs. Torrence, Shaffer, Nygreen, and Buhner, as well as others with whom I had worked, Bob Morris understood the confluence between affective and cognitive development in college students, and he understood the importance of collaboration across academic and administrative boundaries to ensure student success. Unfortunately, the relationship between Bob and the dean of academic affairs, Marion Mochon, was rocky at best. A chain-smoking cultural anthropologist from Wisconsin, Marion's interpersonal communications skills left a lot to be desired. For some reason, she had serious disdain for my supervisor, Bob, and made no secret about it. Yet she also took a liking to me and appointed herself as my mentor. We were both confident in ourselves as people and professionals and could go toe-to-toe in discussions, often disagreeing without being disagreeable.

Approximately three months into my role at IU Northwest, I was summoned to a meeting in Chancellor Danilo Orescanin's office. Accompanied by Dean Mochon, Dan wasted no time getting to the point. "Charlie," he said, "We are pleased with the quality of your work and delighted to have you as a member of our leadership team. As you know, the university is experiencing some serious budget challenges. After careful consideration and consultation, I have decided to reorganize the university by combining Academic Affairs and Student Services and appointing Marion as dean of academic and student affairs. I'd like for you to serve as associate dean of academic affairs with responsibility for all aspects of student affairs, effective immediately. Since I have not spoken with Bob yet, I ask that you treat this conversation as a confidential matter."

I hadn't seen this scenario emerging, and I didn't quite know how to respond. However, I managed to say that while I was prepared to do anything I could to be helpful, I was genuinely concerned about Bob and did not want him to think I'd done anything to undermine him. Both Dan and Marion responded by insisting that I refrain from assuming responsibility for any aspect of the restructuring. They noted that budgetary considerations aside, the working relationship between the two of them and Bob was not going well and that he was fully aware of it. Recognizing that I had an obligation to advocate on my own behalf, I asked whether the new responsibilities were accompanied by an increase in salary. Dan immediately responded no but said that he'd think about it. Six months after assuming my new duties, I was given a modest annual supplement of $1,500, even though the merger generated in excess of $300,000 annually for the campus.

I left the meeting with Dan and Marion in something of a daze—more like a state of shock! My respect for Bob and my personal ethics would not permit me to not apprise him of my recently concluded discussion with Dan and Marion. Bob assured me that he knew something was brewing and that I was not a part of the move to oust him. A consummate professional with real class, Bob told me that he was prepared to do everything possible to help me succeed in my new role. Part of me wanted to tell Dan and Marion that I wanted nothing to do with the restructuring, but with a baby due in three months, a newly signed apartment lease, student loan payments due, and less than $1,000 in the bank, I was between a rock and a hard place. And so I chose the best path forward from a list of imperfect options. Thankfully, Bob got a respectable severance package and a good job four months after leaving IU Northwest. He asked me to serve as a reference for him, and I did so without hesitation. Two years later, still in his early fifties, Bob died of lung cancer. The scourge of cancer is unrelenting!

As associate dean for academic affairs, my new portfolio included all student services activities: university division, admissions, student financial aid, student activities, career planning and placement, TRIO programs, registrar, developmental education, and seemingly everything else that no one else wanted to do. Rather than complain, I fully immersed myself in doing everything in my power to create and sustain a culture of caring, akin to the one that had enveloped me as a student at AM&N more than a decade earlier. My first step was to surround myself with a cadre of talented people who shared my values and had an uncompromising commitment to student success. Rather than looking outside for talented administrative colleagues, I turned to those already affiliated with the university. Their ethnic background didn't matter; I just wanted talented, hardworking people around me, for whom caring was color blind. I promoted Blacks to directorships in Admissions, Financial Aid, and University Division.

Within three years of my arrival at IU Northwest, there was an unimaginable amount of change. The chancellor had completely reorganized the campus and later accepted a position as vice president for university relations at Indiana University, operating out of Bloomington; Bob Morris had negotiated a severance package to his satisfaction; and Marion Mochon had taken medical leave. Before taking her leave, Marion nominated me for the 1981–82 ACE Fellows Program. I was selected and spent the year at Chicago's Roosevelt University and at IU Bloomington. Within a year of nominating me for the ACE Fellows Program, Marion died of an undisclosed illness while on leave. One of my greatest regrets was not having the opportunity to personally thank her for her mentorship and advocacy on my behalf.

In addition to my work at IU Northwest, I was the university's go-to person when it came to involvement in community affairs in Gary. As IU Northwest's highest-ranking Black administrator, I was frequently called on by churches and community-based agencies to speak at major events and to serve on various committees and boards. In 1980, I was elected president of the board of directors of the Urban League of Northwest Indiana. That same year, I was appointed to the Gary School Board by Mayor Hatcher. Principled and determined to do what was in the best interest of pupils in the Gary schools, I worked tirelessly amid an environment of grafts and kickbacks between contractors and school board members.

One Friday afternoon while I was clearing my desk and making preparations to attend the National School Boards Association convention in San Francisco, a FedEx courier delivered an envelope to me. It contained twenty crisp $100 bills, with a note that said, "Here's a little something to make sure you enjoy your stay in Frisco. There's more where this came from if you vote the right way on the bus contract that's up for approval in a couple of weeks." Infuriated, I surmised that the money and accompanying note came from a fellow school-board member, Tom, who had been lobbying me to vote for a particular transportation contractor. I picked up the phone, dialed his number, and told him that I didn't require a bribe to enjoy the meeting in San Francisco.

"I'm returning the money," I said, "and if you do this shit again, I'm reporting your ass to the school board attorney, district attorney, Indiana attorney general, and anyone else who'll listen to me. My vote is not for sale. Do I make myself clear? Is there any damn thing you don't understand about what I'm saying to your crooked ass?"

Never without a Christian cross on his lapel, Tom knew I was angry as hell and wasn't about to impugn my character over a $2,000 bribe. Acknowledging that he was the school board member who sent the money, he apologized profusely.

When our delegation arrived at the airport in San Francisco, we were met by a limo driver for the bus company, who drove us to a posh hotel. Upon arrival at the hotel, we were greeted by several attractive women (prostitutes, I surmised), who had been hired by the bus contractor to do anything necessary to make us happy. I refused to avail myself of their services, and two weeks later, I voted for the contractor with the best proposal, which wasn't the company that sought to bribe me and my fellow board members.

Two years after the attempted bribe from the bus contractor, I was subpoenaed by a Lake County grand jury to testify about alleged graft and contract kickbacks in Gary in general and within the Gary School Corporation in particular. Words cannot convey how happy I was to testify that I had not been a part of any kickback schemes. As the questioning proceeded, it became increasingly clear that Mayor Hatcher was the real target of their inquiry. It felt even better to be able to candidly answer that I had no knowledge of any attempt on the part of the Mayor Hatcher or the superintendent of the Gary School Corporation to fix contracts. That was in 1987, and I haven't heard from the district attorney since.

* * *

Serving as a full-time senior university administrator and a tenure-track faculty member at the same time was far more difficult than I ever envisioned. Despite the 24–7 requirements associated with being an administrator, I managed to present two to three papers annually at national conferences and to serve as the chair of the Gary School Board, the president of the Urban League of Northwest Indiana, and a member of the Community Advisory Board of the *Post-Tribune* newspaper. In addition, I was expected to teach at least one class each semester. How I managed to fulfill my university and community responsibilities without losing my grip is beyond me! The depth, breadth, and significance of my campus, community, and national efforts notwithstanding, most faculty members on the IU Northwest Promotion and Tenure Committee had a very traditional and narrow view of the requirements of a tenure-track faculty member, and I didn't meet them.

In fact, there were some members of the committee who held it against me that I was an administrator. Of course, since IU Northwest was an urban, community-based institution, I was convinced that my scholarly and service activities were consistent with what faculty members at such an institution should be pursuing. Each semester, I taught a graduate course in educational psychology to a group of teachers who seemed more concerned with what would be on the exam than with what they were learning and how it applied to their work. My research focused on the impact of basic literacy skills on employment opportunities of urban youth. In the summer of 1983, I spent what felt like countless hours assembling my dossier for submission to the chair of the department. By a narrow vote, my colleagues recommended that I be tenured and promoted. The chair of the Division of Education concurred and forwarded all materials to the campus Promotion and Tenure Committee, which voted by a narrow margin in my favor. By that time, Marion Mochon was dead, a new academic dean (a closet racist and sexist) was on board, and Dan Orescanin had accepted a new position as IU vice president of university relations and was operating out of the central university administration in Bloomington.

Part of the IU Northwest promotion and tenure process entailed sending the candidate's dossier to at least two faculty scholars and researchers at comparable institutions. In my case, the dean chose to ignore my suggestions and those of the division chair and instead sent my dossier to researchers he knew at Harvard University and the University of Cincinnati. Of course, neither institution was remotely comparable to a community-based institution like IU Northwest, with less than five thousand students. Interestingly, the University of Cincinnati faculty member wrote a generally positive letter on my behalf, while the Harvard faculty member, as one would expect, had very few positive comments about my work. Seemingly pleased with the outcome of the review, the dean called to tell me that the results of the external review had arrived and that he was not prepared to recommend me for promotion or tenure. He suggested that I resign and seek a position at another university.

Two weeks later, I received a personal call from the acting chancellor requesting that I meet with her to discuss the dean's negative recommendation. Rather than meet with me in her office, we met in a conference room in the university library. She began by telling me how much she respected me and how racist and sexist the dean was. However, given his negative recommendation, the chancellor noted that she was not prepared to recommend me for promotion or tenure.

She continued by telling me about the IU president's positive impression of me. She suggested that I forgo a negative vote and resign my tenure-track position while retaining my administrative post. Looking the chancellor dead in the eye, I said, "Chancellor, my record is equal to or greater than most of my colleagues in the Division of Education. I feel I have earned the right to be promoted and tenured. I have a four-year-old son. I don't ever want to look at him and say that I took the easy way out by resigning rather than do what I thought was right. So you do what you feel you need to do, and I'll do what I need to do."

With that, I got up and walked out of the room with my head held high. After all, Mama had told me to hold my head up high when I walk through a storm. I had nothing to apologize for when it came to my professional accomplishments. On April 10, 1987, I received a letter from IU president John Ryan informing me that at its April 4 board meeting, the IU Board of Trustees had granted me tenure as a faculty member at IU Northwest. Unbeknownst to the dean for Academic Affairs, chancellor, or anyone at IU Northwest, just before receiving President Ryan's letter, I was offered the position of vice president of student services and enrollment at one of the largest and most respected two-year colleges in the country, which I eventually accepted.

* * *

As a baby boomer who came of age during the turbulent 1960s, I readily admit that I had little interest in becoming an extensively cited academic scholar. Hell, I felt that America was in dire need of transformation with respect to racial equity and equality, and I wanted to do my part to change things now, not fifty years from now. To the extent that I could use research to frame and articulate a rationale for change, I valued research. However, I had no interest in attending national meetings and listening to scholars read academic papers to each other.

Living and working in a racially segregated midwestern industrial city, I was more concerned about the steps needed by students, parents, public school administrators, and university officials to increase college access and success. I had absolutely no interest in comparing, for example, the performance of Black and White students on the ACT or SAT, or the extent to which the two groups took advanced placement (AP) courses. I was more concerned with making sure that Black students in Gary schools had *access* to courses that awarded dual high-school and college credit than I was in how well Black and White students performed on the AP exam. Yes, I was more concerned with getting more Gary students in and successfully through programs in nursing, teacher education, allied health, accounting, and medicine, for example, than I was in why they didn't pursue those disciplines at higher levels. I was far more interested in the *how* than I was in the *why* that motivated student behavior.

Indiana University Northwest was a lot like Gary—racially segregated—and all but a handful of my White colleagues shared my desire to change that. Regrettably, not many members of Gary's Black middle class exhibited an interest in challenging the status quo either. They didn't seem concerned enough by the small number of Black faculty, staff, and students at IU Northwest to challenge the chancellor or the IU Board of Trustees to do better. How could a majority-Black community not demand that a predominately White institution in its midst do a better job of enrolling more Black students and hiring more Black faculty and staff?

When I arrived at IU Northwest in 1978, the student enrollment was 23 percent Black, according to the 1978–79 IU Fact Book. Today, nearly forty years later, the university's enrollment is down to only 17 percent Black, although the city of Gary is 84 percent Black.[5] Similarly, the number of Black faculty remains meager, in no way reflecting the city's population, and there are no Black members of the university's executive leadership team. These realities stand in contrast to an era when the campus employed a Black female chancellor as well as a Black vice chancellor, dean, and several senior administrative employees.

* * *

For as long as I can remember, my leadership journey has been marked by two important features: management by walking around (or MBWA), and simply going for a walk when I needed to clear my head while dealing with a difficult situation. At noon on a particular fall day in 1986, I decided to forego lunch and head to the Dairy Queen just a block from my office at the corner of Thirty-Fifth and Broadway in Gary to treat myself to a cone of soft-serve ice cream. Upon arrival, I was greeted by Dr. Lynn Merritt, a nationally acclaimed chemist who had retired a few years earlier as a faculty member and dean of the Graduate School at Indiana University. Lynn was now serving as interim chair of the Department of Chemistry at IU Northwest.

After greeting each other and engaging in small talk about the gorgeous weather, Lynn said, "Charlie, I want you to know that John Ryan has his eye on you. He has taken note of your leadership abilities and is prepared to appoint you to a major leadership position at Indiana University in the very near future."

I thanked Lynn but didn't dare tell him about my candidacy for a position at Sinclair Community College. I didn't see Lynn again until 1998, when I assumed my duties as IU's vice president of institutional development and student affairs. At that time, I was a member of the parish council at Bloomington's First United Methodist Church, where it turned out that Lynn was also a member. Shortly after our brief reunion, I read in the local newspaper that Lynn, my behind-the-scenes advocate, had passed away.

I admit that I wasn't fully aware of Indiana University's rich history related to diversity until I talked with my homie, friend, and mentor, the late Jimmy Ross, IU's director of student financial aid, who was among the first Blacks to serve as a senior-level administrator at a Big Ten university. While I met many of IU's Black graduate students from HBCUs in the South, I did not have a full appreciation of the contributions they made to the tapestry of diversity that exists at IU today!

Florida Agricultural and Mechanical (A&M) University, Tennessee Agricultural and Industrial State College, Jackson State, Alcorn State, Alabama State, Alabama Agricultural and Mechanical University, North Carolina College, Allen College, Wilberforce College, Benedict College, Langston College, Central State College, Tougaloo College—all now universities—were just a few of the places from which Blacks came summer after summer to take graduate courses at Indiana University Bloomington (IU Bloomington). I will never forget how pleased I was to meet so many Black graduate students when Jeanetta and I arrived on campus in June 1970. Like us, they were people who believed in the power of education and had an unwavering commitment to Black colleges. Unlike us, however, they left spouses behind to spend the summer at IU living in un-air-conditioned rooming houses or campus dormitories while struggling financially to make ends meet.

With few outlets for social interactions, they gathered at Jimmy's house for parties that lasted well into the wee hours of the morning or at the infamous Hole on Bloomington's west side. Owned and operated by a Black chapter of the Elks International, the Hole was just that—a hole in the ground. By the time the chapter completed the basement, it had run out of money and couldn't finish the first floor of the building, and so they set about the business of using the basement level to host parties, dances, and other social events in the Black community.

The Hole was unable to compete with restaurants and hotels that welcomed Black patrons. I recall that the Hole closed in the late 1980s and reopened for a short while a decade later when a group of men from IU and the Bloomington community tried their hand at revitalizing the place. Although the top floor had been constructed by that time, the Hole was not a place where *sophisticated* Black intellectuals at IU felt comfortable. In fact, the IU archives don't even have a record of its existence! If only walls could talk, they would recount the history of the Hole and the role it played in providing a place of comfort and a safe haven for those of us who made our way to IU for graduate study before the PWIs in southern states welcomed us.

* * *

"Charlie," the voice on the phone said, "this is Ned Sifferlen, vice president of instruction at Sinclair Community College in Dayton, Ohio. As chair of the search committee for vice president of student services, I'm calling to let you know that you're one of two finalists for the position. A few of us would like to visit you at IU Northwest and to talk with a few of your colleagues and subordinates. Here is a list of people we'd like to meet with. Can you arrange those meetings for us?"

I was surprised and pleased at the same time by the phone call; this was the first time I'd been involved in a search of this nature. I proceeded to arrange the meetings requested by Ned, and two weeks later, I received a call from Sinclair's president, David Ponitz, offering me the position at a salary more than $25,000 above my IU Northwest salary. The only problem was that David wanted me to begin my duties immediately. I explained to him that teachers in Gary were on a strike and that as chair of the Board of School Trustees, I could not afford to accept another position or announce my departure before the strike was settled. As a former superintendent of schools in Michigan early in his career, David understood my predicament and offered me the position of vice president at Sinclair with a start date of April 15, 1984.

Commencing my duties in the middle of the semester meant that Jeanetta, a high school mathematics teacher, and Rashad, a kindergartner, would not be able to complete the spring semester in an orderly fashion if they moved with me. For three months, I made the four-hour weekend commute between Centerville, Ohio, a Dayton suburb, and Gary. In addition to the stress of the commute, this was a very tense period in our lives as a mass killer, Alton Coleman, and his accomplice, Debra Brown, were on the loose in the Chicago and Gary areas.

Living several hundred miles away and worrying about the safety of my family meant that I had a lot of sleepless nights. Admittedly, I can't fully comprehend what it must have been like for Jeanetta and Rashad, who found themselves living behind double-locked doors every day from sundown to sunup. We were all excited, delighted, and relieved when we were reunited as a family in Dayton in June 1984. After a crime spree across six midwestern states and eight murders between May and July 1984, Alton Coleman and Debra Brown were apprehended in July of that year, and Coleman was executed by lethal injection in Ohio in 2002.

* * *

Holding two graduate degrees in higher education administration and armed with a decade of work experience at urban colleges and universities, I was well prepared for the position of vice president for student affairs at Sinclair Community College. Although I had never worked at a community college, the mission of this sector of institutions appealed to me in large measure because of the focus on workforce development and an unabashed commitment to serving the educational needs of historically underrepresented populations.

Unlike such states as Illinois, Ohio, Michigan, California, and New York, Indiana did not have a particularly strong community-college system but chose instead to establish a statewide technical-college system, Indiana Vocational Technical College, later known as Ivy Tech. During the presidencies of Herman B Wells at IU and Frederick L. Hovde at Purdue University, more than a half-dozen regional campuses were launched around the state. Some were under the management of IU, while others were managed by Purdue or, in some cases, jointly by both institutions.

The name Indiana University–Purdue University Indianapolis is a reflection of the educational and political dealing that has played out in Indiana for the better part of seventy years. IU and Purdue regional campuses offered a full range of associate degree programs until 2008, when that degree function was largely transferred to Ivy Tech Community College.[6] During my tenure at IU Northwest, between 40 to 50 percent of all students were enrolled in associate degree programs. Ivy Tech is now Indiana's largest public postsecondary institution and the nation's largest singly accredited, statewide community-college system, serving nearly two hundred thousand students annually.

* * *

Although not as bad off as Gary, Dayton was in the throes of economic turbulence when I arrived in 1984. The local economy was heavily tied to Wright-Patterson Air Force Base, General Motors, International Harvester, Mead Paper Company, and Standard Register, all of which were experiencing a decline. Local business and elected officials depended on Sinclair College to play a leading role in the area's economic recovery, and its energetic and visionary leader, David Ponitz, was leading the way. Without a doubt, David was the most talented leader with whom I'd had the opportunity to work during my four decades in higher education. He never stopped learning, and he pushed his executive leadership team not to settle for anything less than excellence.

As a new vice president at the college, I made sure I got to the office early on April 15, 1984. Just as I was getting settled, I was greeted by President Ponitz, who brought with him a basket of fresh rolls baked by his wife, Doris, a model of what it meant to be a presidential spouse without upstaging her popular husband or playing second fiddle to him either! Like my friend Beverly Nygreen had done in 1971, Doris took an active role in helping us find a home rather than simply a house. She scoured one neighborhood after another, searching for the perfect home for the Nelms family. When we found it and the movers delivered our belongings, Doris was there with homemade pizza and beer for us and brownies for Rashad. I get goose bumps just writing about how fortunate I've been to have had so many wonderfully supportive people in my life. In fact, I paused from my writing to telephone David and Doris to thank them for being great role models and mentors for me and Jeanetta.

The agenda awaiting me upon arrival at Sinclair was full, to say the least. Not only was I vice president for student affairs, but I was also appointed acting vice president for administration with responsibility for human resources, technology, and library services, among other functions. The college's enrollment was down a few hundred students, and my executive leadership team was in a panic to increase it. Members of the presidential cabinet were convinced that we needed to do two things: first, hire a new director of admissions and recruitment and, second, market more extensively via television, radio, and newspaper. I sought to make the point about the importance of offering academic programs desired by students and the need to improve the quality of caring and the services offered by the college. Up to this point in my career, I'd never had access to the financial resources required to communicate a consistent, coherent, and compelling message to prospective students about the value education would add to their lives. With an improvement in the quality of services, caring, and marketing, Sinclair's enrollment increased from approximately 16,500 students to over 18,000 in a period of just three years.

As community activists, it didn't take long for Jeanetta, Rashad, and me to become fully immersed in the Dayton community. We enrolled Rashad in a neighborhood Montessori school, where his classmates came from all over the world. Except for Boy Scouts, Rashad seemed to enjoy all aspects of his new life in Dayton. Jeanetta settled into her job teaching mathematics at E. J. Brown Middle School, a few blocks from home, and later at a high school in downtown Dayton. We joined Jack and Jill, a family-oriented social club founded for the purposes of sponsoring social, cultural, and intellectual activities for Black children at a time when they could not participate in White events. In addition, Jeanetta affiliated with her sorority, Alpha Kappa Alpha, America's oldest sorority, while I started paying on a life membership with my fraternity, Black Alpha Phi Alpha, the oldest Black fraternity in the country. As a former school board member in Gary, Indiana, I was sought out by the Dayton Board of Education and asked to become a member of the Dayton Education Council, an entity designed to increase community engagement in K–12 education. I accepted the invitation and soon became chair of the council.

At Sinclair, things were moving along nicely. David and my administrative colleagues were cooperative, and they exhibited a level of support and cultural competence that was refreshing and greatly appreciated compared to IU Northwest. Perhaps the thing I liked most about my colleagues at Sinclair was their willingness to tell you when they disagreed and to do so in an honest and civil manner. I can truly say that for the first time in my professional life, I didn't feel marginalized, attacked, or disrespected by my colleagues. Thanks to the leadership of President David Ponitz, we always found a way to disagree without being disagreeable.

Although we weren't exactly on cruise control, life was good at Sinclair Community College. In addition to my extensive campus and community engagement, the business community took note of my accomplishments, and Bank One, Dayton invited me to become a member of its local community advisory board. I readily accepted the invitation and proceeded to do everything within my power to increase the bank's lending practices in the Black community.

* * *

I knew all this progress was too good to be true. One Saturday afternoon in April 1985, our home phone rang, and it was most unusual to hear the voice of my sister Christine on the other end of the line.

"Charlie," she said, "I'm calling to let you know that Papa died this morning."

Incredulous, all I could think about was my mama, who'd been Papa's rock for more than fifty years. A hardworking man of few words, Papa always deferred to Mama, even when he had a different opinion. My goal was to get to Crawfordsville as quickly as I could to comfort Mama, who was my rock. In consultation with our siblings, I and my sister Carrie, who lived in Michigan, made the funeral and burial arrangements. Papa was laid to rest in Paradise Gardens, an all-Black cemetery in Edmondson, Arkansas, established by a small group of subsistence farmers and sharecroppers in the mid-1950s.

Strangely, Papa's death did not impact me in the ways I had anticipated. He died unexpectedly of an apparent heart attack, and I did not have time to contemplate the possibility of his death. While I was saddened, I was happy that he had been spared a lengthy period of suffering and pain. A few months before his death, I'd bought Papa a nice suit that he'd never worn. Why he saved it, I'll never know, but he was buried in that new suit with one of my favorite neckties. Although Papa never told me or my siblings that he loved us, he showed it in ways that every child would be blessed to experience. I have honored Papa and Mama by making sure that their little farm never ends up in the hands of White people and by establishing the Nelms-Sherrod Scholarship Endowment in their honor and in my mother-in-law's honor at the University of Arkansas at Pine Bluff.

Since leaving the farm and heading to college in 1965, I have not missed a single year of returning home to check on the farm and to feel Mama and Papa's spirit. Although Rashad barely got to know my parents before they died, I've regaled him with stories about them and the lessons they taught me about life and living. When he was experiencing a rough time as an undergraduate and again as a law school student at the University of Michigan, I shared with him stories about Papa and Mama's determination. I told him the same thing my parents told me: Always do your best. That's all any of us can do, and at the end of the day, that's all that's required of us.

* * *

As I came to the close of my third year at Sinclair Community College, I was on the radar of several search firms trying to interest me in a college presidency at a PWI. While I was flattered, serving at a PWI wasn't exactly in line with where I saw myself. One winter day, I received a call informing me that I had been nominated for the chancellorship of my alma mater UAPB. After consulting with Jeanetta and my longtime mentor L. A. Torrence, who was still a member of the UAPB leadership team, I decided to accept the nomination and followed up with a letter of interest and a list of references. Within three weeks of receiving my letter, I was contacted by the search firm informing me that I was a finalist for the position and inviting me for a campus interview. I was pleasantly surprised and wasted no time in expressing my delight in being a finalist.

Word spread quickly within the alumni ranks about my candidacy, and some of my classmates began lobbying the president of the University of Arkansas system, Ray Thornton, a former member of Congress, on my behalf. While I had a wonderful conversation with President Thornton, I returned to Dayton fairly certain that I was not his candidate. Consequently, I was not surprised when I received a call from his chief of staff informing me that Dr. Charles Walker, a UAPB alumnus, distinguished scholar, and dean of pharmaceutical science at Florida A&M University had been offered and accepted the UAPB chancellor position. He served the university well for a period of six years before being brought down by overspending and a cheating scandal in athletics.

One month after President Thornton's UAPB decision, I was contacted by the chair of the search committee for the chancellor's position at IU East in Richmond. Although I felt it was a waste of time, I decided to accept the nomination and submit a letter of interest and a list of references. Within a few weeks, I was invited for a round of interviews with people on campus and in the community. I knew that I was doomed when Dr. Howard Schaller, chair of the search committee and dean of the business school at IUPUI, began the luncheon discussion with approximately thirty business and community leaders by saying, "Thank you for joining us today.

In conducting the search, we've complied with all of the university's affirmative action requirements, and I am pleased to have you meet our first finalist, Dr. Charlie Nelms, vice president at Sinclair Community College in Dayton, Ohio."

In disbelief over how I was introduced, I sucked it up, put a big smile on my face, and began by telling the group how delighted I was to be back in Richmond after having served on the faculty staff at Earlham a decade earlier. I know that Mama and the spirit of those who nurtured me were standing invisibly by my side exhorting me to do my best. That day I was not only representing myself; I was representing everyone who'd helped me become the person I was in 1987. They were Black, White, gay, straight, disabled, young, old, educated, uneducated, foreign born, and nearly every other designation imaginable. They cared about me, and I was standing tall on their shoulders.

As I concluded my interview and headed back to Dayton, I thought about my conversation with Dr. Lynn Merritt a few years earlier when he had said, "Charlie, John Ryan has his eye on you." Lynn was right. Several weeks after my interview, President Ryan's special assistant, Dr. Gene Farris, called to inform me that I was a finalist for the position and President Ryan wanted to meet with me at the Hilton Hotel near Logan Airport in Boston. John and his wife, Pat, were on their way to Afghanistan on university business, and he wanted to get the search wrapped up before his retirement in June 1987. Over a hearty meal, with wine and a few shots of scotch, I had one of the best conversations I ever had with anyone about a job!

"Charlie," President Ryan said, "you know I'm retiring in a couple of months. While you are my candidate of choice, I want to give my successor, Tom Ehrlich, provost at the University of Pennsylvania and president-elect at IU, the opportunity to meet you before I submit your name to the trustees for consideration. I need you fly to Philadelphia on Wednesday and meet with Tom. Can you do that for me?"

Barely able to contain my excitement, I called Jeanetta immediately after my conversation with John, and she booked a flight to Philadelphia for Tuesday, one day after my return to Dayton.

Upon reaching Philadelphia, I took a cab to the University of Pennsylvania and found my way to Tom Ehrlich's office. Tom began the conversation by noting that while he was sure I had many wonderful attributes, he preferred a candidate with more traditional academic credentials. However, he trusted John Ryan's instincts, and he looked forward to working with me to move the IU East campus forward. Over lunch in the Faculty Dining Club, Tom and I talked about our own aspirations for Indiana University and the Richmond campus, respectively. Following lunch, Tom gave me one of the most harrowing rides of my life to the airport. He was known for moving his hands around when he talked, and I was convinced that he would sideswipe another car any minute!

Not long after meeting with Tom, I received another call from Gene Farris to discuss the terms of my appointment as chancellor and professor of education at IU East. I was offered a salary of $2,000 less than I was making at Sinclair. I called my old mentor from my days at IU Northwest, Dan Orescanin, to seek his counsel. After I shared my dilemma with him, he said simply, "Let me look into it, Charlie." True to his word, Dan looked into it, and my offer was revised to reflect $2,000 more than my Sinclair salary.

Tom Ehrlich and I commenced our tenure at IU the same day, July 1, 1987, and we concluded our leadership assignments together on June 30, 1994. Together, with the help of numerous colleagues, we did our part to move the IU East campus forward. The two of us—Tom, a Jewish guy from Cambridge, Massachusetts, and me, a country guy from the Arkansas Delta—made believers out of many who may have had doubts about our fit at Indiana University. I am forever grateful to Tom for his mentorship and friendship, which brings to mind Pete Seeger and Lee Hays's well-known song "If I Had a Hammer." We used our voices, energy, and action to hammer out the dangers of ignorance and hate—and to hammer in love and justice for people from all walks of life.

9

HOLDING FAST

"Hey, Charlie, this is your big sister, Carrie! Jeanetta told me about your new gig. I'm calling to congratulate you and let you how proud I am of my little brother. Be sure to let me know the date of your installation so I can submit my request for a couple of vacation days. Again, congrats, and loads of love."

As word of my appointment as chancellor spread, congratulatory calls, telegrams, cards, and flowers poured in from around the country. None was more special, however, than the one I got from my sister and best friend, Carrie. While chopping and picking cotton many years earlier, we had shared our little secrets with each other and sought advice on how to deal with our crushes. Carrie was the one who delivered my love letters to my girlfriends in high school, and she was my confidante throughout college. She knew of my plans to propose to Jeanetta before anyone else, and I knew about aspects of her life that no one else did. Whether dealing with a relationship gone bad or struggling to pass statistics at Michigan, Carrie was never too busy to take my call. Thus, her call to congratulate me was more than an ordinary call.

When I was appointed chancellor at IU East in 1987, there was but a handful of Blacks serving as chancellors or presidents at predominately White institutions. John Ryan made history by having the courage to appoint me, and I made history by accepting his invitation to serve. With my appointment, I became the first Black and the youngest person to be named chancellor of any IU regional campus. Suddenly, everyone embraced me and claimed me as his or her own, including the director of the ACE Fellows Program, who previously had been convinced that I should obtain tenure as a faculty member before applying for the program. Her predecessor, along with Dan Orescanin and Marion Mochon, stood firmly behind my candidacy and opined that although I was a nontraditional candidate, I had the skills and attributes required to lead a university rather than simply preside at one. I am forever grateful to the men and women who stood firmly behind my candidacy and did everything possible to ensure my success following my appointment.

*   *   *

As one might imagine, my appointment was not universally embraced. The candidate who was a finalist with me, Dr. David Fulton, an affable, liberal White fellow who'd spent his entire career at IU East, took not getting the position relatively hard. The situation was further complicated by the fact that he was the university's director of administration and finance, with a bevy of faculty, staff, and community leaders in his corner. Within the first sixty days of my appointment, David acted out in ways against me that left a lot to be desired. Finally, one day I invited him to meet with me over lunch.

"David, I said, "I know you've served the campus well for nearly twenty years and were disappointed when you didn't get the job. I applaud you for your steadfast commitment to IU East, and I readily acknowledge that I may not fully grasp the extent of your disappointment at being passed over for the position. You and I both know that I didn't appoint myself! After a lengthy process involving numerous university constituencies, I was appointed by the president and confirmed by the trustees. Whether you like it or not, there is only one chancellor, and I'm that person. I respect you and believe we can work together. If, however, you can't work with me, I will be happy to write a letter of recommendation on your behalf. For me, trust and mutual respect are nonnegotiable in maintaining a productive working relationship."

Needless to say, the next fifteen minutes of our conversation were both awkward and tense. David acknowledged his deep disappointment but disavowed any effort on his part to undermine me. As he was a longtime faculty member, I knew that David was close friends with a small group of senior faculty who had some pretty strong thoughts about who should be chancellor—and that person definitely wasn't me. From that day forward, David and I enjoyed an excellent working relationship. I nominated him for the ACE Fellows Program and paid his full salary while he spent his fellowship year at Metropolitan State University in Denver. In 1994, when I resigned to became chancellor at University of Michigan–Flint, I supported David's candidacy for chancellor of IU East, and he was appointed to the position and served until retiring twelve years later. When Chancellor Emeritus Fulton died in September 2016, I and many others in the IU community mourned his passing.

* * *

Soon after my conversation with David, details of behind-the-scenes shenanigans related to my appointment began emerging. It was alleged that a small group of senior IU East faculty members had sent a message to President Ryan through one of his special assistants stating that they did not believe the campus or the city was ready for a Black chancellor. I heard from a very reliable source that Ryan responded by saying, "If I wait for everyone to be ready, there will never be a Black chancellor. Except for his race, Charlie's background is as strong as or stronger than those who have preceded him."

The second alleged incident dealt with whether or not I, as a Black person, would be allowed to join the all-White Forest Hills Country Club, founded in 1931 and located in one of the most scenic settings I have ever seen. The only things Blacks were permitted to do at the club were cook, caddy, clean up, and cut the grass. Concerned that some members of the club would object to my membership, I was told by a member of the club at the time that a group of White corporate executives put the question of my membership on the board's agenda before I ever submitted an application. When discussing the item, they made it clear that if I submitted an application, they expected it to be approved. They further noted that if my application was rejected, they would pull their own memberships, along with those of employees who worked in their companies.

When I arrived in Richmond in 1987, most Blacks lived in the North End or in a subdivision near Earlham, neither of which offered homes appropriate for entertaining prospective donors or hosting social events. To make certain that there were no issues related to us purchasing a home in a subdivision offering a better selection of homes, the area's leading realtor and developer, Paul Lingle, assigned one of his top agents to work with Jeanetta and me. We chose a home under construction in Hunter's Point and settled in among a group of business owners, physicians, engineers, and corporate executive, most of whom had moved to Richmond from elsewhere. Except for being called the N-word once or twice or getting into fights with the boys who used that word, Rashad enjoyed a comfortable, civil, and cordial relationship with his playmates and classmates. When he graduated from high school in Michigan in 1997, several friends from our old neighborhood and his high school made a special trip to wish him well.

* * *

"I have a complaint, and I want to speak with the chancellor right now!"

I had been on the job barely six months, and standing in front of me in the reception area of my office was an irate White man of about six feet nine inches and nearly three hundred pounds. Ranting and raving about the university's refund policy, there he was demanding a full refund of every penny he'd paid for his classes.

He wasn't quite sure of what to say or do when I replied, "Sir, I am the chancellor. Would you like to step into my office and tell me what this is about?" Incredulous, he replied, "Are you sure? I didn't know the chancellor was colored!" Maintaining my composure, I proceeded to listen to his complaint. The student didn't like the faculty member or the class, and I had no interest in engaging in a battle with him. I walked him to the bursar's office to complete the paperwork for a full refund. He was always cordial when I saw him around town, and I had the pleasure of presenting him with his degree approximately five years after our initial meeting.

My extensive experience in higher education notwithstanding, being a member of the faculty staff at Earlham over a decade before assuming my duties as chancellor at IU East served me well. A year before my IU East appointment, Dick Wood, a former professor of religion and philosophy who'd gone on to serve as provost at Whittier College, was named president of Earlham. Dick and I enjoyed an excellent working relationship during the early years of our career, and he was eager to help us in any way he could. Although less than 20 percent of Earlham's 1,200 students were from Indiana, Dick was actively engaged in community leadership roles in Richmond.

Connor Prairie Museum in Fishers, Indiana, was under Earlham's management, and Dick was well acquainted with executives at the Lilly Endowment and with Morris Mills, an Earlham College graduate, businessman, and powerful Republican leader in the Indiana legislature. On several occasions, Dick and I made the trip to Indianapolis to lobby members of the Indiana General Assembly and the Indiana Higher Education Commission in support of funding for facilities and academic programs for IU East. Earlham was one of the founders of IU East and provided space and management expertise to the institution in its formative years. Without a doubt, Dick was the most ardent supporter and advocate I could ever wish for. When I accepted the chancellor's position at UM–Flint, the first person who looked at our house bought it and requested immediate occupancy. We spent two months house-sitting for Dick and Judy Wood while they were in Japan. Their friendship was priceless!

While IU regional campuses bore the Indiana University name, many faculty at the flagship campus in Bloomington did not consider them as equals. Like the runt of a litter of pigs, it was always a struggle to get enough sustenance for regional campuses to survive, let alone grow into the types of institutions envisioned by the faculty and the leaders of the communities in which they were located. When I was appointed at IU East, regional-campus chancellors were not accorded the privilege of an inauguration or installation. That changed a year later with the appointment of Dan Cohen as chancellor at Indiana University South Bend, who had a red-carpet inauguration fit for royalty.

* * *

"I've heard a lot of wonderful things about my predecessor, Dr. Glenn Geokre, and I commend him for the great work that he, Alex Schlitz, and Fred Ghrosmeyer, all of my predecessors, did to bring the campus to this point in its life cycle. I have no plans to try to fill Glenn's shoes; we don't wear the same size. I promise to do what my mama, who's here this evening from Arkansas, admonished my siblings and me to do many, many years ago. She said simply, 'Do your best,' and that is my promise to you. I will do my best, and with your help, I'm confident that the university will continue to move forward. Thank you for coming out in such large numbers to welcome Jeanetta, Rashad, and me. Godspeed and good night."

That was the extent of my inauguration speech as chancellor of IU East. The Forest Hills Country Club was packed with people from all ethnicities and social classes, many of whom had never been afforded the pleasure of attending an event there. From the beginning, I made it clear that I did not want to have multiple receptions welcoming me to the community. I only wanted one, and I wanted everyone to be invited and welcomed with outstretched arms. My request was granted, and one wall separating Blacks and Whites for more than half a century had at least been cracked. Nevertheless, thirty years later, it remains to be shattered. During our seven-year tenure at IU East, Jeanetta and I never hosted a social or cultural event without every element of the community being invited. More often than not, they responded affirmatively to the invitation to join us.

Inasmuch as my appointment was John Ryan's last senior leadership appointment before retiring in 1987, I did not have the privilege of working with him. But we remained in contact until his death a few years ago. During the time that I shadowed him as an ACE Fellow, John exhibited three leadership qualities that resonated profoundly with me and that I sought to emulate during my chancellorships. First, he was a kind and gracious man whose ego appeared to be intact. I never heard him swear at or pull rank on anyone, and he went to great lengths to share with those who disagreed with him the rationale for his decisions. Second, he didn't take credit for the university's accomplishments; he always talked about what *we* did—it was never about what *he* accomplished. Third, he was a man of enormous courage who embraced diversity and equity before it enjoyed much of the acceptance it does today.

Nearly all of the currently existing diversity initiatives on the Bloomington campus were launched during John Ryan's tenure as president. The chief architects of those programs were Dr. Herman Hudson, vice chancellor for Afro-American Affairs, and Dr. Ken Gros Louis, chancellor of the Bloomington campus, who worked tirelessly to change the profile of the student body. (Afro-American was widely used at IU and throughout higher education in the 1970s and 1980s.) The values expressed were reinforced by an array of initiatives for increasing enrollments of international students and creating a supportive environment for LGBTQ students, strategic financial investments in scholarships for minority students, and grow-your-own minority faculty efforts. "Grow your own" is a concept that recognizes that the pool of academically prepared ethnic minorities and women is limited and that colleges and universities must identify, educate, and mentor prospective faculty members.

Of course, John Ryan will always occupy a special place in my heart for having the courage to appoint me, a Black man, as chancellor at IU East, IU's least ethnically diverse campus, against the advice of a powerful group of faculty.

* * *

In the months immediately preceding my appointment at IU East, IU trustees voted to change the mission of the campus from a two-year educational center offering associate degrees to a fully accredited, comprehensive baccalaureate-degree institution. John's charge to me was to make that happen without compromising the quality standards of Indiana University. Of course what we did not discuss in any detail was the challenge of achieving these lofty goals absent the availability of requisite human, fiscal, and physical resources.

As the campus's chief executive officer, it fell to me to make a clear and compelling case to IU trustees, IU deans who controlled academic programs and who fought with every fiber in their bodies to restrict access to bachelors and master's degree programs, legislators who controlled the purse strings, and donors at the local level who were not IU East graduates and whose commitment could not always be relied on for support. With the help of a core group of stalwart supporters, we succeeded in convincing enough decision makers of the efficacy of the institution's new mission, and resources began to flow. During my seven-year tenure, IU East was the fastest-growing college in Indiana.

* * *

One guest said to another, "Who's that guy over there who keeps speaking and shaking hands with people?" The other guest replied, "Oh, you haven't met him? He's the head nigger in charge, HNIC."

Angry and incredulous, the only Black member of the IU East Board of Advisors called to apprise me of a conversation he'd overheard between two guests at the IU School of Business Economic Outlook Forecast Luncheon. The guest who responded derisively to the questioner turned out to be a retired business executive and founder of the campus. Although I'd never had any negative interaction with him, he had a reputation throughout Richmond's Black community for being a racist. While he never allowed any of his racial predilections to impact his financial contributions to the campus, no matter how hard I worked and how successful the campus was, I always felt that I was being measured against the accomplishments of my White predecessors, in whose selection he had allegedly played a major role. The purpose of the call from the Black board member, who was also my friend, was to tell me to watch my back and not to trust the person who referred to me as the HNIC. From that point forward, I never had a conversation with that particular founder without thinking about his overheard racist description of me.

During my time at IU East, I developed a solid reputation for being a bridge builder who worked effectively across regional, political, racial, class, and educational boundaries. My work ethic, optimism, community engagement, and effectiveness in meeting the goals articulated in the campus's strategic plan resulted in my election to the board of directors of First Bank Richmond, Reid Hospital and Health Care Services, and the Chamber of Commerce—all of which were firsts for Black. At the state level, my most rewarding activities included serving as a founding member of the boards of the Indiana Youth Institute and the Indiana University Center on Philanthropy, the forerunner to today's Ruth Lilly Family School of Philanthropy.

There were times when I felt I would fall under the staggering weight of my workload, but with the love and support of my family and a few close friends, I managed to keep moving forward. In an effort to stem the tide of the impact of a major economic recession in East Central Indiana, IU East opened instructional centers in Connersville and New Castle in the early 1990s. Under my successor David Fulton's leadership, two devoted IU alums, Danny and Patti Danielson, made a major gift to IU East to construct a facility to enable IU, Purdue, and Ivy Tech to offer courses leading to associate and bachelor's degree programs.

* * *

It was September 1970, the fall semester had just gotten underway, and the influx of Black graduate students who'd been on campus just a month earlier had returned to their respective HBCU campuses, where they would spend the academic year teaching. The following summer, they'd return to Bloomington to reclaim their dorm rooms in the Graduate Residence Center or in one of the little green, university-owned mobile homes. Those who couldn't afford either of those options took up residence in a rooming house on Bloomington's north side, where most of the Black families lived. In 1970, the Bloomington campus numbered less than 2 percent of the total student body, or fewer than one thousand students. Following a student protest in 1968 led by twelve Black football players, who later became known as the IU Twelve, the university administration made a commitment to take steps to recruit more Black students and faculty.

Rozelle Boyd and Mrs. LaVerta Terry, both community leaders in their own right, were hired to create the Groups Scholars Program (GSP), which would recruit promising minority students, primarily Black and Latino, throughout the state. Boyd directed the program while Terry served as assistant director. Deans Boyd and Terry were joined by a group of early adopters from various administrative areas and academic disciplines who budgeted funds to support students financially, as well as those who designed and taught courses that addressed the academic deficiencies that some students had in the areas of writing and mathematics.

In its fifty-year history, GSP has evolved into one of IU Bloomington's signature programs for serving the higher-education needs and aspirations of first-generation college students from low-wealth backgrounds. It admits more than four hundred students annually and boasts an alumni base of nearly twelve thousand persons, who now reside and work around the globe. Core features of GSP include a mandatory summer-residential program where students take nine credit hours of collegiate-level course work; access to academic, career, and personal advising; participation in a life skills seminar; guaranteed financial support for four years; and opportunities to participate in study abroad programs. Eligible GSP participants may receive additional financial support through the Hudson-Holland Scholars Program and the Twenty-First Century Scholars Program, as long the total amount of funding awarded does not exceed the cost of attendance.

* * *

Having been an active participant and observer of IU's diversity efforts for nearly five decades, I am struck by how little many of today's administrators, faculty, staff, and students know about the university's rich history in this arena. IU has been blessed with a core group of luminaries who provided the vision, focus, and leadership that enabled the university to lay claim to being a leader in American efforts to diversify the academy. I have had the privilege of knowing, working with, and being mentored by many of those individuals.

Herman B Wells, who served as IU's eleventh president from 1937 through 1968, is recognized as a pioneer in all aspects of diversity at IU. Although diversity and equity as we know them today were not in vogue during much of Wells's presidency, he took decisive action, in some cases using the popularity of Black athletes, to desegregate living and eating quarters on campus and in the city. He was responsible for removing the Reserved signs from the Commons dining table, and he asked the most popular African American athlete, Rooster Coffey, to swim in the pool at the busiest time, thereby effectively desegregating it. Wells reportedly told local restaurateurs if they did not serve Black students, he would prohibit all students from patronizing their establishments.

Wells was also the first president in the Big Ten to recruit an African American basketball player, and IU was the first Big Ten university to have African Americans on its golf and baseball teams. In the late 1940s, Hoosier legend Bill Garrett became the first African American to play varsity basketball in the Big Ten, and IU football star George Taliaferro became the first African American to be drafted to play in the National Football League. Wells's autobiography, *Being Lucky*, is worth reading for a greater understanding of the leadership challenges he faced.

In addition to efforts from the top, some IU students organized themselves to fight segregation and discrimination. Established in 1938, the Student Religious Cabinet was a progressive interfaith and interracial organization whose members wrote letters to protest discrimination toward African American students at IU and at other universities.[1] Concerned with issues of war, race, and religion, they were active in the Bloomington community and beyond. In the 1940s, the Bloomington chapter of the American Veterans Committee (AVC) was comprised of male students attending IU on the GI Bill, and they were active in civil rights and desegregation. AVC was later the target of McCarthy-era purges.[2]

* * *

Long before the popularity of internationalization in higher education, Wells welcomed international students from around the globe. Considering the time, Wells's most daring initiative was providing a safe place for Professor Alfred Kinsey to conduct his controversial research on human sexuality. I first met Herman in 1978 and maintained continuous contact with him until just before his death in 2002. Each time I changed jobs, I got a handwritten congratulatory note from Herman wishing me well. When I returned to IU as vice president in 1998, Herman was never too busy to see me when I needed to seek the advice of a sage, without any expectation of reciprocation. The most important lesson I learned from Herman was the importance of exercising the courage of one's commitment.

Herman was one of the invaluable mentors at IU who influenced my leadership journey. Another, Professor August W. Eberle, was a tough and demanding IU faculty member who took a special interest in the academic success of Black graduate students in higher education administration, many of whom were HBCU graduates. During his twenty-year tenure as professor and department chair, Eb, as he was affectionately called, chaired countless thesis committees, including mine.

Eb's Marine Corps–style haircut and gruff manner might lead one to erroneously conclude that he was an ultraconservative political type from the mountains of Tennessee. Although he spent administrative stints at the University of Chattanooga and at Oak Ridge Associate Universities, Eb exhibited a high level of cultural competence and a commitment to racial equality. He was a man who did not mince his words; he said what he meant, and he meant what he said.

I gave Eb a copy of a draft of the first three chapters of my doctoral thesis just before the Christmas recess in 1976. Ten days later he handed it back to me with this note in red cursive: "You haven't followed the *Thesis Guide* by Dougdale, and your writing stinks. Come to see me if you're serious about writing a quality thesis." Peeved and dejected, I paid Eb a visit right away. Wearing a big smile, he began by saying, "Now that I have your attention, let's get to work." I learned many lessons from him, but two have stayed with me throughout my leadership journey: refrain from judging people based on how they look and equality is not a substitute for excellence.

Herman C. Hudson was the epitome of what it means to be a luminary. Legally blind from his youth, he earned three degrees with honors from the University of Michigan: a bachelor's, master's, and doctorate. Before coming to IU in 1968, Hudson held teaching and administrative positions at Kabul University in Afghanistan, the University of Puerto Rico, and Florida A&M University. Named vice chancellor of Afro-American Affairs in 1969, which made him the highest ranking Black person on the Bloomington campus, Hudson was the architect of an impressive array of academic, research, instructional, outreach, and scholarship programs that still exist today.

Hudson was in high demand as a consultant, as leaders at Big Ten and Research 1 universities sought to emulate Indiana University's success. Among the programs created by Dr. Hudson and funded by IU were the Department of Afro-American Studies; the African American Arts Institute, consisting of the three performance groups: Choral Ensemble, Soul Review, and African American Dance Ensemble; the Mathematics and Science Scholarship Program; the Minority Achievers Program; and the Faculty Strategic Hiring Initiative, in partnership with the Bloomington campus chancellor Dr. Ken Gros Louis. Although he retired from active leadership before the Neal-Marshall Black Culture Center was constructed, Dr. Hudson was a major force behind its creation. Dr. Hudson taught me and his other protégés the importance of being strategic, collaborative, and persistent. Those lessons served me well as a three-time chancellor and vice president of Indiana University.

Jimmy L. Ross, who died much too young at age sixty in 2002, was among the first Blacks nationally to hold a major administrative leadership position at a predominately White university. A native of Arkansas and graduate of UAPB, an HBCU, Jimmy served as the first Black director of the IU Office of Scholarships and Financial Aid from 1973 to 1988. Jim, as friends called him, never met a stranger, and his home served as friendship central for both domestic and international graduate students. His house reminded me of the one Sam Walter Foss wrote about in his epic poem "House by the Side of the Road." This poem is about friendship without regard to boundaries or circumstances of any kind, and captures the essence of those who befriended me at IU.

Jimmy knew exactly how state and federal student-financial-aid rules worked, and without breaking the rules, he stretched them to the limits as he sought to help low-income students stay in college. Active in the National Association of Student Financial Aid, Jimmy was regularly called on to advise legislators at the federal and state levels as they sought to develop legislation to make various programs more effective and responsive to students. Jimmy taught me the true meaning of courage and the lesson that life is to be lived, not feared. He also helped me to appreciate that diversity and equity is about more than Black and White; it is about LGBTQ people, Latino populations, international students, foster children, and so much more.

Ken Gros Louis, who had Native American ancestry, is someone it seems I have always known. A nationally recognized scholar in English and comparative literature, Ken held numerous leadership roles at IU, including department chair, dean of the College of Liberal Arts and Sciences, vice president of the Bloomington campus, vice president of the Indiana University multicampus system, chancellor of IU Bloomington, vice president for academic affairs, and ultimately university chancellor, a position held by only one other person in the university's long history, Chancellor Herman B Wells. During his four-decade-long IU career, Ken championed numerous causes related to diversity, equity, and inclusion for ethnic minorities, women, and members of the LGBTQ community. A person of great personal warmth, Ken worked collaboratively with Rozelle Boyd, Herman Hudson, me, and others to launch nearly all of IU's existing diversity initiatives.

No matter how tight budgets were, Ken always managed to realign Bloomington budgetary priorities to improve conditions for historically underrepresented students. Ken was the lead advocate for the creation of the vice president of institutional development and student affairs position that I would occupy for nearly a decade. He understood the importance of my portfolio, which included more than diversity, and he added one of the university's most respected programs in the mix, the Honors Division, later renamed the Hutton Honors College. From Ken, I learned the importance of maintaining cordial working relationships even with people who do not share your values and views. But most importantly, I came to appreciate at the deeper level the art of compromise. Ken passed away in 2017 and will be missed by all of us who had the pleasure of knowing him.

Myles Brand was a man of great intellect, integrity, compassion, and quiet warmth. I first met him while serving on the IU Presidential Search Committee, which led to his appointment as the university's sixteenth president. His first day as president was my last day as chancellor of IU East. The IU Board of Trustees was meeting on the East campus, and I was given the opportunity to address the board. I thanked them for the opportunities they'd accorded me and challenged them to do a better job of living out their avowed commitment to diversity by diversifying the board and the leadership ranks of the university at all levels.

Little did I know that four years later, Myles would ask me to leave my position as chancellor of the University of Michigan–Flint to fill a newly created university-wide vice-presidential position with a broad portfolio, including diversity and equity, and regional campus chancellor searches, among numerous other responsibilities. Without much fanfare, Myles and I crafted a strategy that won over the trustees to support a $7.5 million, multiyear, tuition set-aside budget line item to improve diversity and student retention on all IU campuses. This marked the first time in the university's history that funds had been earmarked for diversity and student retention on all campuses.

As president, Myles was my supervisor, but he was my friend as well. When we disagreed with each other, we did so without being disagreeable. For six months I served as special assistant to the president and later as vice president for Student Development and Diversity. From Myles, I deepened my appreciation for the art of negotiation and using clearly articulated objectives against which to measure progress. We never agreed, though, on deploying disincentives when members of the university's management team failed to meet their diversity targets.

Cora Smith Breckenridge earned her undergraduate degree in 1959 and her master's degree in 1963, both from IU. She became the first Black person to serve on the IU Board of Trustees when she was elected by IU alumni voters in 1997. A speech and language pathologist in the Elkhart School System, throughout her campaign for a seat on the board and in her subsequent years of service following her election, Mrs. Breckenridge was a passionate, compelling, and unwavering advocate for diversity, equity, and inclusion. She was often the lone voice until she was joined by Dr. Clarence Boone Sr., a Black physician from Gary, who was appointed in 2004. Both Breckenridge and Boone were respected alums with distinguished records of community service and the ability to work across racial and economic boundaries.

Their pleas resonated with enough other board members to make diversity more of a trustee agenda item. Trustee approval of the $7.5 million, multiyear, tuition set-aside budget line item was reflective of the board's commitment. In 2006, the board approved but never funded the proposal *A Comprehensive Strategy: Increasing the Enrollment of Underrepresented Minorities on the Bloomington Campus*. Mrs. Breckenridge's persistent and passionate advocacy conveyed to those of us who did the heavy lifting in diversity and equity every day that we had allies at the highest levels of university governance who were not willing to play nice to keep the peace. With Mrs. Breckenridge's loss to another candidate in 2006 and the end of Dr. Boone's term in 2009, trustee voices for diversity declined significantly.

* * *

"Dr. Nelms," said the voice on the phone, "this is Dr. Harriet Wall, chairperson of the chancellor's Search and Screen Committee at the University of Michigan–Flint. I'm calling to inform you that you have been nominated for the position and we want to encourage you to become a candidate. The closing date for applications is right around the corner, and you need to move rather quickly if you wish to be considered."

I thanked Dr. Wall for her call and asked if she had time for a few questions, to which she replied, "Of course, please feel free to proceed."

I began by asking a series of questions. The most urgent were, what happened to your last chancellor? Was he fired, did he retire, or did he take another job? What are the most important challenges currently facing the

University of Michigan–Flint? Does the institution have a budget deficit? Is the enrollment up or down? How would you characterize the relationship between the chancellor and the faculty and staff? How would you characterize campus morale? What attributes and skills are you seeking in your next chancellor?

As the conversation continued, I sensed that the search committee chair was not prepared for an undeclared candidate to be asking such probing questions; after all, she was calling just to let me know I'd been nominated. On the other hand, I was trying to assess whether there was a reasonable fit between the campus and me before agreeing to be a candidate.

"Dr. Wall," I finally said, "the University of Michigan–Flint sounds like a place with enormous potential. I'd be grateful if you'd share with me a copy of the position profile and announcement, and I'll let you know right away if I decide to become a candidate. I'm not trying to be difficult, but I have a great job already and do not wish to become an applicant just because I've been nominated. This an important decision for the committee and for me." Vowing that she fully understood, Dr. Wall promised to email me the requested information and did so immediately.

After reviewing the information, I telephoned my longtime friend and colleague Jim Renick, who had been chancellor at the University of Michigan–Dearborn for two years or so. I asked if he could give me the real scoop on UM–Flint. He gave me a quick overview of the campus politics and the way that a small group of senior faculty had conspired to try to force out the last chancellor, a Black male. Jim continued by saying how great it was to work with Jim Duderstadt, the University of Michigan's president. When pressed, he spoke candidly and extensively about Flint's deteriorating downtown, the poor quality of its public schools, the area's near-total reliance on General Motors for economic sustainability at a time when the auto industry was fighting to survive, White flight from Flint, and what he perceived as an unwillingness of many faculty to embrace the opportunity to serve a more diverse student body.

Renick's observations and insights proved invaluable in my decision making about pursuing the position and in my ultimate decision to accept President Duderstadt's invitation to join his leadership team when he called me several months later. Renick and I concluded our conversation by observing that UM–Flint was a politically charged place with enormous potential for transforming the city of Flint, as well as the region from which students were drawn.

"Charlie," Jim said, "UM–Flint needs a courageous and experienced leader, and that's why I nominated you. Man, it would be fun having you here!" Armed with Jim's insights and encouragement, I emailed Dr. Wall to inform her that after conversations with Jeanetta and a few trusted colleagues, I was submitting my application right away for the position. She thanked me. Two weeks later, she called me to say, "Congratulations, Dr. Nelms. You're one of seven semifinalists for the UM–Flint chancellor, and I'll call later in the week with potential dates for an airport interview with the search committee."

The chancellor's search process at UM–Flint differed from the one at IU East in three important ways. First, UM–Flint used a national search firm, Academic Search Consultants, to solicit feedback from various university constituencies regarding challenges and opportunities facing the university, to recruit desired candidates, and to vet finalists for the position. Second, the search committee held confidential interviews with seven candidates at a hotel near Detroit International Airport in order to arrive at a list of five candidates to invite to the campus. Third, the campus interview felt like a daylong inquisition, as I stood in front of one group after another, responding to canned questions about my leadership style and experiences as well as my views on faculty governance and unionization, teaching loads, casinos, and academic budget priorities, among other topics.

As I worked my way through interviews with various UM–Flint groups, word quickly spread that I was a personable, passionate, and experienced leader who had done his homework on the university and the community and that I was more interested in being a change agent than in simply being the next UM–Flint chancellor. I was surprised by the questions people did *not* ask me, such as, what experience have you had recruiting and retaining a diverse population of students, faculty, and staff? What role should urban universities play in addressing the challenges faced by the communities in which they are located? What strategies might we pursue to strengthen UM–Flint's profile and brand rather than living in the shadow of University of Michigan–Ann Arbor (UM–Ann Arbor)? What role do you think faculty should play in helping to achieve UM–Flint's mission? What opportunities do see for collaboration between UM–Flint, Mott Community College, and the General Motors Institute? What experiences have you had in developing university and business partnerships to promote economic development?

The interview process at UM–Flint was far more faculty centric than it was at IU East. What I perceived to be a prevailing faculty-first attitude had stymied UM–Flint's growth for decades. Unfortunately, those close to the institution refused to acknowledge this reality—or to concede that they were part of the problem.

After being heavily recruited by colleges and universities around the country, in May 1994, I was offered and accepted the position of chancellor at the University of Michigan–Flint, effective August 1, 1994. Aside from the challenges I inherited at UM–Flint, Jeanetta and I faced a far more personal and fundamental dilemma: where to send our only child, Rashad, to high school. Our options included Flint Public Schools; Powers Catholic High School in Flint; Cranbrook Upper School in Bloomfield Hills, Michigan; and Detroit Country Day School in Oakland County, north of Detroit. Fully cognizant of the pros and cons of our choice, we chose to send Rashad to Flint Central High School, a magnet school focused on the humanities and fine arts, and to enroll him in advanced science and math courses at Flint's Northern High School.

We concluded that we could not be authentic advocates for strong public schools if our child was attending a private school. A career math teacher, Jeanetta worked tirelessly to compensate for what Rashad did not receive in the course of the school day at Flint Central. Although he graduated with honors from Flint Central, and he did the same at Michigan, I'm not sure the price he paid by not attending a better and more comprehensive high school was worth it. Plus, at the end of the day, I'm not sure our advocacy had an impact on the quality of education provided by Flint schools.

* * *

By the time I reached the point of my inauguration as the fourth chancellor of UM–Flint, I had concluded that my tenure wasn't likely to be a lengthy one. Not only were there critical questions I was not asked during the interview, but also there were major university problems not fully revealed between the time I was a candidate, was offered the job, accepted the position, and assumed my duties. Some of the challenges included the strained relationship between the university and the Black community; the lack of broad-based engagement between academic units on campus and relevant community and corporate entities; systemic problems in admissions, financial aid, and academic advising; lack of a high-quality service culture on the part of staff throughout the campus; and the brewing fight among city officials, the university, and the Mott Foundation over a proposal to repurpose property less than one hundred yards from the UM–Flint campus for use as a casino.

City and labor union officials, as well as untold numbers of Flint citizens, favored the proposal, while officials at the Mott Foundation and UM–Flint vigorously opposed it. My predicted short tenure was predicated on the belief that decisive action was needed on so many levels that if I made the bold decisions required to unleash the university's vast potential, my detractors would far outnumber my allies. Convinced that playing it safe wasn't in the best interest of the university, the community, or myself, I set about the business of strategically doing what I felt needed to be done while respecting the rights of others to disagree with me. I had the support of two critical allies, University of Michigan president James Duderstadt and Mott Foundation president William White.

Unintimidated by the challenges I faced as UM–Flint's chancellor, I made it my business to get to know every university constituent possible, including junior and senior faculty members, university secretaries, members of the custodial staff, groundskeepers, students and alumni leaders, pastors of churches of all denominations, directors of homeless shelters, school principals, YMCA/YWCA officials, Chamber of Commerce and corporate leaders, newspaper and television reporters, and elected officials.

My style of leading was uncomfortable for some members of the internal university community who expected me to follow traditional communication protocols, even if those protocols were unresponsive to the needs of a contemporary urban university. Within my first four months on the job, I spoke at dozens of churches and community events. I didn't just drop in and out; I tarried to talk with those in attendance while insisting they call me Charlie, not Dr. Nelms. This request was in keeping with my exposure to Quaker values and practices at Earlham some twenty years earlier.

* * *

My inauguration as the fourth chancellor of the University of Michigan–Flint took place October 21, 1994, at Whiting Auditorium in Flint's Cultural Arts District. More than three thousand university delegates, family members and friends, local citizens, UM–Flint faculty and staff, university regents, Flint business and educational leaders, and members of Michigan's philanthropic, religious, and political communities were there to wish me well. The people I loved most—Mama, Jeanetta, Rashad, and my siblings—were all there to cheer me on.

As I rose to give my inaugural remarks, I felt the spirit of Papa and all of those on whose shoulders I stood. Although many of them were long ago deceased, in the moment in which I was speaking, they were very much alive; I was their connection to the present. The Indiana University delegation was led by former first lady Ellen Ehrlich and supported by several IU vice presidents, including my friend and advocate Terry Clapacs, along with a large delegation of colleagues from IU East. The next day, the *Flint Journal* newspaper carried a front-page article and color photo of me in full academic regalia. The headline read, "Excellence without Equity Is Hollow!"

With the inauguration behind me, I set about the business of continuing the work I was called to do. With a $100,000 grant from one of the university's strongest supporters, Bill White, president of the Charles Stewart Mott Foundation, a strategic-planning process had been launched under the leadership of Dr. Larry Kugler, professor emeritus of mathematics and acting chancellor, prior to my arrival. I didn't give the planning committee a blank check; I provided a charge that forced the committee to focus its efforts on those areas that I felt would set the campus on a course of transforming itself into a more relevant, responsive, and excellent institution.

Drawing on the recommendations of the Strategic Planning Committee, two new schools were created: Education and Human Services, and Nursing and Health Profession Studies. The Mott Foundation agreed to underwrite the costs until the units became financially self-sufficient. The Mott Foundation gifted several strategically located properties to UM–Flint, which were either repurposed for academic purposes or demolished. One of those properties, AutoWorld, was an indoor theme park built to attract tourists and trigger the "rebirth" of Flint, according to Michigan's then-governor James Blanchard, and Flint's mayor and others wanted to transform it into a casino. It was featured in Michael Moore's 1989 film *Roger & Me,* which used satire to explore the serious impact of General Motors auto-plant closures on Flint and the region. AutoWorld was imploded live on CNN in 1997.[3] The site is now a UM–Flint building that houses the schools of Education and Nursing as well as a center with early childhood education and day care.

The Educational Opportunities Initiatives office was established in 1995 and served as the administrative coordinating unit for all UM–Flint precollegiate outreach and collegiate activities designed to increase educational access and success for minority and first-generation students. Tendaji Ganges, a national leader in education from preschool through college completion (P–16), was recruited from Illinois to run the unit. Tendaji set about the business of establishing an array of community and minority P–16 outreach programs serving over two thousand students annually. In 2015, a new chancellor arrived at UM–Flint, and within a few weeks, one of the smartest, most effective, and committed educators I've ever known, Tendaji Ganges, was out of a job. Less than a year following his departure, Tendaji was dead. Despite his nearly twenty years of exemplary and dedicated service, the university didn't even bother to send his family a resolution, the document sent by a university to the family of the deceased acknowledging the persons' service and expressing condolences, which is typically read at the funeral or memorial service.

* * *

In the spring of 1996, after two years at UM–Flint, I received a surprising call. "Charlie, this is Jim Duderstadt. I'm calling to let you know that I have decided to step down as president at Michigan, effective immediately. The regents and I have reached an impasse in our relationship, and I believe it's in everyone's best interest for me to retire and return to the faculty after a sabbatical. I'm pleased to note that Homer Neal, vice president for research, has agreed to serve as interim president until a person is named. I don't believe your work will be impacted by this change, and I hope you'll remain with the university. You're doing a great job and we need people like you."

And with that, I became less certain about my future at UM–Flint. Jim was an extraordinary leader who understood the big picture as well as the nuances of the academy. The only thing I could say was, "Thank you, Jim, and I look forward to working with you no matter what role you're in." I hung up the phone and walked across the hall to one of my most trusted colleagues, Chief Financial Officer Dorothy Russell, to share with her the devastating news I'd just received from President Duderstadt. We both knew that he understood the need to transform UM–Flint into a different type of institution and was not swayed by the self-serving whining of the faculty, who preferred a smaller version of UM–Ann Arbor in Flint!

An internationally acclaimed physicist, Homer Neal earned bachelors and master's degrees from Indiana University and his PhD from Michigan. Early in his career, he served as dean of research and sponsored programs at Indiana, until accepting the position of provost at SUNY Stony Brook. As Michigan's vice president of research, Homer presided over a massive research portfolio and was one of the most respected administrators in his profession. While he accepted the regents' request to serve as Michigan's acting president, he indicated he had no interest in becoming its permanent president.

Today, when I tell people that at one point all of UM's campuses were headed by Blacks and not one Black person is in those roles today, they are incredulous. Homer oversaw the Ann Arbor campus along with the total system, while Jim Renick served as chancellor at the Dearborn campus and I was at Flint. Homer's transition into his temporary presidential role was seamless, and he proved to be one of my greatest supporters and allies throughout my stay at UM–Flint.

I was an activist leader at UM–Flint and refused to acquiesce to the wishes of the Faculty Senate, which wanted to weigh in on everything. I knew that without strategic change, the university could compete neither for students, legislative, nor philanthropic support. So with the support of UM's central administration, I didn't take no for an answer and proceeded to do what needed to be done, even if faculty did not agree. After all, my role was to lead, not simply preside, over the wishes of the faculty.

Admittedly, there was a great deal of head butting at times, with some faculty taking their case directly to members of the Board of Regents. When approached by individual regents, I shared with them the racist tendencies of complaining faculty, of which they were unaware or unwilling to accept. Needless to say, I expended an enormous amount of energy and goodwill trying to work with faculty, many of whom wanted the university just the way it used to be while the world around it was constantly changing.

* * *

On a gorgeous Sunday afternoon in September 1997, the phone rang, and I picked it up without looking at the caller ID. It was my sister Carrie, who I thought was calling to discuss our planned trip to Michigan's upcoming football game. But I sensed from her voice that something was awry.

"Charlie," she said, "after nursing what seemed like a cold for several weeks, when we got back from the family reunion, I decided to go to urgent care here in Southfield. I'm calling to let you know that they ran some X-rays, and I've been diagnosed with stage four lung cancer."

I was in shock and said, "There must be a mistake. You can't be serious. This is not something to joke about."

She replied, "Charlie, I am not joking. I have been told that I should start chemotherapy right away!"

I was devastated and bewildered, and I told her how sorry I was to hear about her diagnosis, especially knowing she didn't smoke and was one of the most health-conscious people I knew. Carrie asked if I'd meet with her and her physician on Wednesday of the coming week, to which I replied yes without hesitation. Rather than meet her at the doctor's office, I picked her up at home and drove her there. The doctor knew that Carrie had invited me to accompany her, and he'd set aside the time to talk with us and to review the diagnosis, as well as her prognosis.

A warm and personable physician, he began by saying how truly sorry he was to confirm the diagnosis of advanced lung cancer. He talked about the added measure of difficulty because Carrie wasn't just a patient but his friend, and he pledged to do any and everything to make sure she received the best care available. Carrie took meticulous notes and understandably had tons of questions that he patiently answered. He understood our decision to seek a second opinion but encouraged us to do so sooner rather than later.

Physicians at the University of Michigan Cancer Center in Ann Arbor confirmed that Carrie did indeed have metastatic lung cancer and agreed with the proposed treatment plan recommended by her physician. The lead oncologist at Michigan concluded the conference by encouraging Carrie to consider doing any travel she may have been putting off because of the unpredictability of lung cancer and how she might tolerate the chemo. Carrie's reply was unbelievable: "Dr. Louis, I have done everything I've ever wanted to do. I want to devote my full attention to beating this darn cancer." And with that, we got up, held hands, and walked out into one of the most spectacular days ever: sunny, breezy, and without a cloud in sight.

For the next several months, I drove Carrie to chemo, and we'd go to lunch afterwards. One day while receiving chemo, she asked, "Charlie, are you happy?" Before I could reply, she said, "Do something that makes you happy!" Several months after receiving that advice, I accepted an invitation from Indiana University's president Myles Brand to lead the university's diversity efforts. When I told Lee Bollinger, Michigan's president, of my decision to resign to do something less stressful, it was because I was convinced that I had done all I could do to put UM–Flint on a course for growth. The state of Michigan and the Mott Foundation had provided much-needed resources, and now seem like a good time to hand off the reins to someone else.

At age fifty-four, on May 12, 1998, cancer claimed Carrie's life but not her indomitable spirit. Until the last two months of life, she continued to work as director of Detroit-Wayne County's WIC program. Most of her colleagues had no idea she even had lung cancer, because she never experienced the severe weight loss that many chemo patients do. While getting Carrie's condo ready for listing with a real estate agent, I came across a world map on a basement wall with color-coded pins of places she'd visited. It was then that I better understood her advice to me as well as her reply to her physician. In memory of Carrie, Jeanetta and I decided to take a European tour before I commenced my new duties as vice president at Indiana University.

* * *

Armed with imagination, preparation, and determination, I embarked on a leadership journey that began in the 1960s and continues even today. That journey has taken me to places I didn't know existed as a boy chopping cotton and to positions that I never knew Black people held. Although I was on the forefront of America's diversity experiment in the 1980s and 1990s, my goal through leadership was equity, nothing more and nothing less. The accomplishments I feel proudest of include nurturing the dreams of others, always being willing to speak truth to power without fear of retribution, modeling the qualities of servant leadership, establishing personal scholarships endowments to enable first-generation students to go to college, joining forces with like-minded colleagues to pursue a progressive higher-education agenda, and never using my position of leadership to uphold the status quo.

I've lost count of the number of times I was the first Black person to do one thing or another. The important question is, did I use the opportunities that I had to advance the hopes, dreams, and aspirations of others? I realized early on in my leadership journey that there would not be a second, third, fourth, or fifth Black leader in a particular position unless I and the other "firsts" invested in others. In 1998, I joined forces with nine other Black college presidents to create the Millennium Leadership Initiative; to date, more than 500 aspiring leaders have participated in the program, 134 of whom have become college presidents.

Hindsight is always perfect, because we have the privilege of viewing things retrospectively from the perspective of experiences we've acquired. Over the course of my leadership journey, I have had more than a dozen actual university president offers, not just nominations, and I never chose the one that paid the biggest salary or had the largest enrollment. I chose the ones that had the greatest opportunity for leadership and service and the ones I considered to be the best fit. Although IU East and UM–Flint were vastly different from each other with respect to size, student and faculty profile, financial resources, and political dynamics, two important lessons have stayed with me long after my tenure. Leadership is not about what you accomplish as an individual but about what people accomplish collectively. Collaboration is the sine qua non, the essential and indispensable ingredient, of leadership.

I learned to dream while chopping and picking cotton more than sixty years ago. It was there in the cotton fields of Crittenden County in eastern Arkansas that I got myself a big dream. The only thing larger than my dreams was my imagination. In the words of the Langston Hughes poem "Dreams," I knew that holding fast to my dreams would give me wings:

> *Hold fast to dreams*
> *For if dreams die*
> *Life is a broken-winged bird*
> *That cannot fly*[4]

As the billows rolled and the manacles of poverty tightened their grip, I refused to let go of my dreams. It wasn't just about me escaping the hopelessness imposed by poverty; I dreamed of helping to create a more equitable world. I dreamed of being a leader for people, who, like me, bore the scars of historic disenfranchisement. I got more help than I ever imagined from people who looked like me, as well as those who did not.

10

THIS SPINNING TOP

"HEY, BROTHER NELMS! THERE'S THIS RUMOR FLOATING AROUND that you're leaving Michigan to return to Indiana, one of the most backward states in the nation. Is there any truth to this story? Surely you know that diversity positions are like dead-end roads leading to nowhere. Is there something you know that the rest of us don't?"

This conversation with my longtime friend Art occurred in November 1997, several months before I accepted Indiana University's invitation to return as vice president. I wasn't the least bit offended by the directness of his comments. Like me, Art had spent his entire professional career at PWIs, trying to make a difference.

Sarcastically, I responded, "Thanks for the encouragement, comrade. I knew there was at least one person who'd understand my reasons for accepting IU's invitation; I just didn't know it would be you!"

After a hearty, howling laugh that would have made a passerby wonder what was going on, I replied, "Comrade, you've been around long enough to know that all that glitters isn't gold. I accepted the UM–Flint position because I felt I could make a difference, and I believe I have. I have planted some trees whose shade I'll never enjoy, and I have created some programs that'll serve the needs of people who look like us for years to come. My terminally ill sister, Carrie, advised me to do something that makes me happy. While I'm not exactly sure what happiness is, my job at UM–Flint has exposed me to an unimaginable level of stress. There are no perfect institutions, but I feel good about returning to one of the places that nurtured my dreams at a critical time in my professional development. I know the people at IU, and they know me, which is important in the context of what they're asking me to do."

Art responded, "Godspeed! You know you can always call on me for support." I called on him many times before and after my decision to return to Indiana University in 1998.

* * *

Back from our two-week European vacation following Carrie's death, Jeanetta and I settled into our rented house located in a forest-like subdivision on Bloomington's far-east side. While it was a fantastic area for me to jog or hike in the adjacent woods, Jeanetta was absolutely terrified when I was away overnight. She was so terrified that she left all indoor and outdoor lights on all night and often fell asleep on the sofa! We knew only one family nearby, IU Bloomington's chancellor, Gros Louis, and his wife, Diana, who lived a quarter mile away.

Jeanetta's fear was further exacerbated when hundreds of White supremacy fliers were left on car windshields on July 4, 1998, just two months after we moved to town. Around the same time, the Klu Klux Klan (KKK) announced plans for a Bloomington march, and they endorsed presidential candidate George W. Bush. The distribution of White supremacy fliers and KKK activities led to the formation of Bloomington United in Diversity, a movement comprised of people from all faiths, races, political affiliations, and socioeconomic classes. The group distributed yard placards proclaiming, "No Hate in Our Yards. Not in Our Town. Not Anywhere."

A year later, on July 4, 1999, White supremacist Benjamin Nathaniel Smith, a former IU Bloomington student, gunned down Won-Joon Yoon, a Korean IU graduate student, as Yoon entered a church located less than two hundred yards from the IU Bloomington campus. A few days earlier, Smith had killed former Northwestern University assistant basketball coach Ricky Byrdsong in Skokie, Illinois. Smith also shot and wounded nine Orthodox Jews in the West Rogers Park neighborhood of Chicago.

While the vitriolic language of the KKK and the murderous actions of Benjamin Smith were of great concern to me, I wasn't about to go into hiding and abstain from engaging in the one pastime that I enjoyed most, jogging. I became more observant of the people and the activities around me. At the same time, I appreciated the stance taken by my neighbors, university colleagues, religious leaders, and elected officials in their unified denouncement of racism in its myriad forms. Even while growing up in the Arkansas Delta, I was never afraid of Klan members, who met in the woods less than a half mile from our house. I figured that people who needed to hide beneath cone-shaped hoods with small openings for their eyes were genuine cowards.

As despicable as the activities of the KKK were, it would be giving this hate group undeserved credit to claim that they influenced President Brand's decision to create the position of vice president I was recruited to fill. It seems that Brand's decision was driven by several salient factors: a desire to demonstrate his commitment to diversity by appointing an executive-level officer who would be an equal among other university vice presidents on the president's cabinet; the desire to achieve a higher level of coordination of various diversity initiatives on the Bloomington campus; and the desire to increase the emphasis on diversity across all IU campuses. I believe it's fair to say that Brand, Gros Louis, and other senior administrators took seriously the demands articulated by members of the student coalition during its campus-wide Unity March on MLK Day, January 20, 1997. The coalition, comprised of all minority groups at IU Bloomington campus, including members of the LGBT community, may not have caused the creation of my position, but they certainly hastened it.

* * *

In October 1997, Stephanie, my administrative assistant at the University of Michigan–Flint, paged me. "Chancellor, there is someone from Indiana University on the phone asking to speak with you. He said his name is Ken Gros Louis. Is he someone you know? Do you wish to speak with him now, or shall I tell him you'll call him back?" Stephanie knew that I was working feverishly to review a major grant proposal to the Mott Foundation and had asked not to be disturbed. Yet she knew of my long association with IU and figured she should ask if I wanted to take the call before telling Ken I was not available. I thanked her and asked that she put the call through.

"Charlie," Ken began, "how're things in Michigan these days? Myles asked me to give you a call to run an idea past you. As you know, there has been quite a stir around diversity on the Bloomington campus in recent months. Much of it, or so it seems, revolves around our director of diversity on the Bloomington campus. In fact, you may have seen the recent article in the *Chronicle of Higher Education* in which Steve Burden and several people at IU are quoted. Having been at IU for a long time, I don't think the article is reflective of the morale here or of the things we've been doing over an extended period of time to enhance diversity. Myles is contemplating creating a university-wide position to oversee diversity, and I told him I thought you're an ideal person, if we can interest you in such a position. We'd like for you to come to Bloomington for a day of consultation with Myles and me at your earliest convenience. At that time, we can tell you more about what we're thinking and get your feedback as well."

I thanked Ken and said I'd get back to him in a few days after talking with Jeanetta and Rashad. Jeanetta and Rashad knew firsthand the growing stress I was experiencing and encouraged me to at least find out what Myles and Ken had in mind. I made a quiet, unannounced trip to Bloomington for meetings with Myles and Ken to get a better sense of just how serious they were about this new position under consideration. Following a candid conversation about the status of diversity at IU Bloomington, I indicated that I'd be interested in the position, with several important caveats.

First and foremost, as a sitting chancellor, I was not prepared to go through a public search process. The Michigan legislature was in the process of considering a bill related to environmental remediation on a parcel of property badly needed for campus expansion, and I could not appear to have one foot in the door and the other one out by participating in a highly publicized search. Secondly, I was in the midst of making some essential structural changes at the university, and I could not have it appear that I was doing so based on personal preferences and motives. (UM–Flint has had three chancellors since I retired, and nearly all of the changes I made are still in place.) Third, I would only consider the position if my portfolio was comprehensive and included a combination of diversity- and non-diversity-related areas. Fourth, as an indication of President Brand's commitment, I asked that he include a financial commitment to the new initiative in the press release announcing my appointment. Finally, I requested that the university absorb the cost of a six-person consulting team of senior leaders from around the country to join me in conducting a comprehensive assessment of IU Bloomington's diversity efforts and to offer their observations and recommendations for improvement.

Within a few weeks of my initial meeting with Myles and Ken, we reached an agreement on my return to Indiana University as vice president of student development and diversity, effective July 1, 1998, making IU the first major research university in the nation to establish such a position. When my appointment was publicly announced in May 1998, the press release included an additional commitment of $1 million from Myles to support diversity initiatives across the university. Those funds were used to leverage other commitments, which more than doubled Myles's commitment during my first two years as vice president.

Having concluded the details of my appointment, my national multiracial review team and I spent three months performing a comprehensive review of IU Bloomington's diversity efforts. Four fundamental assumptions guided our work, and we publicly communicated them as our work got under way. We wanted the entire university community to know that we were serious about our work and that we weren't there to do the predetermined bidding of the university administration. They were the following:

1. The Indiana University administration was committed to improving the current situation on the Bloomington campus regarding the recruitment and retention of faculty, staff and students of color.
2. The president of Indiana University and the chancellor of the Bloomington campus were willing to hold key administrators in academic and nonacademic areas accountable for expanding and enhancing diversity activities and resolving issues of equity.
3. Deep and long-term institutional change was needed in order to achieve the results that the university had committed to achieving.
4. The optimum climate had to be a supportive and nurturing one. Rather than being marginalized and isolated, students, faculty, and staff from all minority groups were to be fully engaged in all aspects of campus life, without having to sacrifice or compromise their racial or ethnic identity.

The review team concluded that IU's advocacy offices model, established in the early 1970s, was inadequate for helping the university achieve the broad goal articulated in the IU Strategic Directions Charter, which called for "ensuring that Indiana University reflects the diversity of American society and supports the achievement of minorities in all aspects of university life." The advocacy offices model was in widespread use at many American colleges and universities during the 1980s and '90s. The model entailed midlevel diversity officers serving a specific ethnic or gender group, for example, Asian, Black, Latino, LBGTQ, and so on. Most advocacy offices were poorly staffed and funded, and the emphasis was on providing social and cultural activities for students. University policies were off limits to those who directed advocacy offices, while funding for scholarships, faculty, and staff hiring remained stagnant.

We suggested that a new paradigm was needed, one in which institutional and individual practices and behaviors at IU Bloomington were reflective of its vision and goals of inclusiveness. Under the distributed leadership model, accountability was to be shared by all university leaders, and collaboration across academic and administrative was expected. Acknowledging IU's rich history of facilitating the educational development of Blacks, we called on the university to rededicate itself to this goal.

The review team met with more than two hundred university constituents and reviewed countless planning documents and annual reports spanning more than two decades. Our report, entitled *20/20: A Vision for Achieving Equity and Excellence on the Bloomington Campus of Indiana University*, offered a succinct list of recommendations, which, if implemented with fidelity, would enable the Bloomington campus to interpolate the future rather than extrapolate the past. Perhaps one of our most salient observations was the fact that there was no need for additional studies. The time had arrived for the university's executive leadership team to stop expecting consultants and external reviewers to do what it clearly had the power to do—enact change.

As the newest member of the president's cabinet, with overarching responsibility for diversity, I refused to let my colleagues off the hook by adopting a lone-ranger mentality. Quite the contrary, I pushed collaboration and distributed leadership across academic and administrative boundaries, and campus and community boundaries, as well as collaboration across gender and ethnicity. My highest priority was to develop effective working relationships not only with my fellow vice presidents but also with deans, key department chairs, and directors. I viewed my role as that of facilitator rather than enforcer.

When a colleague expressed reluctance or reticence about the applicability of diversity to his or her area, I assumed the role of executive coach, all the while abstaining from characterizing that colleague as an opponent to diversity. My role was to make that person both an advocate and a collaborator. While there were varying degrees of engagement, each of the vice presidents launched one or more significant diversity initiatives. When I was told that the applicant pool did not include women and people of color, I challenged my colleagues to start a grow-our-own program. Accepting the challenge, the vice president for technology, Michael McRobbie, started a year-long internship program for minorities, women, and first-generation students. He made sure that each participant was provided with outstanding supervisors and mentors.

While I enjoyed an excellent working relationship with each of IU's vice presidents, Ken Gros Louis and Terry Clapacs were most influential in my decision to return to Indiana University. When I was chancellor at IU East, Ken had been my go-to person when negotiating with IU Bloomington deans and the Indiana Higher Education Commission to gain approval for new degrees. Similarly, Terry Clapacs had been a true collaborator when it came to enhancing IU East campus aesthetics and getting approval for new facilities.

Also, reconnecting with Dr. Herman Hudson was a real joy. Well into his seventies and still working part-time, Herman was a master strategist who was never reluctant to share his ideas with me over bourbon after work. At his eulogy several years later, I described my mentor and friend as the only blind person I'd ever known with twenty-twenty vision. Herman's impact on enhancing diversity at IU Bloomington was indelible and irrepressible. One of my greatest accomplishments as vice president was to recommend to President Brand, Chancellor Gros Louis, and the IU Board of Trustees that two scholarship programs that Herman had established, the Minority Achievers Program and the Mathematics and Science Scholars, be renamed the Hudson-Holland Scholars Program to honor Herman and his collaborator, James Holland, a professor of biology. Herman embraced and mentored me from the first time I met him in 1970. He enthusiastically welcomed me as vice president because he knew that I shared his unwavering commitment to equity *and* excellence.

Each day that I served as IU's vice president for student development and diversity and vice chancellor of diversity on the Bloomington campus was action packed; there was seldom a lull in activities or a dull moment! I was fortunate to be assisted in my work by a talented group of men and women who shared my passion for enhancing diversity at all levels of university operations. Professor Edwardo Rhodes, from the School of Public and Environmental Affairs; Professor Gloria Gibson, professor in the Folklore and Ethnomusicology Department; Frank Motely, assistant dean at the IU Maurer School of Law; and Vicki Roberts, assistant dean of African American Affairs, all agreed to join the new diversity team.

Recognizing the need to tell the IU diversity story more persuasively and proactively, author Nadine Pinede came on board as director of communications, while Mike Wilkerson and Jack Schmidt took on the task of grant development and special projects, respectively. Professor Karen

Hanson served as the first dean of IU Bloomington's Hutton Honors College, while Victor Borden assumed a university-wide role as associate vice president for university planning, institutional research, and accountability. I am proud to say that our work group was the most diverse of any in the entire university. In assembling a work group, I felt strongly that our staffing pattern should reflect the type of diversity expected of others. In a word, I had to walk the talk, and that is exactly what I did!

Without specifying which areas should be included, when I was appointed vice president and vice chancellor, I simply requested that my portfolio be diverse and not limited to units that served only minority populations. Recognizing the reality of politics in the academy, I trusted Chancellor Gros Louis to do the right thing with respect to determining which nondiversity units should become a part of my portfolio. Of course, there were no volunteers! While many Indiana University faculty in the 1980s and 1990s expressed support for diversity, they did not want their academic programs to be misperceived or denigrated by placing them under an administrator with responsibility for diversity. After much discussion, and to the consternation of many faculty and staff members, Ken decided that the Honors Division should be moved from the College of Arts and Sciences to my supervision as vice chancellor of diversity on the Bloomington campus.

The decision was not well received by many faculty and staff in the Honors Division, including the director and the associate director. Someone either mistakenly or intentionally copied me on an email where faculty took exception to including Diversity and Honors under the same administrative umbrella. "Why," they asked, "would the administration include its most respected program under the same structure as its least respected one?" Per Ken's request, I met with Honors Division faculty, staff, and students on numerous occasions to discuss our collective aspirations for Honors and the best way to proceed with procuring the financial resources needed to strengthen Honors.

To aid in our decision making, I invited the deans of the Honors Colleges at the University of Minnesota and the University of Illinois to conduct a comprehensive review of IU Bloomington's Honors Division. Based on their recommendations, the Honors Division was transformed to an honors college and later renamed the Hutton Honors College. This was in honor of Edward L. Hutton, who funded the construction of the $3.5 million Hutton Honors College and was generous in funding several other scholarships and endowments, including $9 million to establish an endowment for the

International Experiences Program. Not long after my retirement in 2007, the Hutton Honors College was moved from under the aegis of the vice president for institutional development and student affairs. The many gains of the Honors College notwithstanding, the academic arrogance of many of IU's academic elites meant that they couldn't fathom the idea of having Honors and Diversity share an administrative tent.

The work of diversity requires perspicacity, patience, and persistence. It also requires focus, follow-through, and strategic investments. There were days when the frustration from stalling tactics and game playing at all levels of the university made me wonder whether the effort was worth it. There were days when I wondered whether I had done as much as I could and if it was time for me to take up my professorship in the School of Education. I came to realize two very important facts. First, privileged White people talk a good game about the importance of diversity, but few are willing to hold themselves and their subordinates accountable for achieving it. Second, the biggest deterrent to diversity is not a lack of money but a lack of will. Although the challenges weren't inconsequential, I knew that I could not give the diversity naysayers the pleasure of seeing me throw in the towel. So I pressed on with the ardor of hope and the certainty that I was making a difference, albeit not as much as I would have preferred. I learned to celebrate small wins without losing sight of the big picture.

My four proudest moments while leading IU's diversity efforts are the dedication of the Neal-Marshall Black Culture Center, the appointment of Mike Davis as IU men's head basketball coach, the appointment of Adam W. Herbert as IU's sixteenth president, and the IU Board of Trustee's approval of a tuition set-aside initiative to increase diversity and student success at all IU campuses. Collectively, these four moments catapulted Indiana University to the front of the Big Ten by demonstrating a tangible commitment to diversity. Within the time frame in which these things were occurring, IU filed an amicus brief in support of the University of Michigan in *Grutter v. Bollinger*. This was a pivotal lawsuit in which the US Supreme Court upheld the use of affirmative action in higher education.

* * *

The excitement and pride was short lived with respect to the appointment of Adam Herbert and Mike Davis as president and coach, respectively. In both instances, it didn't take long for opposition forces to manifest themselves, which led to the departure of both Herbert and Davis. While it's not unusual for presidents and coaches to be fired or forced out, the tactics employed by the faculty were unprecedented in recent Indiana University history. Many would argue that both decisions were race neutral, but that's definitely not the perception of IU Black alumni with whom I have had the opportunity to interact.

* * *

"Vice President Nelms, this is Rob from the Black Student Union calling to share our profound disappointment with you."

"And what may I ask is the source of your profound disappointment?"

"Dr. Nelms, I thought the Neal-Marshall Black Culture Center was built for Black people. If that's the case, why can't we use it whenever we want to? Every time we try to use the Grand Hall or Bridgewater Lounge, we're told that both have been reserved. And when we walk past the building, we see it overflowing with White folks! Since they own all of the other buildings on campus, why can't we have just one?"

This was in 2003, when a growing number of students had expressed concerns similar to Rob's and were allegedly contemplating a march to make those concerns public. I began by patiently sharing with Rob that none of the buildings on campus was owned by a particular group—they were all owned by Indiana University and ultimately the state of Indiana. While certain buildings or parts of them may be designated for specific uses, public spaces were open to all campus groups without regard to race or ethnicity.

I asked Rod a simple question that neither he nor his fellow complainers had thought through very well, if at all: "When attempting to reserve a meeting room or reception hall in the Student Union Building or in the School of Education, for example, how would you feel if you were told that those particular spaces could only be used by White students?"

Rob's immediate response was, "Oh, that's different!"

I pushed back, "Can you tell me a bit more about those differences? Are you saying that only Black people should use the Black Culture Center? Have you or your fellow students attempted to reserve space in the Black Culture Center well in advance of an event rather than dropping in a day or two before a planned event?"

Unhappy with my line of questioning, Rob angrily informed me that he was not only calling Amos Brown, a popular radio personality at WTLC in Indianapolis, but all of the television stations! I encouraged him to feel free to share my telephone number with Amos or anyone else who wanted to discuss campus facility-use policies in general and those at the Black Culture Center in particular.

It didn't take long for my old friend Amos Brown to call to, as he put it, "get your side of the story." Remembering me from my days as chancellor at IU East, Amos often called me as Mr. Chancellor when he wanted to press a point, and he wasted no time doing so when he called. A couple of times I responded to him with a question: "Amos, what do you think I would do if a Black student attempted to reserve space and was told that the space could only be reserved by White students? In the thirty-plus years that you've known me, have you ever known me to do anything intentionally to discriminate against anyone, Black or White? Amos, you and I both know the answer to the question is no, and I'm not about to start now. As IU's chief administrator for diversity, my job is to promote excellence, equity, and integration, not racial segregation!"

For all of the right reasons—ethical and legal—I held fast to my position that we could not promote living and learning by restricting the use of the Black Culture Center. In 2016, nearly two hundred events were held in the center, and they attracted more than sixty thousand guests according to figures from the Black Culture Center. The controversy over who should use the Neal-Marshall Black Culture Center would not be the last philosophical difference I would have with Black students and others of goodwill.

* * *

"Why should we have to take classes in a room with members of the KKK staring down at us from a mural that you call a work of art? What we see when we look at the painting are concealed identities of White hate-mongers who appear poised to jump out the painting and lynch us at any minute. If you really cared about how we feel, you would cover up that crap or take it down. If this is such great art, why don't you put it in the art museum where it belongs?"

Passions soared on all sides relative to whether panels of the Benton murals in Woodburn Hall auditorium should be taken down, with the controversy attracting national media coverage. Yet the overwhelming majority of IU students had no idea who Thomas Hart Benton was or what the message was he sought to convey with the murals he was commissioned to paint. The massive mural series depicted the cultural and industrial history of the state of Indiana and was the dominant feature in the Indiana Pavilion at the 1933 World's Fair in Chicago.

Benton is said to have spent weeks traveling the state interviewing Hoosiers and deciding what to include and what to leave out. Many were unhappy with his depiction of Hoosier politics and his depiction of the faces of well-known politicians and businessmen on the bodies of drunks, card players, and other marginal folks. Conservatives thought his political interpretations were too friendly to labor and hostile to management; in part, that's because his style as an artist always glorified manual labor. The panel that was controversial in 2003—the depiction of the Klu Klux Klan—was upsetting to many in 1933 as well. The feeling then was that the KKK had been driven out of power in Indianapolis and it was best to forget it. True to his commitment not to leave anything out, Benton included Native Americans being displaced in the early panels, punishments and whippings, and the ugly, belching, smoky steel mills in Gary. So it was fitting that he included the KKK; it was indeed a dominant force in Indiana for a period of time.

Shortly after commencing her duties in 2003, IU chancellor Sharon Brehm was inundated with demands that the murals be moved immediately from Woodburn Hall. Sympathetic to the concerns of students and committed to advancing ethnic diversity on campus, Sharon did not want to be derailed by this issue before barely getting started. She was leaning toward acquiescing to student demands, while many of her administrative colleagues, faculty, and staff members were encouraging her not to remove the mural from Woodburn.

I led the list of administrators opposed to taking it down. My reason was simple: the history of Indiana is inextricably linked to the KKK, and we can ill afford to forget or whitewash that reality. To the dismay of many students, Chancellor Brehm chose not to take the mural down and settled on a threefold strategy. First, a descriptive plaque was placed alongside the mural identifying the artist and explaining its historical significance. Second, a video was produced and shown on the first day of class every semester. A staff member from the Office of Diversity Education or the art museum would be there to facilitate a discussion about the mural or respond to student questions. Third, Chancellor Brehm established an Art Acquisition Fund to be used to acquire works of art by minority and women artists. A companion activity included a student design competition to develop diversity banners for placement throughout the campus. This compendium of strategies, I believe, allowed the university to make the Benton mural controversy a teachable moment rather than one that further divided the campus community. The words of poet W. H. Auden capture well my thinking on the matter of art, diversity, and censorship: "Great art is clear thinking about mixed feelings."

* * *

The twenty-first century got off to a wonderful start for Jeanetta and me personally. Rashad, our only child, graduated with honors from the University of Michigan and was admitted to several excellent law schools, including Michigan, Duke, the University of Southern California, Indiana, and Iowa. He settled on Michigan, with the idea of becoming a civil rights attorney. By the time he completed law school, he had completely changed his mind about practicing law. International humanitarian work had been on his radar for several years, due in large measure to his participation in the Model United Nations program while in high school. After law school, he went off to spend a year working as a policy officer with the UN World Food Programme. Fourteen years later, he's still with the program and has literally traveled all over the world. Currently based in Rome, Rashad serves as Human Resources officer and special assistant to WFP's executive director. Jeanetta landed her dream job as director of the Twenty-First Scholars Program at IU Bloomington, a position she would retire from in 2008 to join me when I became chancellor at North Carolina Central University.

* * *

"Charlie, quickly, turn on your television if you don't already have it on! A plane just crashed into one of the towers of the World Trade Center in New York City. Another crashed in Pennsylvania, and another one just hit the Pentagon. Hurry, turn the TV on and call me back in a minute!"

The frantic call was from my colleague Vicki Roberts, who served as associate vice president on my leadership team. It was Tuesday morning, September 11, 2001, my fifty-fifth birthday, and I had just walked in the door after completing a ten-mile run to mark this important milestone in my life. I was stretching on my exercise mat and wondering how much longer my lower back and knees could take the fierce pounding on the asphalt. After all, I had been running six-to-eight miles a day since I was twenty-five years old. I did as Vicki requested and turned the TV on. I watched in utter horror as CNN and all of the other stations repeatedly showed clips of an airplane intentionally flying into the World Trade Center. As I listened to one expert after another, it seemed that they had more questions than answers.

They were unified in their belief that the plane incidents in New York, Pennsylvania, and Washington, DC, were all connected. There was no doubt in their collective minds that these were terrorist acts perpetrated by terrorist leaders from halfway around the world, with all fingers pointing to the Middle East. As devastating as the loss of American lives was, the attack demonstrated that the United States was vulnerable and not the safe haven so many of us Americans had convinced ourselves it was.

After a brief conversation with Vicki, I felt the need to grieve among those with whom I shared a mutual commitment to improving the quality of life for all humans. I hastily showered, got dressed, and made my way to campus in time for an impromptu convening of the cabinet by Myles. We agreed that we should not cancel classes but rather proceed with business as usual. To do otherwise would inadvertently cede power and control to the terrorists!

Little work got done on September 11, 2001, as I made my way to various offices in my division to reassure colleagues that fear and hate were not effective tools for meeting the challenges that faced us as a nation and a university community. That evening, I joined several hundred students, faculty, staff, and administrators for a peace vigil in Alumni Hall. Instead of listening to speeches extolling the virtues of democracy, we shared our innermost feelings about love of country, and we recommitted ourselves to being the change agents America needed to become a better place. That was the first birthday I ever remember celebrating without a meal and the company of family and friends. To this day, I refuse to refer to September 11 as 9/11. I tell people that it's my birthday and I had it long before terrorists took their best shot!

Not everything was negative in September 2001. *Time* magazine named IU Bloomington as the top student-centered research university in America. The authors commented favorably on IU Bloomington's efforts to create and sustain a culture of caring and support for students. The Groups Scholars Program, the Faculty and Staff for Student Excellence Mentoring Program, CultureFest, and the various culture centers were among the programs singled out for recognition. My passion and hard work notwithstanding, I took no credit for this national recognition of IU's focus on the quality of the undergraduate student experience. I thanked my colleagues across the university for their persistent support of students across the boundaries of race, class, academic discipline, and zip code. Even without accolades like those in the *Time* article, every day is the right day to put students first in all that we do.

* * *

It was the fall of 2003, and I'd been in my position for five years. Things were moving along smoothly, even with a few of the hardcore diversity doubters beginning to believe. Whether they had a genuine interest in diversity and equity or were primarily concerned with the hit that IU's image had taken just a couple of years earlier because of KKK demonstrations, the Benton mural discord, and the murderous acts of Benjamin Smith, at least I felt our work was gaining support. Regional campus leaders and members of their faculty and staff expressed appreciation for being included in the diversity dialogue, but they were more appreciative of the matching minigrants that my office provided to them from the $1 million Myles made available when my appointment was announced. I think many of my regional-campus colleagues had prematurely concluded that all of the funds would go to the flagship in Bloomington and to IUPUI. Our matching-funds approach ensured that campus leaders had some skin in the game, undergirded by a financial incentive signaling the importance of diversity from a central-university administrative perspective.

When the tuition set-aside initiative to support diversity and student success was developed and approved by IU trustees, regional campuses were included. The two most important deliverables to result from our One University approach to diversity was the revitalization of the annual Enhancing Minority Attainment Conference at IU Kokomo, which I, along with my friend Benjamin Johnson and my colleague Phil Rutledge, founded in 1991. This two-day conference brought together campus teams of eight to ten participants to learn about diversity best practices from researchers and practitioners around the country. The annual nature of this convening also provided an opportunity for campus teams to work at developing or refining their objectives and strategies for achieving higher levels of diversity and equity, with more than two hundred participants from Indiana University, Purdue University, Indiana State University, and other public and private institutions in the state.

A second important deliverable to emerge from our One University approach to diversity was our partnership with Indiana University's Faculty

Academy on Excellence in Teaching (FACET). Partnering with FACET allowed us to delve into the heart of diversity from the perspective of teaching and learning. Underwritten by my office and coordinated by a faculty committee with members from all IU campuses, interdisciplinary faculty teams came together annually to consider effective strategies for integrating diversity, equity, and social justice into the curriculum.

It has long been my belief that the curriculum is the most universally-available-yet-underutilized vehicle for addressing diversity and equity. Until and unless universities better equip all instructional staff—tenured, nontenured, adjuncts, and TAs—with the skills they need to teach more effectively, they will continue to place diversity in an administrative bucket to be attended to by administrators, who are not equipped to ensure that students graduate college equipped to live, lead, and work in a global world. No matter how many high-profile speakers colleges and universities invite to campus, they are not substitutes for the role that faculty members should play every day!

* * *

When Myles announced at a 2002 cabinet meeting that he had been named president and chief executive officer of the National Collegiate Athletics Association (NCAA) and would take the helm in January 2003, quite candidly, my emotions ranged from shock, surprise, disappointment, and excitement. At first, his appointment struck me as rather odd, but on deeper reflection, I could see why a person of Myles's vast intellect, experience, and courage would be tapped to lead the NCAA. The organization was at a critical juncture in its life cycle, with increasing pressure to halt the "spending arms war," improve the academic performance and graduation rates of student athletes, reel in noncompliant coaches, and do a better job of addressing gender inequality in all aspects of intercollegiate athletics, among other challenges.

If anyone could tackle these big-ticket issues, it would be my mentor, colleague, and friend Myles Brand, a person of impeccable integrity with an indefatigable work ethic and experience leading a large, multicampus institution like Indiana University. With the firing of IU's iconic basketball coach Bobby Knight, Myles had shown the courage to do what he believed was right and in the best interest of the institution. Never in my long career in the academy had I seen a leader endure as much hateful criticism and threats to his physical well-being as I witnessed in Myles's case. A case study in composure and resolve, Myles just kept moving forward.

Two or three months after Miles started as head of NCAA, I received a phone call. "Charlie, this is Jerry Parker. As you may know, our firm facilitated the search that led to the appointment of Dr. Brand as president and CEO of NCAA. Since coming aboard, Myles has done some reorganizing and is looking for a senior vice president of education and membership services. He respects you and your work immensely and is interested in the possibility of you joining him at NCAA. He asked us to follow up to see if you might have an interest in the position."

I replied, "Wow, what a pleasant surprise. I have enormous respect for Myles, and although I'm not looking for a job, the position is one that I'd be willing to take a look at." After talking with Jeanetta and Rashad, I applied for the position, went through a quiet search, and was offered the position six weeks later by Myles.

My NCAA contract arrived via FedEx a couple days after the verbal offer from Myles. In addition to a salary approaching $100,000 more than I made at IU, the position included perks the likes of which I never knew existed. I hand delivered the contract to my attorney, who reviewed it and called to say that everything appeared in order; I could sign it, if that was what I wanted to do. I signed and returned the contract to Myles right away. In fact, that weekend Jeanetta and I made a trip to Indianapolis to look at housing options.

A week after I signed the contract with NCAA, my longtime friend Adam Herbert called from Jacksonville, Florida, to say that he was in the final stages of contract negotiations with the IU Board of Trustees to become the seventeenth president of the university and he wanted to tell me how excited he was about the prospects of working with me. After my heart skipped a beat, I congratulated him and proceeded to wish him well! I told Adam that I'd just signed a contract to join Myles Brand as senior vice president at NCAA and would not be here when he arrived. He asked that I at least give him an opportunity to talk with me and to see what he could do to make it worth my while to stay at IU.

Following my conversation with Adam, I called to inform Myles that I'd be staying at IU to work with Adam. Needless to say, he was not a happy camper and told me so in a polite but firm manner. I responded that my decision was influenced by my desire to ensure the success of IU's first Black president, even if it meant forgoing a significant increase in salary and the opportunity to work with him at the national level. Ever the gentleman and diplomat, Myles said he understood and wished me well.

When Adam Herbert was inaugurated on April 15, 2004, eight months after he'd arrived in Bloomington to lead IU, I felt like the proudest person at IU, even though I had just turned down the opportunity to increase my salary by more than $100,000 annually. The money honestly didn't matter. I reasoned that if Adam could succeed at IU, this would open the doors of opportunity for Blacks to serve as presidents at other major research universities around the country. With Adam's appointment, IU, one of my alma maters, was on a demonstrable diversity ascent, and I was blessed to be a part of it. With Adam's appointment, Blacks at IU had scaled two of the least likely walls in the academy: head men's basketball coach and president of the university. As my colleagues, Blacks and Whites alike, left the press conference where Adam was introduced, we gave each other a thumbs-up. We were convinced that IU had hired a president of enormous personal warmth, intellect, and articulateness who would serve the university well for the foreseeable future.

Within the first six months of President Herbert's arrival, I sensed that his presidency might not proceed as smoothly as I had hoped. While there is always a predictable amount of speculation about the composition of a new president's leadership team—who is in and who is out—President Herbert quickly decided to request the resignation of Dr. Sharon Brehm, vice president and chancellor of the Bloomington campus, the first woman to serve in this position. Brehm's resignation lead to the appointment of her predecessor, Dr. Ken Gros Louis, as acting chancellor. While Chancellor Brehm's resignation generated mixed reactions from the faculty, it was President Herbert's decision not to offer the chancellor's position to the popular dean of the College of Arts and Sciences, Dr. Kumble Subbaswamy, that generated a highly publicized negative response from the faculty. It seems that every grievance, real or imagined, the faculty had about the university and Herbert's leadership was unleashed. In fact, some members of the faculty took a vote of no confidence in the president and communicated their displeasure to the Indiana University Board of Trustees.

A major aspect of Adam's recovery strategy entailed restructuring the university. He eliminated the Bloomington campus chancellor's position and created the position of provost to manage the day-to-day affairs of the campus. Dr. Michael McRobbie was named interim provost while retaining his positions as vice president for research and vice president of information and technology. In 2007, three years after taking the position, Adam announced his decision to retire as president of Indiana University, and following a national search, Dr. Michael McRobbie became the eighteenth president on July 1, 2007.

Although President Herbert's tenure was shorter than the national average for college presidents, he can be credited with several major accomplishments during his presidency:

- Expansion of undergraduate and graduate opportunities in STEM for minorities and first-generation students by establishing the IU/HBCU Summer STEM Program
- Creation of a university-wide, merit-based scholarship program to attract and retain talented Indiana high school graduates. IU trustees voted to name the program Herbert Presidential Scholars in his honor.
- Establishment of the Women and Minorities Business Procurement Program
- Completion of the Mission Differentiation Initiative, realigning the mission of the core campuses, IU Bloomington and IUPUI, and the mission of regional campuses
- Realignment of the athletics budget and the upgrade of facilities
- Working to strengthen admissions standards on the Bloomington campus and increase undergraduate enrollment

Beyond concrete programmatic initiatives, Herbert's appointment sent a powerful message to IU alumni, Blacks in particular, that the trustees were open to the possibility of appointing talented personnel across racial and cultural lines. Regrettably, at the moment of writing this book in 2018, over two decades after my appointment, I believe there are no Blacks serving as full academic deans at IU Bloomington, IUPUI, or any of the regional campuses. Vice President James Wimbush, the only vice president on the university side of the ledger, has the additional title of dean of the University Graduate School.

Preparing to retire from IU in 2007, I took stock of its diversity agenda and could not help but marvel at the progress the Bloomington campus and the system overall had made in a short span of nine years. I am grateful for the support of countless colleagues across the university who value diversity and equity not because it looks good but because it's the right thing to do.

A partial list of Indiana University's diversity accomplishments from 1998 to 2007 includes the following:

- Construction and dedication of the Neal-Marshall Black Culture Center
- Transformation of the Honors Division to the Hutton Honors College
- Creation of CultureFest
- Expansion of diversity education
- Creation of the Adam Herbert Scholars Program
- Revitalization of the Enhancing Minority Attainment Conference and collaboration with FACET
- Conversations on Race Series, an initiative funded by the Charles Stewart Mott Foundation
- Launch of the Black Male Initiative
- Initiation of a targeted marketing program in selected Indiana cities
- Collaboration with the School of Education to expand minority recruitment and outreach
- Increase of the number of students participating in the Groups Scholars Program
- Collaboration with the School of Business to launch the Junior Executive Leadership Program
- Collaboration with the School of Health, Physical Education, and Recreation, now the School of Public Health, to establish a grow-your-own faculty initiative
- Expansion of the Hudson Holland Scholars Program to include students in the Group Scholars Program
- Establishment of the Ghana study abroad program
- Collaboration with the vice president for administration to establish the Women and Minorities Business Procurement Initiative
- Collaboration with the Indiana Higher Education Commission to establish the Twenty-First Century Scholars Program at IU Bloomington
- Launch of a diversity training program for instructional staff
- Collaboration with the Maurer School of Law to file an amicus brief in support of the University of Michigan in the case *Fisher v. Michigan*
- Establishment of a K–12 statewide outreach initiative for minority and first-generation students
- Strengthening of IU's presence at the Indiana Black Expo Summer Festival

- Collaboration with campus chancellors to establish a tuition set-aside program to support diversity and student retention
- Establishment of the Indiana Project on Academic Success, with funding from the Lumina Foundation
- Completion of the Mission Differentiation Study, leading to the clarification of the role and mission of the regional campuses and IUPUI, one of two core campuses along with the Bloomington campus.

I list these accomplishments with a sense of gratitude for the opportunity I've had to do my part in making a difference. The legendary Howard Zinn, author *A People's History of the United States*, wrote these words that continue to inspire me:

> To be hopeful in bad times is not just foolishly romantic. It is based on the fact that human history is a history not only of cruelty, but also of compassion, sacrifice, courage, kindness. What we choose to emphasize in this complex history will determine our lives. If we see only the worst, it destroys our capacity to do something. If we remember those times and places—and there are so many—where people have behaved magnificently, this gives us the energy to act, and at least the possibility of sending this spinning top of a world in a different direction.[1]

* * *

While sitting on the sofa in my office amid boxes of books, plaques, gifts, and notes for my memoir, I dozed off. I was waiting for the moving van to come and retrieve my belongings for our relocation to Durham, North Carolina, the place we'd call home for the next five years. In that brief nap, I dreamed of Mama and Papa and all the people who had nurtured my dreams as a young boy in the Arkansas Delta. In my dream, I saw Papa smiling broadly and Mama saying, "You see, Charlie, I told you that you could be anything you wanted to be." I was abruptly awakened by my assistant, Storme Day, who announced, "The movers are here."

As they lifted the heavy boxes of books, I thought about my sister Carrie and her admonition a decade earlier to do something that made me happy. While I still didn't know exactly what happiness was, I could say with certainty that my tenure at IU had been fun, I'd done my best, and I had made a difference in the process. I didn't know exactly what North Carolina Central University, my new employer, would be like, but I felt Carrie's spirit propelling and encouraging me to do something that made me happy. And that was exactly what I was preparing to do. Even if I failed,

I had the privilege of having a long and successful career, and IU would always be a place I could return to.

We were headed north on Highway 37 toward Indianapolis, where we'd pick up I-70 East on our drive to Durham. Jeanetta, in her sweet casual way, asked, "What are you thinking about, Pootz? If you had it to do all over, would you move to Bloomington or stay in Flint? What would you do differently? What did you learn worth passing along to others?"

"Jeanetta," I replied, "I've had enough tests to last a lifetime, and I'm not interested in taking one today."

Not inclined to push me, she knew that I would respond at different points along the way before stopping in Knoxville, where we'd spend the night.

When I'd had some time to ponder her questions, I responded, "Jeanetta, I've been thinking a lot lately about how blessed I truly am. I'm not lucky; I am blessed, and there's a big difference in the two! Indiana University is anything but perfect, but I've met some wonderful and supportive people here. And I'm going to miss some of them more than others. As I head off to chase new dreams and new avenues of happiness, I'm pleased that I accepted Myles Brand's invitation ten years ago. There were a few times of late when I found myself thinking maybe I should have kept my commitment to join him at NCAA. But I believe I stayed at IU for the right reasons. I honestly can't think of anything I'd do differently, except spend more time with you. I'm a workaholic, and that's my only regret, really.

"As for lessons that I learned, there are two. First, about the only thing you can do by yourself is read a good book! What I'm saying is, relationships matter in all leadership positions but especially when it comes to diversity. You must establish authentic relationships with colleagues and leverage them if you expect to get the results you desire. Second, you must pace yourself. People have been culturally and racially insensitive for eons, and they're not going to change overnight. So you have to be patient and persistent at the same time if you want to create substantive and sustainable change.

"Since I'm driving and can't fall asleep without killing us and other defenseless drivers, I think I want to just be quiet and listen to some blues on Sirius Radio. Would that be OK? Heck, you're falling asleep anyway!" I finished.

Jeanetta replied, "I wasn't asleep. I heard everything you said."

I didn't want to test Jeanetta's excellent memory, and we both chuckled. I kept on driving, and I know she nodded off for sure, because I heard changes in her breathing. Between listening to B. B. King and the other blues greats, I said to myself, "Charlie, you followed Mama's advice. You did your best, and that's all that matters."

Although Jeanetta was fully asleep by now, I just had to say, "Miss Jeannie, I'd do it all over again!"

11

FULL CIRCLE

"THE EAGLE IS NO COMMON, ORDINARY BARNYARD FOWL." This phrase was coined by Dr. James E. Shepard, president and founder of the National Religious Training School, now North Carolina Central University, more than a century ago. This mantra stuck, and today's students and alumni do not hesitate to invoke it when they want to convey the difference between their beloved NCCU and other HBCUs. As Jeanetta and I welcomed platform guests and other dignitaries to historic Shephard House on the morning of February 22, 2008, it dawned on me that I was the bridge between the past and the future for this venerable institution. It was I, a farm boy from the Arkansas Delta, who was entrusted with keeping and nurturing Dr. Shepard's dream. I would use his words to remind my colleagues and students alike that excellence is an expectation, not an option!

A gentle rain fell on that warm February day as delegates, faculty, and platform guests processed to McDougald-McLendon Arena, where I would be installed as the tenth chancellor of North Carolina Central University. The last person in the procession, I was greeted with high fives by pedestrians and "Best wishes for success!" from drivers inching along Lawson Street on their way to the nearby parking area. Wanting to greet everyone, I had to be encouraged by my chief of staff, Susan Hester, to keep up! As we entered McDougal, the atmosphere was electric, ebullient, and energizing. For a moment, it felt as though I was soaring on the wings of eagles. Resplendent in colorful academic regalia representing universities from all corners of the world, the faculty and the delegates gave me an ovation fit for royalty. Even though it was only pomp, I allowed myself to enjoy it. On Monday, I knew it would be back to the daily grind of addressing the long-term challenges impacting Dr. Shepard's university.

The audience was comprised of nearly every constituent group one can imagine: NCCU trustees and members of the UNC Board of Governors;

elementary school students; corporate and elected officials; alumni; church congregations; delegates from other colleges and universities; delegations from the University of Michigan and Indiana University; and family members and friends, among countless others. They all came bearing the gift of goodwill.

The guests who stole the show were a group of children from Shepard Elementary School who sang "I Believe I Can Fly" to prolonged applause and a standing ovation. The person who traveled the farthest was our son, Rashad, who came from Rome. Although they were long deceased, my sister Carrie and my parents were with me in spirit, sitting on the front row, all broadly smiling their approval. Of course Papa, a man of few words, would have reveled in telling Mr. Ed, the White landowner who loaned him money to make a crop in Arkansas, that all of his kids turned out well, especially Little Black Bear (Aunt Minnie's childhood nickname for me), who would shortly be sworn in as chancellor of the nation's oldest public historically Black liberal arts college.

McDougal Arena was filled with more than six thousand patrons, well above the legal limit, all dressed in their Sunday best! A half-dozen representatives brought greetings that exceeded by far the two minutes allotted, while an NCCU alumnus, District Court Judge A. Leon Stanback, administered the oath of office. After the NCCU choir sang my favorite song, the spiritual "Lord Hold My Hand," I took to the podium to give one of the most important and best delivered speeches of my career. I wrote it personally. Except for my chief of staff and NCCU's director of communications, no one had the slightest idea of what I would say when I ascended to the podium. The title of my twenty-five-minute address was "In Pursuit of Excellence: A Return to the Basics."

I began my remarks by noting that NCCU had a rich, vibrant, and deeply rooted history for which we should be very proud. But the operative focus now, in 2008, was not where we had been but rather where we were headed. We had to demonstrate through the quality of our programs and services that we were competitive, relevant, and responsive. My vision for North Carolina Central University was anchored in the belief that the true measure of an excellent university was defined by the success of its students and alumni, not in the recitation of its rhetoric or in the repetition of its rituals. NCCU must educate character-centered students who could think critically and analytically and could communicate exceptionally well orally, in writing, and interpersonally. We had to educate students who had an appreciation for other cultures and a passion for creating a more equitable world for all of its inhabitants.

I went on to say that I had been in higher education long enough to realize that vision without focus was nothing more than illusion. Therefore, I believed we must focus on five areas. First, we must raise the expectations we had for ourselves—everything and everyone. Second, we must embrace collaboration internally and externally. Silo attitudes must be replaced by transparency, cooperation, and collaboration. We must see ourselves as members of the North Carolina Central University community, not as mere inhabitants of departments, divisions, schools, a university group, or a community group. We had to replace the silo paradigm if we expected to achieve new levels of excellence and responsiveness. Third, we must become more strategic in the investments we made in academic programs and services. Our focus had to be on initiatives that would enable the university to improve quality and achieve new levels of distinction and distinctiveness. Fourth, it was essential that we made more effective use of current resources while procuring new ones. Fifth, we must create and nurture a stronger sense of community within NCCU. Respect and civility were vital hallmarks of this heightened sense of community. Cynicism must be replaced by caring and optimism. Disrespect must be replaced with self-respect. The attitude of "each person for himself or herself" must be replaced by attitudes of mutual well-being for all members of the NCCU community.

As I ended my remarks, I issued an invitation to key constituent groups to invest in my vision for the future of NCCU. I invited students to double their determination, self-discipline, and resolve to succeed by graduating. I challenged them to raise their expectations for themselves by making graduation their destination or finding another institution that would better meet their needs. I invited faculty to deepen their commitment to teaching the students we had rather than wishing they were more like the students they were. And I invited my administrative and staff colleagues to invest in my vision for NCCU by serving the needs of students as though they were responding to the needs of their own children, family members, and neighbors. Finally, I invited elected officials to invest in my vision by appropriating funds consistent with the mission of the university and its aspirations for achieving new levels of excellence and responsiveness. Excellence had a price!

As the installation ceremony ended and we recessed to the reception in the Walker Athletic Complex, for a brief instance, the rain stopped and the sun emerged, as though welcoming us to a new era for James E. Shepard's National Religious Training School. I waded through the crowd of reception guests. Too excited to eat, I took a bottle of water and made a point of stopping to greet each guest. I couldn't believe my eyes when in the distance I spotted my mentor and friend Vic Josey, a justice-loving White man from Richmond, Indiana, who not only welcomed me to Richmond when I was named chancellor of IU East in l987 but also made sure with his wife, Faye, that we were never alone as the Christmas holidays approached each year. Jeanetta and I would always be at their house singing Christmas carols to an out-of-tune piano.

Next to my family, I was most delighted to see Vic and my friends Bob Emerson and Judy Samuelson from Flint. They, like August Eberle, Bob Shaffer, John Ryan, Myles Brand, and a host of other Whites, renewed my faith in the human race at a time when I needed it most. As the reception ended, Jeanetta, Rashad, and I retreated to the chancellor's residence for a few hours of relaxation before welcoming out-of-town friends and family for a catered meal punctuated by music, libations, jokes, and laughter. Inspired by my invitation to invest in my vision for NCCU, some wrote checks that evening, while others did so when they returned home.

* * *

Between 1987 and 2007, I received ten presidential offers: four from HBCUs and six from PWls. Before retiring, I had the privilege of serving as chancellor of three comprehensive, master's-level public universities: two PWls and one HBCU. I retired from the HBCU in 2012 and received offers from two additional ones in the years immediately following retirement. Sensing my personal struggle in deciding whether or not to accept an HBCU presidency, my son, Rashad, asked pointedly, "Dad, what are you afraid of? You know that these institutions, like all others, have more problems than you can ever solve. So if it's something you really want to do, I'd encourage you to accept the next HBCU presidency that's offered to you or stop getting in these searches."

As I approached retirement, I knew Rashad was right, and so when UNC president Erskine Bowles invited me to serve as chancellor of NCCU, without hesitation, I said yes. Once I assumed the chancellorship, I discovered a broad range of challenges that neither Erskine nor the university trustees bothered to mention during my interview. In retrospect, I don't believe they were deliberatively deceptive; rather, they were simply unaware of the true state of the university.

* * *

Beginning with our very first year of marriage, Jeanetta and I had discovered the employment hassles that dual-career couples face. An intelligent, articulate, and passionate woman, Jeanetta never viewed herself simply as the wife of the dean, vice president, or chancellor. When introduced as such by others, she would smile graciously, extend her hand, and say with emphasis "I am Jeanetta Nelms. It's a pleasure meeting you." Having made her point, she proceeded to have a good conversation with the person, never to be introduced in that way by that person again.

Jeanetta encouraged me to accept the NCCU chancellorship, and in doing so, she indicated her willingness to retire from her dream job as director of IU Bloomington's Twenty-First Century Scholars Program to join me in Durham, North Carolina, six months after I commenced my duties. She did so with the understanding that we would keep our home in Bloomington, along with a car, so that she would always have a home of her own. Keeping our house was consistent with the advice given to me by my mentor David Ponitz many years earlier.

"Charlie," David would say, "always keep your own house, and always keep you some 'go to hell' money. There may come a day when you'll need both." I followed that advice, and we were never without our own house. When I retired as chancellor five years later, we didn't shed any tears as we exited the NCCU chancellor's residence, a six-thousand-square-foot ranch-style house with gorgeous curb appeal located on a golf course. It was an impressive house, but we knew it as a home in dire need of updates and repairs that most taxpayers couldn't phantom!

As a former marathon runner, I discovered at a young age the importance of getting off to a good start if you wanted to have a successful run. Within six weeks of commencing my duties as chancellor, I appointed an NCCU Transition Advisory Committee (TAC), comprised of five national experts and practitioners in higher education. The TAC was tasked with conducting a comprehensive review of the challenges and opportunities facing the university and offering recommendations for consideration in undergraduate excellence, student services, academic-program mix and quality, and community and economic development, among other areas.

The Transition Advisory Committee followed my advice and didn't take a full year to complete its work. After numerous conversations with key stakeholders, data analysis, and team deliberations, I was presented with a succinct report focused on the university's strengths, challenges, and opportunities, along with team findings and recommendations in the areas reviewed. The committee ended its sixteen-page report by identifying five areas of highest priority. To ensure transparency and to build trust, the report was shared with members of the chancellor's executive leadership team, the Council of Academic Deans, and the Board of Trustees. Including travel and modest honorariums, NCCU paid less than $25,000 for invaluable advice from a panel of national experts that could easily have cost more than $150,000 had they not been my professional and personal colleagues who shared my commitment to HBCUs. The findings and recommendations of the TAC, along with a newly developed strategic plan, served NCCU well during my tenure and continues to be the foundation of what has come to be known as Eagle Excellence.

Each of the ten institutions I was invited to lead over the course of my career possessed a unique set of attributes as well as challenges. Some faced persistent fiscal- and enrollment-management problems, while others struggled to meet accreditation standards and provide students with a consistently high-quality educational experience. But whether public or private, a common challenge has strangled the progress and stability of HBCUs, and that challenge is a lack of money. During my interview for NCCU chancellor, no one bothered mentioning the budget overruns on the new cafeteria, which were so severe that there were no funds to purchase cooking equipment or furniture for the building. No one bothered talking about air-conditioning systems that didn't work properly or the abrupt electrical power outages that disrupted everything from computer systems to the animal labs in the Julius Chambers Biomedical Biotechnology and Research Institute. And for sure, no one remembered to say anything about the fact that NCCU was operating an unapproved campus at New Birth Baptist Church in Lithonia, Georgia. It was against this backdrop that I assumed my duties as the tenth chancellor of North Carolina Central University.

It was August 2007, my first month on the job. As Vice Chancellor and Chief of Staff Susan Hester, Special Assistant to the Chancellor Betty

Willingham, and I made our way toward the entrance to Eggleson Hall, a newly renovated high-rise residence hall, the line of people waiting to either check in or catch the elevator was at least one hundred students deep. Since the signage was poor or nonexistent, it wasn't clear which line was for what activity. The chaotic scene was reminiscent of the baggage claim experience that Rashad and I had at Russia's Moscow International Airport in 1989. No one seemed to be in charge! Disturbed by what I saw, I asked Susan to find out what was going on and to work with the acting vice chancellor for student services to develop and implement a remedial action plan immediately. Furthermore, I added, "No matter the cost, I want an elevator service representative here ASAP, and I expect the person to make the repairs and remain here until he's sure that the elevator is functioning properly."

Not waiting for the return of the sole elevator that worked, I introduced myself to anxious freshmen and their parents and announced that I was there to do more than welcome them; I was there to help them move in. Followed by a newspaper reporter and TV cameraperson, I picked up two large plastic containers and proceeded to walk up six flights of stairs to the student's room. Wringing wet in my Bermuda shorts and NCCU Welcome Week T-shirt, I repeated this scenario for several hours before moving on to another residence hall to meet and greet new students and to help them move in. Athletically, I was in tip-top physical condition, and most students struggled to keep up with me. As I dropped off the students' belongings, I jokingly told them that I was helping them move in so I would know where they lived and could come find them if they skipped classes! On a more serious note, I told them how pleased we were that they had chosen to enroll at NCCU and I looked forward to presenting them their degree in four years.

The media dubbed me the "Move-in Chancellor," but they quickly realized that my efforts to help students move in was not a photo op or publicity stunt. Rather, it represented my genuine commitment to strengthening NCCU's culture of caring by modeling my expectations. In my second year on the job, and henceforth, more than one hundred university employees, athletes, and student leaders joined me in helping students move in. What people didn't know was that the origin of this commitment could be traced back to my days as a student leader at the University of Arkansas at Pine Bluff, followed by my tenure at every institution with dormitories.

Located in the heart of a neighborhood that was once home to Black bankers, insurance executives, teachers, professors, physicians, dentists, attorneys, and other middle- and upper-middle-class Blacks, today the housing stock around NCCU is deteriorating and in need of attention and care. Nearly all of the original homeowners are now deceased, and their descendants have migrated to suburban subdivisions or to nearby towns surrounded by preferred schools, restaurants, and other amenities sought by middle-class families. The NCCU song "Alma Mater" sings of "the sloping hills and verdant green. The lovely blossoms' beauteous sheen," apt descriptors of the roughly sixty-five acres of land on which the campus is housed. Lacking the financial resources to purchase surrounding properties, the campus is landlocked.

Founded in 1909 by Dr. James Shepard as a private institution, the college was acquired by the state of North Carolina in 1923 and renamed North Carolina College for Negroes. Today, the university enrolls over 8,500 students in baccalaureate and master's degree programs, as well as the JD in law and a PhD in biotechnology. The university has an annual operating budget exceeding $100 million and a full- and part-time workforce of approximately 3,000 employees. The university operates two major research institutes, the Julius Chambers Biomedical Biotechnology Research Institute (BBRI) and the Biomanufacturing Research Institute and Technology Enterprise (BRITE). BBRI focuses on minority health-disparities research related to cancer, cardiovascular disease, and hypertension, while the focus at BRITE is on pharmaceutical sciences, from research and discovery to production.

* * *

"Chancellor Nelms, this is Beverly. We have a serious financial problem, and I was wondering if you are available to meet with the budget people and me in an hour?"

Provost Beverly Jones served as acting chancellor for the month immediately preceding my arrival. A smart and personable woman, she was an NCCU alumna and the first African American woman to earn a PhD in history from the University of North Carolina. Beverly had been a candidate for the position and had quite a few campus and community residents supporting her candidacy. Before consenting to meet with the group, I inquired about the nature of the problem to be discussed, whereupon Beverly replied, "Chancellor, we may not be able to make August payroll."

I nearly fell out of my chair. After all, it was just yesterday, my first day on the job, that Beverly, the NCCU budget director, the internal auditor, and I had met with President Bowles and the UNC vice president of finance to discuss several 2006 audit exceptions. When President Bowles asked if there were any more issues he should be aware of, all of my colleagues from NCCU answered no. And just twenty-four hours later, I was being told that the university might not be able meet its payroll commitments. What a way to start a new job! I indicated to Beverly that I'd be at the meeting and requested that the board chair be included in the conversation. No way was I, as a two-day chancellor, about to take the blame for a problem that had been in the making for months.

The payroll debacle was embarrassing but not fatal. I learned later that since payroll checks were issued from a centralized state account, with a billback to various state agencies, it was not possible for hundreds of NCCU checks to bounce. I took a deep breath and steadied myself for the next distraction, which came my way in just a matter of days. It was in the form of a former employee in Information Technology protesting his dismissal for sharing pornographic materials with a colleague at North Carolina State University. That was followed by the resignation by a senior staff member in Academic Affairs who allegedly signed off on a contract to a former girl-friend and who hired his nephew.

The grand distraction involved the operations of an NCCU degree-granting outreach program in Lithonia, Georgia, at a church pastored by a former NCCU board member. Although the operation was unauthorized, a comprehensive review by a panel of academic experts revealed that the courses and degrees offered met the same academic standards as on-campus degree programs. The US Department of Education demanded a repayment of $1.7 million in financial aid distributed to students enrolled in classes at the unauthorized site. As for the students, they met the requirements for receipt of financial assistance, and there were no allegations of improprieties.

* * *

The distractions and the challenges notwithstanding, I inherited an institution with enormous brand recognition and potential in North Carolina and beyond. The question was how to achieve that potential, given the cumulative effects of historic underfunding on the one hand and contemporary budget cuts on the other. My analysis of the state of affairs at NCCU, reinforced by the excellent work of the Transition Advisory Committee and the university's Strategic Planning Committee, convinced me that we needed to reposition the university for qualitative growth rather than continue to bring in record numbers of new students each year who lacked the preparation, motivation, self-discipline, and commitment to succeed academically.

The first step entailed increasing admissions and persistence requirements by making it mandatory that all newly admitted students have at least a 2.5 GPA and all continuing students maintain a 2.0 GPA. Faculty agreed overwhelmingly, while many NCCU alumni and a few members of the Board of Trustees felt that as an HBCU, we had an obligation to provide access for underprepared students. I argued that given the UNC Board of Governor's embrace of performance-based funding, whereby student persistence and graduation were the dominant metrics, NCCU needed to be creative and strategic in its approach to serving underprepared students by embracing an intrusive (by which I mean required) culture of academic support, redesigning gateway courses, and placing greater emphasis on teaching and learning.

As predicted, the adoption and enforcement of more rigorous admissions and persistence requirements led to a drop in enrollment of more than 300 students in the fall of 2009. By the fall of 2011, not only had the university recovered from the enrollment lost due to tougher standards, but also enrollment was up by 200 students. With a stronger academic profile, in the fall of 2012, NCCU reached an overall enrollment of 8,637 students. The cumulative GPA for entering students was 2.98, and the GPA for continuing students improved dramatically. In a very short span of time, NCCU became one of the premier public HBCUs of choice.

In 2015, NCCU was named the third-highest-rated public HBCU in the country and the second highest among North Carolina HBCUs. Among seventy-two HBCUs ranked, NCCU placed twelfth overall in the listings published annually by *U.S. News & World Report* magazine. *Washington Monthly* magazine's annual college guide and rankings recently placed NCCU nineteenth in its list of the Best Bang for the Buck Colleges in the Southeast.[1] It wasn't long before both HBCUs and PWIs in North Carolina followed suit by raising admissions and persistence standards. What angered some opponents of my strategy for elevating the stature of NCCU soon became a source of pride for all.

* * *

As NCCU approached its centennial celebration, Dr. Kevin Rome proposed that we create an initiative to recruit and nurture the academic success of Black males, and the Centennial Scholars Program was born. The program was predicated on the premise that Black males were underperforming academically and that lamenting it was not a strategy for changing this reality. Rome developed a program that met the "I Test": intellectual, intentional, intrusive, integrated, and interesting. Participants were told that inside each of them resided a scholar and that the aim of the Centennial Scholars Program was to nurture and support their intellectual, social, leadership, and cultural development. The program started with a cohort of fifty-nine students in 2009 and had grown to over five hundred by the fall of 2012. In 2010, the university established a Women's Center and created an intentional initiative for female students as well.

While increasing admissions and persistence standards were important first steps in ensuring the long-term success and competitiveness of NCCU, it was clear that much more needed to be done, beginning with a comprehensive review of the quality and the mix of curricular offerings. Equally important, we needed to review all administrative policies and practices to reduce redundancy, inefficiencies, and costs.

Once I reached this decision, I appointed an Academic Program Review and Restructuring Commission, chaired by Dr. Bernice Johnson, associate provost, professor of human sciences, and former dean of the University College. Mr. Wendell Davis, vice chancellor for administration and finance, chaired the Process Improvement and Efficiency Commission. Both commissions were comprised of faculty, staff, and administrators who enjoyed the respect of colleagues across academic and administrative boundaries. In my charge to each commission, I emphasized the importance of being thorough, objective, inclusive, fair, and transparent. In addition, I encouraged them to make optimal use of institutional research data to aid in developing recommendations for consideration by all entities in the decision-making queue.

After six months of data review and analysis, interviews with constituent groups, open forums, and commission deliberations, the Academic Program Review and Restructuring Commission recommended that twelve academic programs be retained, six programs be merged or restructured, five programs be eliminated, one new major be created, and the College of Science and Technology (CST) be merged with the College of Liberal Arts to form the College of Arts and Sciences.

In my charge to the Process Improvement and Efficiency Commission, I requested that they identify $1 million in base cost reductions to enable reallocation of funds to support the academic mission of NCCU.

The commission recommended reductions in excess of $1.5 million. Selected examples of areas cited for improvements and savings included the following: implementing People Admin Software, $190,000; relinquishing Banner education software maintenance agreements, $100,000; optimizing enrollment in selected General Education Curriculum courses by using larger classrooms and increasing class size, $27,000; streamlining processes in the office of Human Resources, $310,000; streamlining facilities-management processes, $300,000; and centralizing trash receptacles and restructuring the office of Health and Safety, $85,000.

After carefully reviewing the recommendations of each commission with members of the university's executive leadership team, I decided which of them I would support and take to the Board of Trustees for consideration and approval. Few people complained about the recommendations offered by the Process Improvement and Efficiency Commission; however, faculty from programs recommended for restructuring or discontinuation exhibited anger and attitudes that were unprofessional and untenable. Despite the trend data from institutional research showing the number of students enrolled and the number of degrees conferred, faculty who opposed the recommendations challenged the accuracy of the data and, ultimately, the motives underlying my recommendations.

The greatest opposition came from faculty opposed to the merger of the colleges of Science and Technology and Liberal Arts to create the College of Arts and Sciences. They argued vehemently that discontinuation of the College of Science and Technology would negatively impact the faculty's ability to obtain research grants from various federal agencies. What they conveniently forgot to remember was the fact that neither grant submissions nor funding increased during the six-year life of CST, which grew out the dismantled College of Arts and Sciences.

The second most virulent opposition came from sociology faculty, who were convinced that every "good" liberal arts college should offer an undergraduate degree in sociology—even if the quality was inconsistent, students could not find jobs or get into graduate school, and the university lacked the resources required to raise the quality. Faculty enlisted the advocacy and support of the American Sociological Association, which took me to task for having the gall to recommend the discontinuation of a bachelor's degree in a critical discipline like sociology—and at an HBCU, of all places! They invoked the words of W. E. B. DuBois and other internationally acclaimed sociologists in making their argument for not only keeping the degree but also investing additional resources. The organization contacted members of the UNC Board of Governors and NCCU trustees, asking them to reject my recommendation on sociology. At the end of the day, my recommendations were unanimously approved by the NCCU Board of Trustees and the Board of Governors.

NCCU offered an undergraduate degree program in computer science through CST and a degree in computer information systems through the School of Business. Neither program had many majors, while those who graduated had difficulty obtaining jobs in one of the most technology-intense regions of the country, North Carolina's Research Park Triangle, located less than five miles from the university. My recommendation that the two programs be merged was characterized as posing a threat to the business school's accreditation from the Association to Advance Collegiate Schools of Business. When I raised the issue of growing national concern about the paucity of Blacks in tech fields, one international faculty member opined that Black students couldn't handle the intellectual rigor of computer science and instead gravitated to the information systems major in the School of Business. The racism of his assertions aside, had he checked enrollment statistics, he would have discovered that there was only a handful of Blacks in that particular major as well.

On every recommendation dealing with academic program changes, small groups of faculty argued that their programs should not be disturbed because any changes would undermine quality, reduce options for students, and lead to a reduction in the number of full-time faculty. Conversely, I argued that given draconian state-budget cuts and the implementation of performance-based funding by the UNC Board of Governors, higher education institutions were in the midst of confronting a "new normal" and could not afford to continue with business as usual.

Moreover, I stressed that NCCU could not be all things to all people and that across-the-board budget cuts were the surest pathway to mediocrity. When making their case against my recommendations, faculty alleged that I hadn't listened to them. Of course, I had documentation to show the number of one-on-one meetings I had hosted, along with the appointments with affected departmental and college faculty, as well as open campus forums. Our records showed that more than one thousand constituents had provided feedback in one form or another. It was evident that I was listening; the problem was my unwillingness to accept the status quo or to take the path of least resistance. Doing so, in my view, amounted to a dereliction of my duties!

* * *

I arrived at NCCU prepared to lead, and my readiness was repeatedly tested in numerous ways. I quickly discovered that there was a lack of alignment between the aspirations various constituent groups had for the university and their willingness to make the necessary investments, financial and otherwise, to make those aspirations a reality. The unwillingness to embrace change, more so than money per se, will continue to be the Achilles' heel of the higher education enterprise. One need only look at how slow higher education has been to embrace the use of technology in the delivery of instruction, as well as in the provision of student services and the performance of administrative functions. The institutions that can ill afford to keep doing business as usual are low-resourced colleges and universities, the category into which HBCUs overwhelmingly fall.

Enhancing NCCU's excellence required that the university offer high-quality academic programs desired by current and prospective students and attract students who could succeed by offering them the financial, academic, and personal support services they needed. It was far easier to articulate needs than it was fulfill them. And changing that calculus required an unprecedented level of cross-boundary collaboration. It also required working with community colleges, as well as other UNC campuses, both HBCUs and PWIs. Athletic fields and basketball courts were the places constructed for competition! This is a lesson that HBCUs as a sector have yet to embrace and act on.

North Carolina is home to ten HBCUs, five public and five private, with countless untapped opportunities for collaboration. I discovered that the leaders were far more cordial than they were collaborative. It seemed that an imminent threat, not the omnipresent threat, was the only thing that commanded our attention. Changes in the Parent PLUS Loan program were an example of an imminent threat, whereas the continuing effects of historic underfunding of HBCUs was but one example of an omnipresent threat that HBCU leaders appeared reluctant to attack in an organized and collaborative fashion, with the engagement of alumni and others of goodwill.

* * *

My assistant, Betty, buzzed me on the intercom to say that one of the trustees, Ed Stewart, was on the telephone and wanted to speak with me for a minute. I asked her to put him through.

"Chancellor," he said, "this is Ed Stewart. How're you doing this afternoon? Chancellor, I had a call a few minutes ago from a parent complaining about housing. She said that her daughter was admitted about a month ago, but when they brought her to campus today, they were told the university didn't have a dormitory room for her. I'm calling to see if you can get her into a room."

I began by indicating that I'd be happy to have someone look into the matter, but it was highly unlikely that I could get her in a room. I said, "The university has over eight thousand students but can only house a little more than twenty-six hundred of them on campus. Since this student was admitted just a month ago, by that time, I'm certain all rooms had already been assigned. Even so, let me have Susan look into the situation and call you back."

This same scenario would play out countless times during my tenure at NCCU. The calls came from trustees, elected officials, alumni, pastors, and students themselves, directly appealing to me to make an exception and get a student into the residence halls. No matter how many times I said I couldn't, it didn't seem to register with the caller.

When I assumed my duties in 2007, the university was leasing an entire apartment complex on a twelve-month basis at an inflated price. All budget shortfalls and property damage incurred by the owner had to be covered by the university. Never in my entire professional career had I seen such a one-sided contract! The owner balked at renegotiating the contract and refused to take me seriously when I said that the university would no longer serve as his cash machine and that starting in the fall of 2008, contracts would be between his company and each tenant.

Immediately, I began receiving calls from NCCU trustees wondering why the university wanted to end the lease, knowing full well that we could not house all students. I explained that the university was subsidizing the contract to the tune of approximately $2 million annually and that NCCU was the only university in North Carolina to my knowledge with this odd housing arrangement. All other universities required students to sign their own leases. Sure enough, we exited the lease without negatively impacting students, and this did force the owner to compete with other apartment complexes for student business.

Despite the chronic housing shortage at NCCU because of financial liquidity issues, neither the UNC General Administration, nor the Board of Governors, nor the Department of State Treasurer would approve the university's request to issue bonds to build student housing. Further, because of ongoing problems encountered on another privately constructed student-housing project at NCCU prior to my arrival, even the most sympathetic of our supporters were hesitant about permitting the university to enter a relationship with a private developer. At the same time, Western Carolina University and several other UNC campuses were doing exactly the same thing we were begging for permission to do! Whoever said the world is fair? After bringing aboard a smart and skilled vice chancellor for finance and administration, the university began addressing its liquidity issues and won approval to construct a state-of-the-art residence hall with a capacity for six hundred students. While it proved very helpful and enhanced the attractiveness of the campus, the university still had a housing deficit of more than two thousand beds.

While there were distractions I faced every single day of my NCCU chancellorship, not being able to make more progress in addressing the housing shortage and my inability to construct a new student-union building to improve the quality of student life were major sources of disappointment for me. No matter how hard my colleagues and I worked, we simply never received the level of support our students deserved. Both of these needs reflect the cumulative effects of historic underfunding and a system's unwillingness to acknowledge and address contemporary inequities.

In addition to the much-needed realignment of academic programs, admissions, persistence, and standards; improvements in the quality of customer services and of technology and facilities infrastructure; and reaffirmation of the university's regional and specialized accreditation, along with a host of other accomplishments, five anchor initiatives during my tenure positioned North Carolina Central University for becoming a stronger institution:

- Investing more than $75 million in new facilities and infrastructure improvement
- Establishing the Division of Research and Economic Development
- Developing and implementing a PhD program in integrated biosciences
- Developing and implementing a comprehensive aesthetic-improvement plan for the campus
- Transitioning intercollegiate athletics from Division II to Division I

As I turned sixty-five years of age on September 11, 2011, I could not help but think about Papa, who had died suddenly at age sixty-nine. And here I was, dancing the night away with some four hundred university constituents who had said yes to the invitation from NCCU's Student Government Association. I had made it clear to them that I had no interest in gifts or cards. Rather, I asked that contributions, which we would match, be made to the Charlie and Jeanetta Nelms Scholarship Endowment.

When the party came to a close, I was questioned about my retirement by my reporter friend from Durham's *Herald-Sun* newspaper. I replied simply, "Neil, I'm having a blast dancing with these young people who're less than a third of my age, and retirement is the farthest thing from my mind." And with that, I gave him a big smile and kept on doing a dance that students probably concluded was from the Age of Dinosaurs, but I was having a blast. The next day I made the front page of the paper looking like an old man on steroids!

As I approached my sixty-sixth birthday in 2012 and came to the end of the five-year commitment I had made to President Bowles when he had hired me to become the tenth chancellor of NCCU, I began thinking about the next phase of my life. Even though I had been burning both ends of the proverbial candle seven days a week, things were moving in the right direction for NCCU. I had come full circle and fulfilled the commitment I made to myself to become an HBCU leader.

Mama was right, and so were Mr. Mozell, Bob Shaffer, Prexy, Torrence, and countless others who'd invested in my career and were vested in my success. If I retired now, it would be on my terms, when things were at an all-time high for the university and for my family and me. I knew for sure that I couldn't and wouldn't go home and sit down on my retiree rocking chair. There's no way I could retire from a lifetime of active engagement that began at the tender age of five. No, I still had a lot of living to do, and I wanted to do it on my own terms and on my own schedule.

* * *

As I prepared to end my leadership journey, I didn't wait to feel Carrie's spirit or to be asked by Jeanetta what I'd learned. On a gorgeous Sunday morning in July 2012 as I walked alone on the golf course, I asked and answered the question for myself. What did you learn on your journey, Charlie? Well, I learned that most dreams are achievable if we have the discipline and the work ethic to pursue them. Work as though everything depended on you and pray as though everything depended on God, and with the confluence of the two, literally anything is possible. And I learned that leadership is not for the faint of heart; you must have courage, commitment, and fortitude. There are no substitutes!

Was it worth it leaving your cushy position as a vice president at a major research university to serve as chancellor of a low-wealth HBCU? Would you do it over again?

Just as I answered yes to myself, a huge buck deer ran across the path I was on, as though it was on a journey that only it could see. I couldn't help but remember our house on the Buck Lake Road, where I'd begun my own journey, so many years ago.

Oh, Lord, you held my hand and guided my feet, and if I had to run this race again, I'd do it in a heartbeat!

NOTES

1. "I'll Fly Away"

1. Henry Louis Gates Jr., "The Truth Behind 40 Acres and a Mule," *The Root*, January 7, 2013, www.theroot.com/the-truth-behind-40-acres-and-a-mule-1790894780.

2. Sylvia A. Harvey, "For Decades, the USDA Was Black Farmers' Worst Enemy. Here's How It Became an Ally," *Yes!* July 8, 2016, www.yesmagazine.org/people-power/the-resurgence-of-black-farmers-20160708.

3. Tadlock Cowen and Jody Feder, "The Pigford Cases: USDA Settlement of Discrimination Suits by Black Farmers," Congressional Research Service, May 29, 2013, http://nationalaglawcenter.org/wp-content/uploads/assets/crs/RS20430.pdf.

4. Ibid.

5. Harvey, "For Decades, the USDA Was Black Farmers' Worst Enemy."

3. Tacks and Splinters

1. Langston Hughes, "Mother to Son," Poetry Foundation, accessed October 6, 2018, www.poetryfoundation.org/poems/47559/mother-to-son.

4. College Bound

1. Erica L. Taylor, "Little Known Black History Fact: Black Is Beautiful," *The Tom Joyner Morning Show*, accessed July 13, 2017, http://blackamericaweb.com/2013/11/26/little-known-black-history-fact-black-is-beautiful/.

8. "If I Had a Hammer"

1. "Adams v. Richardson, 1972," The State of History, North Carolina State University Special Collections Research Center, accessed July 13, 2017, https://soh.omeka.chass.ncsu.edu/items/show/288.

2. Chris Arnade, "White Flight Followed Factory Jobs out of Gary, Indiana. Black People Didn't Have a Choice," *The Guardian*, March 28, 2017, https://www.theguardian.com/society/2017/mar/28/poverty-racism-gary-indiana-factory-jobs.

3. "Merrillville, Indiana," Wikipedia, accessed July 13, 2017, https://en.wikipedia.org/wiki/Merrillville,_Indiana#cite_ref-9.

4. Bill Dolan, "2005 Study, Census Show NWI Is Most Segregated Metro Area in the Country," *Indiana Economic Digest*, December 10, 2006, www.indianaeconomicdigest.com/main.asp?SectionID=31&subsectionID=217&articleID=30924.

5. "IU Northwest Fast Facts, Fall 2016," Indiana University Northwest, accessed July 13, 2017, www.iun.edu/institutional-effectiveness/fast-facts/index.htm.

6. Doug Lederman, "Hoosier State Gets Coordinated," *Inside Higher Education*, May 16, 2008, www.insidehighered.com/news/2008/05/16/indiana.

9. Holding Fast

1. Shannon Larson, "The Student Religious Cabinet—a Student Organization Concerned with Overcoming Religious and Racial Differences," *Blogging Hoosier History*, Indiana University Archives, February 28, 2013, https://blogs.libraries.indiana.edu/iubarchives /2013/02/28/student-religious-cabinet/.

2. Allison Haack, "American Veterans Committee—Bloomington Chapter," *Blogging Hoosier History*, Indiana University Archives, December 16, 2014, https://blogs.libraries .indiana.edu/iubarchives/2014/12/16/c570/.

3. "AutoWorld (Theme Park)," Wikipedia, accessed 7 October 2018, https://en.wikipedia .org/wiki/AutoWorld_(theme_park)#References_in_popular_culture.

4. Langston Hughes, "Dreams," American Poetry Society, accessed 7 October 2018, www .poets.org/poetsorg/poem/dreams.

10. This Spinning Top

1. James Ridgeway, "The World According to Howard Zinn," *Mother Jones*, January 31, 2010, accessed October 7, 2018, www.motherjones.com/politics/2010/01/world-according -howard-zinn/.

11. Full Circle

1. "*U.S. News & World Report* Names NCCU as a Top HBCU," North Carolina Central University, September 10, 2015, http://www.nccu.edu/news/index.cfm?id=2AFCDE74-15C5 -F8D8-3AC555C89AE185F3.

CHARLIE NELMS is currently Senior Scholar at the American Association of State Colleges and Universities and Center Scholar at the Center for Postsecondary Research, Indiana University School of Education, as well as retired Chancellor of North Carolina Central University and Vice President for Institutional Development and Student Affairs Emeritus at Indiana University (IU). A native of the Arkansas Delta, Nelms has devoted his life to equalizing opportunities for disenfranchised peoples. During his long tenure at Indiana University, he held leadership positions on several campuses, including associate dean for academic affairs at IU Northwest, chancellor at IU East, and vice president of IU. In retirement, he works with historically black colleges and universities to strengthen leadership and governance.